DEMOCRACY IN ACTION

KRISTINA SMOCK

DEMOCRACY IN ACTION

Community Organizing and Urban Change

COLUMBIA UNIVERSITY PRESS ■ NEW YORK

COLUMBIA UNIVERSITY PRESS
Publishers Since 1893
New York, Chichester, West Sussex
Copyright © 2004 Columbia University Press
All rights Reserved

Library of Congress Cataloging-in-Publication Data
Democracy in action : community organizing and urban change /
   Kristina Smock.
      p. cm.
   Includes bibliographical references and index.

   ISBN 0-231-12672-7 (cloth)
   ISBN 0-231-12673-5 (pbk.)

   1. Community Organization—Case studies.
   2. Community development, Urban—Case studies.
   3. Political participation—Case studies.

HM766 .S66 2003
361.8 22   2003055764
                                                   CIP

Columbia University Press books are printed on permanent and
durable acid-free paper
Printed in the United States of America

c 10 9 8 7 6 5 4 3 2 1
p 10 9 8 7 6 5 4 3 2 1

*All names of organizations, individual participants, and neighbor-
hoods have been changed.*

*All the citations to information derived from the World Wide Web
were accurate at the time of writing. Neither the author nor Columbia University Press is responsible for Web sites that have changed
or expired since the time of publication.*

To my parents, Audrey and David,
my sister, Erica, and my husband, Marc

CONTENTS

TABLES

ACKNOWLEDGMENTS

THIS STUDY was motivated by my work as a community organizer in the early-
to mid-1990s. I owe a great deal to the many residents and organizers with
whom I worked during that time. They taught me about the rewards, the
challenges, and the value of community organizing and inspired me to write this
book.

I am also indebted to the hundreds of organizers and residents who are por-
trayed in this study and whose privacy must be protected through anonymity. They
opened their doors to me, allowed me to share in their work, and helped to make
my fieldwork rich and thought provoking. I am especially grateful to the more than
200 people who generously gave their time to be interviewed for this study.

Many people have contributed to the development of this book through their
input, analytical contributions, and support. Allan Schnaiberg, Al Hunter, and
Orville Lee provided valuable feedback on the dissertation upon which this book
is based. In the process of converting the dissertation to a book, I received feedback
and advice from Wendy Espeland, Robert Fisher, Randy Stoecker, David Pellow,
Michelle Van Natta, Herb Rubin, Sandy O'Donnell, Ellen Schumer, Kirk
Nowlen, James Mumm, David Smock, Erica Smock, Marc Jolin, and many others
too numerous to mention. My editors at Columbia University Press, John Michel
and Leslie Bialler, as well as several anonymous reviewers, helped me to improve
the manuscript and skillfully shepherded the book through the production
process.

My friends and family provided moral, intellectual, and logistical support
throughout this endeavor. My parents inspired me to take on this project and provided advice and encouragement throughout the experience. My in-laws shared
their home during the final stages of writing. My sister provided ongoing feedback
and moral support. And many wonderful friends tried to help me keep things in
perspective.

Most importantly, I owe a special thanks to my husband, Marc Jolin, who has
lived this book with me, and whose astute insights, careful editing, painstaking
dedication to this project, and unflagging emotional support have sustained me
throughout this journey.

PART I
INTRODUCTION

CHAPTER 1

POPULAR DEMOCRACY AND URBAN CHANGE

Chanting and cheering, seventy-five residents of Chicago's Westridge neighborhood crowded the sidelines of the local youth soccer league's championship game. As they watched the players race across the well-kept fields, the residents exchanged exuberant smiles despite the late-November chill. This was a watershed day, and not just because their children had made it to the season finale.

Six months earlier, the park where they were standing had been a desolate patch of concrete and dead grass where few ever ventured. Parents had steered their children away from the block-long stretch, and the sight of any activity in the park during daylight hours was rare. Then a teenager was shot and killed on the park's deserted basketball courts, and residents decided it was time to take action.

With the help of community organizers from the Westridge Organization of Neighbors (WON), the residents developed a coordinated strategy for reclaiming their park. After some initial research and several planning sessions, they approached the city's Parks Commissioner to demand improvements to the park's recreational programs and facilities. When they got no response, dozens of residents brought their children to the Commissioner's house to play soccer on her front lawn. Their actions got the city's attention, and after a series of negotiating meetings, the residents secured a commitment for thousands of dollars worth of improvements to the park's sports programs, its fieldhouse, and its grounds. Galvanized by their victory, the residents launched the area's first youth soccer league at the park, staffed entirely by parent volunteers.

Through their collective actions, Westridge's residents turned an abandoned park into a vibrant community resource. More importantly, the experience transformed residents' perceptions of what it means to live in a democratic society. "It's fabulous to see what power people can have," one neighbor reflected. "People have a tendency to sit back and say 'oh yeah, the alderman's supposed to do this, and the police are supposed to do this, and this is what they're supposed to do, and if I just be quiet that will happen.' And it doesn't. You have to hold them accountable. And you can do it. You have the right to do it."

■

Every day, in cities across the United States, organizations like WON are making democracy a reality for urban residents. Bringing ordinary people into public life, often for the first time, these organizations are revitalizing popular participation in disenfranchised communities. Through a process commonly referred to as "community organizing," organizations like WON enable urban residents to identify shared problems, develop a vision for the future, and implement collective solutions to achieve their goals. By empowering residents to gain control over the social and political arrangements affecting their communities, these organizations enhance the quality of life in hundreds of urban neighborhoods.

This book analyzes the techniques that organizations like WON use to achieve their goals. Building on the lessons of almost a century of experimentation, community organizing groups have developed an array of different methods for engaging disenfranchised residents in public life and solving urban problems. *Democracy in Action* explores the five dominant models of community organizing in use today, based on the stories of ten very different organizations working in economically and racially diverse urban neighborhoods. Through a detailed comparative analysis of each model's approach to the core elements of the organizing process, the book offers important lessons about participatory democracy, social action, and the process of urban change.

WHY ORGANIZE?

Before exploring the differences between models of organizing, it is important to understand the broader role of community organizing in contemporary urban life. Scholars of American society have long emphasized the connection between vibrant civic institutions and a healthy democracy. Recent academic studies and media polls documenting declining rates of civic involvement have thus generated much hand-wringing about the state of participatory democracy and community life. In 1985, Robert Bellah's *Habits of the Heart* touched a national nerve with the pronouncement that American individualism had undermined our traditional sense of public commitment. Building on the momentum of this landmark study, in the early 1990s a group of prominent academics and politicians calling themselves "communitarians" (Etzioni 1993) warned that the erosion of our sense of civic responsibility threatened the very fabric of our society. In 2000,

Robert Putnam's *Bowling Alone* confirmed these fears with statistical evidence of a steady decline in public participation over the past fifty years and a compendium of data demonstrating the negative impacts of this decline.

While these trends are cause for concern, they are in many ways just the visible manifestation of a much broader problem. A significant portion of our nation's population has *always* been excluded from meaningful participation in the democratic arena. And as our society becomes more economically and socially stratified, this pattern has only worsened.

To be truly inclusive, a democratic society must be built upon a foundation of genuine political equality. Citizens must have equal access, not only to the voting both, but also to direct participation in the public decision-making process. Democracy flourishes when people come together as equals to deliberate over their common affairs, make decisions about public priorities, and influence the social and economic arrangements that shape their everyday lives.

But in a society with vast social and economic inequalities, this kind of genuine public engagement is hard to attain. In the United States, disparities in financial resources, social status, education, and other resources confer political advantages on the most privileged and effectively exclude a sizeable portion of our populace from meaningful public participation. Our electoral system is increasingly driven by the interests of corporate contributors and economic powerholders. The traditional channels for civic participation in the policy making process are frequently dominated by an economic and political elite. And in our increasingly globalized and privatized society, many of the critical decisions affecting our quality of life are made outside of the formal political process altogether, in arenas that are closed off from popular participation.

If we are to create a more democratic society in the face of these trends, we must develop mechanisms through which ordinary people—especially society's most disenfranchised members—can impact the social and economic conditions affecting their lives. The ability to create such mechanisms, both within the political process as well as outside of formal political channels, is what makes community organizing so important. Community organizing groups have been working for almost a century to build residents' skills as public actors and engage them in collective action to achieve their common goals. By bringing America's most disenfranchised residents into public life, community organizing expands the democratic process, enabling urban residents to influence public decisions and build vibrant communities that serve their needs.

THE ORGANIZING PROCESS

What makes community organizing such an effective vehicle for engaging urban residents in public life? Although no two organizing efforts ever look exactly alike, all effective organizing initiatives share certain common features that distinguish community organizing from other approaches to urban change. These core features will provide the framework for comparing the models of organizing that are the subject of this book:

- **Building individual capacity—developing local leaders:** Community organizing enables individual residents to become actively involved in public life by developing their capacities as leaders. Using a range of different techniques, community organizing groups work to expand residents' skills, knowledge, and sense of self-efficacy. In addition, they provide residents with the opportunity to exercise these skills by taking on public roles and responsibilities within the community and the broader public sphere. Through this process, community organizing transforms ordinary people into effective public actors.

- **Building community capacity—networks and social capital:** In addition to building individual leadership skills, community organizing strives to develop the collective capacity of the community as a whole. Through the organizing process, residents get to know their neighbors and build lasting social networks within the community. These networks expand the neighborhood's social capital—the norms of trust and reciprocity that enable the community to work together on common goals. Furthermore, by linking these networks to external resources and support, community organizing increases the capacity of the networks' members to achieve their shared goals.

- **Building a community governance structure:** In order to work together effectively, the members of a community must be able to make collective decisions about the neighborhood's needs. Community organizing groups build democratic governance structures at the neighborhood level that enable residents to deliberate about their common affairs and make decisions about the community's priorities. By fostering popular participation in community decision-making, these governance structures create microcosms of genuine democracy at the neighborhood level. And by facilitating the development of a shared vision for the community's future, they make collective action possible.

- **Diagnosing and framing the community's problems:** Community organizing groups don't just develop the community's *capacity* for collective action, they *harness* this capacity by working with residents to diagnose the neighborhood's problems and identify appropriate solutions. By providing a framework that residents can use to reflect on and make sense of their experiences, organizing groups shape the way that residents define and interpret community problems. Furthermore, by helping residents to identify causal explanations for their grievances, the organizations shape the strategies that residents adopt for addressing these problems.

■ **Taking collective action for community change:** Once residents have developed strategies for change, community organizing groups coordinate the implementation of these strategies through grassroots projects and campaigns. By engaging residents in the public arena, these collective action initiatives make political and economic institutions more responsive to residents' interests and needs. And by facilitating concrete solutions to the neighborhood's problems, they help to improve residents' quality of life.

■ **Widening the scope: Organizing for broader social change:** In some cases, organizing also goes beyond its community-based focus to contribute to broader social structural change. It does this by building the foundational infrastructure for broader movement building and by providing the spaces for residents to reflect on their experiences and develop a collective vision for society.

MODELS OF COMMUNITY ORGANIZING

While all effective community organizing initiatives share the same core elements, the contemporary community organizing arena includes hundreds of different groups using a wide range of methods and techniques for putting these elements into practice. The primary approaches to community organizing over the past decade can be categorized into five distinct models: (1) the power-based model; (2) the community-building model; (3) the civic model; (4) the women-centered model; and (5) the transformative model. These models can be distinguished by the way they approach each of the core elements of the organizing process, and the relative emphasis they place on each of these elements within the overall organizing project.

Democracy in Action explores the differences among these five models and their implications for participatory democracy and urban change. The analysis is based on an examination of the experiences of ten contemporary community organizing groups—two case studies for each model. I conducted the research for this study in Chicago and Portland, Oregon in 1998 and 1999.[1] My fieldwork included participation in more than 270 meetings and events for the different organizations—small group planning meetings, committee meetings, strategy sessions, public meetings, protests, actions, and celebrations. I also observed staff meetings and in-house trainings and spent time with individual organizers and leaders.

In addition to observing the organizations' day-to-day activities, I participated in trainings on each organization's approach. Most were intense, multi-session workshops lasting several days. I also examined training manuals, newspaper articles, meeting minutes, newsletters, annual reports, and meeting handouts from each group.

To capture the insights and reflections of the organizations' staff and participants, I conducted 168 interviews with two to three staff and twelve to fifteen members and leaders from each group. The interviews averaged about forty-five minutes in length and focused on participants' personal experiences in the organizations, their opinions about local neighborhood issues, and their assessments of various aspects of the organizations, including internal power dynamics, decision-making, organizational structure, leadership development, external relationships, and membership recruitment.

I also interviewed more than thirty veteran organizers, funders, and academics to get their insights and perspectives on the different approaches to organizing. And I participated in numerous informal discussions among organizers and activists about the relative merits of the different approaches.

OVERVIEW OF THE BOOK

The book is arranged thematically, with each chapter comparing the five models' approaches to one of the essential elements of the organizing process. The analysis draws out the key strengths and limitations of each model, revealing important insights about how to build a more democratic society and strengthen disenfranchised communities.

Chapter 2, the second half of the introduction, overviews the core principles and characteristics of the five models and introduces the ten case study organizations.

Part II begins the substantive analysis with several chapters that examine how the case study organizations bring residents together and build their capacity for collective action. Chapter 3 explores the case study organizations' efforts to develop individual residents' leadership skills and their capacity to participate effectively in the public sphere. Chapter 4 analyzes how the organizations develop the capacity of the community as a whole through the creation of social networks among residents and institutions. Chapter 5 evaluates the case study organizations' efforts to create formal governance structures for community priority-setting and decision-making.

Part III examines the case study organizations' efforts to create concrete improvements in local residents' quality of life, and the effectiveness of their distinctive strategies and techniques. Chapter 6 describes the frameworks different organizations use for diagnosing the neighborhood's problems and defining appropriate solutions to these problems. Chapter 7 evaluates the impact and effectiveness of these varying approaches through a comparative analysis of the case study organizations' campaigns. Finally, chapter 8 examines whether community organizing has the potential to contribute to broader social structural change and, if so, which models are most likely to realize this potential.

Part IV, the conclusion, highlights the lessons and insights that can be gleaned from the book's comparative analysis. It summarizes the overall strengths and limitations of each model and then offers practical suggestions for how these insights might inform efforts to strengthen democracy and create urban change.

Each chapter is followed by a summary table that reviews the main comparisons among the models. Some readers may prefer to read the tables prior to beginning each chapter. A list of all the tables is included on page ix.

CHAPTER 2

MODELS OF COMMUNITY ORGANIZING: AN OVERVIEW

MY INTEREST in different models of community organizing stems from my experiences as a community organizer and neighborhood activist over the past decade. In the early 1990s I became involved as a resident participant in a local community organizing initiative in Portland, Oregon. After years of working in the social services sector, I was exhilarated by this grassroots, democratic approach to solving urban problems. Inspired by my experiences, I found a job as a community organizer in a nearby neighborhood. The experience was a transformative one, and from it I developed a passionate interest in both the theories and the practice of community organizing. After working as an organizer for two and a half years, I moved to Chicago—long considered to be the capital of modern day organizing—where I continued to work as a consultant, activist, and researcher with a variety of different community organizing initiatives.

Over the course of these experiences, I was continually amazed and intrigued by the diversity of approaches used by the groups I was involved with. Each organization seemed to espouse a different theory of change. And each had a distinctive set of techniques for achieving its goals. Almost every organization I worked with was convinced that its approach was *the* "right" or "best" route to urban change. But my own experiences, as well as my observations of other groups around the country, made it clear that, in fact, every approach had unique advantages, as well as distinct drawbacks and limitations.

Eager to deepen my understanding of these different approaches to organizing, I searched the academic and practitioner literature for research on

---

All the names of the case study organizations are pseudonyms. In some cases I have used the real names of regional and national networks with which the organizations are affiliated. This is for identification purposes only. My use of the present tense when talking about the case study organizations refers to the time period during which I did my research. My observations and analysis are based on the organizations' work during this time frame, as well as information about the organizations' histories that I was able to glean from interviews and written materials.

the relative merits of different organizing methods and techniques. Although I discovered a number of excellent studies of organizing, I found few systematic empirical comparisons of *different* organizing approaches.

The literature on community organizing is dominated by case studies of single organizations (e.g. Delgado 1986; Medoff and Sklar 1994; Slayton 1986; Stein 1986; Stoecker 1994; Warren 2001), or of multiple organizations utilizing the same approach (e.g. Boyte and Riessman 1986; Eisen 1994; Rabrenovic 1996; Rivera and Erlich 1992). These case studies provide useful information about the characteristics and impacts of particular organizations, but they don't enable us to systematically compare the wide array of different organizing approaches in use today. The comparative analyses that do exist focus primarily on the core characteristics and theories of change that distinguish particular approaches, rather than on an empirical analysis of their actual implementation (e.g. Delgado 1994; Robinson and Hanna 1994b; Rothman 1968, 1996; Rubin and Rubin 1992). And the few comparative studies that *are* based on empirical research—most notably, Robert Fisher's *Let The People Decide* (1994)—typically rely on secondary sources rather than first-hand observations. Consequently, while these studies offer valuable insights into the most public and visible aspects of different organizations' work, they can provide only limited information about the organizations' internal dynamics and day-to-day operations.

In an effort to address this gap, I decided to undertake a systematic empirical comparison of the wide variety of organizing approaches in existence today. To create a framework for my analysis, I developed a five-model typology reflecting the dominant approaches to community organizing over the past decade:

- Power-based model
- Community-building model
- Civic model
- Women-centered model
- Transformative model

While my categorization of the models was inspired by several existing typologies (Fisher 1994; Robinson and Hanna 1994b; Stoecker and Stall 1998; Rothman 1968, 1996; Delgado 1994), it was based primarily on my own observations and experiences in the organizing field.

Breaking down the existing universe of organizing approaches into five distinct models makes it possible to do a systematic assessment of the diversity of available approaches. As is the case with any typology, the five models operate more as ideal types than perfect reflections of reality. Most community organizations are complex and multifaceted and cannot easily be placed into neatly defined boxes. However, almost all community organizing groups can be identified as being oriented primarily towards one of the models, or as an amalgam of two or more specific models, each of which contributes distinctive elements to the organization's approach. The five models thus provide an analytical framework that can be used for evaluating the vast majority of community organizing groups in existence today.

In order to assess the real-world consequences of these different models, I conducted an in-depth case study analysis of each approach. Given that variations exist *within* each model as well as between them, I studied two organizations for each model. The *primary* case study for each model is the closest reflection of the ideal type that I could find. The *secondary* case study serves as a foil, demonstrating the breadth of potential variations within the model itself. Comparing two cases for each model enabled me to separate the aspects of the organizations' work that flow from the principles of the particular models from those that relate to idiosyncratic elements such as individual personalities or neighborhood context.

For an ideal type analysis to work, the case study must serve as the literal embodiment of a particular model. To ensure that my case studies were accurate representations of the different models, I looked for organizations that were recognized and respected for their work by their peers. My goal was to identify organizations that were strong examples of each approach, without being organizational superstars. Each organization needed to reflect both the successes *and* the challenges experienced by organizations utilizing that particular approach.

To ensure parity in the breadth and scope of the case study organizations' work, I narrowed my selection to organizations that do neighborhood-based organizing in low- and moderate-income urban communities. Each organization works within a specific geographically defined "turf" to involve residents in solving local problems. The organizations don't start with a predetermined set of issues, but instead take their goals from the residents themselves. And they strive to engage residents and community members as leaders in achieving these goals.

All of the organizations, with the exception of two secondary cases, are located in Chicago in medium to large, economically and racially diverse urban neighborhoods. As the birthplace of modern community organizing, Chicago has a rich organizing legacy and is host to a wide range of organizing groups. Based on my own observations as well as extensive conversations with veteran organizers, funders, and academics around the city, I identified eight Chicago organizations as my principal case studies. For two of the models, however, Chicago offered a fairly narrow range of examples to choose from. To broaden the available options, I expanded my study to include two secondary cases from Portland, Oregon, a city with a legacy of neighborhood activism, but a somewhat different organizing environment.[1]

My analysis of the ten cases provides a foundation for making sense of the vast diversity of community organizing initiatives in existence today. The cases offer detailed insights into the philosophies and principles that characterize each model of organizing. And their experiences translating these principles into practice illuminate the nuances and complexities, as well as the potential real-world ramifications, of each approach. The ideal type analysis makes it possible to predict how the models' different principles, or "logics," are likely to affect the on-the-ground work of specific organizations, whether those organizations embody a single model or an amalgam of several models. And it provides a framework for evaluating which approach—

OVERVIEW OF THE MODELS AND CASE STUDIES

TABLE 1 The Models and Case Studies

Model	Primary Case Study	Secondary Case Study
Power-based	Westridge Organization of Neighbors (WON)	United Neighborhood Institutions of the Eastside (UNITE)
Community-building	Port Angeles Collaborating Together (PACT)	Central Orland Organizing Partnership (CO-OP)
Civic	Cranston Association of Neighbors (CAN)	Chicago Alternative Policing Strategy (CAPS)
Women-centered	Parents in Leadership and Organizing Together (PILOT)	Templeton Leadership Circle (TLC)
Transformative	Justice Action Group (JAG)	Center for Reflection, Education and Organizing (CREO)

Note: The order in which the models will be presented throughout the book will vary depending on the substance of the analysis. The order is never intended to reflect the relative worth of the different approaches, but instead is meant to facilitate comparisons among specific features of their approaches.

or combination of approaches — is likely to be most effective, given a specific context, constituency, or issue.

THE POWER-BASED MODEL

The power-based model is rooted in the theories of Saul Alinsky (1946, 1971) and has been the dominant approach to organizing in the United States for much of the past century.[2] At the core of the power-based philosophy of organizing is the belief that urban problems stem from residents' lack of power within the public sphere. Espousing a pluralist conception of the political system, the model's proponents believe that goods and resources are allocated through a public bargaining process in which competing interest groups battle it out for what they need. Within this system, decisions are made based on the raw calculus of power. As one power-based organizer put it, "If you don't have power you can not create change. It's not that the system isn't working, it's that the system is predicated on power."

Because low- and moderate-income residents aren't as organized as other interest groups and don't have access to traditional sources of power such as money, their neighborhoods are typically not well represented in the interest group process. Without the clout to fight for their interests at the public "bargaining table," the model's proponents argue, urban residents' priorities and needs are typically overlooked when decisions are made that affect their neighborhoods. To solve this problem, proponents say, urban residents must be organized into large, well disciplined "people's organizations" that can advance the community's interests in the public decision-making arena. As Alinsky explained, "A people can participate only if they have both the opportunity to formulate their program, which is their reason for participation, and a medium through which they can express and achieve their program. This can be done only through the building of real People's Organizations in which people band together, get to know one another, exchange points of view, and ultimately reach a common agreement which is the People's Program" (Alinsky 1946: 196).

Once the community is organized, proponents say, it must engage in public confrontation with powerholders in order to win a seat at the negotiating table. Arguing that change isn't possible without conflict, power-based organizations rely on aggressive, in-your-face tactics to pressure political officials and economic elites to accede to the community's demands. Through a public demonstration of their power-in-numbers, the organizations aim to become respected players within the interest group process in order to win material benefits for their communities.

Primary Case Study of the Power-Based Model: WON

The Westridge Organization of Neighbors (WON) is a community-based organization dedicated to improving the quality of life for residents of Chicago's Westridge neighborhood. Founded in 1978, the organization's mission is to fight for the community's interests within the public sphere by building a base of resident power in the neighborhood. In the words of one of the organization's staff, "Our sole purpose is to help people to build power in the neighborhood and to develop leadership in the neighborhood that will take a greater role in the public life of the neighborhood, that will have a greater voice in things that affect their everyday lives."

In order to accomplish this mission, WON has six paid organizers who operate behind-the-scenes to build the organization's membership and coordinate resident-driven action campaigns. The organizers knock on doors throughout the neighborhood to talk to residents, identify their interests, and recruit them to get involved. "The [purpose] is to get leadership from people that live here," one member explained. "To get them together and say what do you think is a problem, and then if you all agree, do you guys want to work on it." The issues that WON works on and its specific goals and priorities are determined entirely by the interests of the participating residents.

In recent years, WON's campaigns have included a battle to secure funding for new school construction to relieve overcrowding at the neighborhood's schools; a campaign to get the city to build a new public library for the neighborhood; a fight with the local alderman to improve the condition of the neighborhood's streets and alleys; a campaign to get the police department to respond to residents' complaints about gangs and drug dealing; and an effort to get the city to replace the neighborhood's aging sewer system.

In all of these campaigns, WON relies on public confrontation with elected officials and political leaders to achieve its goals. One organizer explained, "Our approach is that we believe that it's important that people are comfortable with aggression, people are comfortable with confrontation, as a means of building power. That's how, through conflict and confrontation, how we achieve real change."

WON is structured as a federation of eight neighborhood-based affiliates. Its membership represents a diverse cross-section of the Westridge community. The majority of the organization's members are Latino families, with smaller numbers of white ethnic and African American participants. WON's core membership includes approximately fifty leaders who are active participants in the organization's ongoing work. In addition, WON is able to turn out 150 to 750 residents for specific actions and public events.

WON is funded primarily through grants from local and national foundations; it also receives a small percentage of its budget from public contracts. It has historically supplemented these external funding sources by running bingo tables several times a week in neighborhoods around the city. The organization is closely affiliated with National People's Action, a national network of more than 300 grassroots organizations which provides its members with training materials, support, and technical assistance.

Secondary Case Study of the Power-based Model: UNITE

The United Neighborhood Institutions of the Eastside (UNITE) is an institutional-membership organization dedicated to building "a successful, multi-ethnic, mixed income community" on Chicago's East side. Founded in 1974, UNITE is composed of more than seventy institutions from within its geographic boundaries. As UNITE's director explained, "The organization is an organization of organizations. Its members are religious congregations, businesses, non-profit organizations, tenant associations, and ethnic mutual assistance associations in the community. The members pay dues . . . every year to belong."

UNITE's mission is to engage residents in the public sphere and to build their power to affect public decision-making about the issues that concern them. According to its director, UNITE works to "teach people the skills of public life, and to create environments in which people can . . . experience their own power, so that wherever they go, wherever they live, they can build relationships with others and act in a powerful way."

In order to achieve this mission, UNITE tries to bring together as many community members as possible into a unified bloc to engage in public action around issues of common concern. The organization has five full-time organizers who work behind the scenes to identify the interests and priorities of the member institutions and their constituents and to coordinate action campaigns to address these concerns. The organizers spend much of their time meeting with potential leaders, developing their skills, and engaging them in UNITE's work. Together, these leaders develop strategic campaigns to create change in the neighborhood by applying public pressure to local officials and power brokers.

UNITE's campaigns reflect the interests and priorities of its member institutions. Recent campaigns have included a battle to increase police accountability and stem police harassment of local youth; an effort to prevent gentrification by fighting for community control over local development dollars; a campaign to create a community oversight board for the local public aid office; an effort to secure public assistance for poor immigrants; and a campaign to win increased public funding for local youth recreation programs. Like WON, UNITE approaches these issues through public confrontation and negotiations with public officials.

UNITE's geographic area is extremely diverse, and UNITE's membership reflects this diversity. Each of the organization's institutional members represents anywhere from five to several hundred individuals who reside and work in the neighborhood. Consequently, UNITE as a whole represents thousands of people. The organization is able to turn out 150 to 1,000 people for public meetings and events, and it has more than fifty active leaders who are involved on an ongoing basis in decision-making, strategic planning, and action. These leaders include a mix of African Americans, whites, Latinos, and Asians, with a sizable number of recent immigrants from Africa, Eastern Europe, and Asia.

Like WON, UNITE is funded primarily through grants from private foundations. The organization eschews any government funding or support, but it supplements its foundation dollars with revenue from membership dues. With each of the seventy member organizations paying several hundred dollars annually in dues, this funding provides a valuable addition to UNITE's operating budget.

UNITE is a member of United Power, a regional coalition of more than 200 Chicago area institutions that is affiliated with the Industrial Areas Foundation (IAF). The IAF, a national network of institutional-membership organizations founded by Alinsky,[3] provides training to UNITE's key leaders and staff.

THE COMMUNITY-BUILDING MODEL

Whereas the power-based model focuses on building residents' clout within the public sphere, the community-building model focuses on strengthening the internal social and economic fabric of the neighborhood itself.[4] Community-building practitioners believe that the fundamental problem facing urban neighborhoods is their lack of internal capacity to address their own needs. This dynamic is attributed to the community's isolation from mainstream economic and political opportunity structures as well as the erosion of more traditional forms of social cohesion and connection in today's inner city.

In order to resolve this situation, the model's proponents argue, urban neighborhoods must rebuild themselves from within: "Socially atomized and increasingly cut off from centralized, unresponsive mainstream economic institutions, [urban] neighborhoods and their residents present a new challenge to organizers. It seems clear that new strategies must stress an organizing process that enhances and builds community, and that focuses on developing a neighborhood's own capacities to do for itself" (Kretzmann and McKnight 1984: 16).

Using an "asset-based" approach to development, community-building organizations work to build collaborative partnerships among the neighborhood's stakeholders in order to strengthen the community's internal capacity to solve its own problems. Every institution and organization with a stake in the neighborhood—nonprofits, businesses, banks, hospitals, public agencies, resident's associations, and churches—is seen as a potential source of assets and resources that can contribute to the creation of a healthier, more sustainable community. In order to develop a shared vision among these groups, community-building organizations engage in a comprehensive planning process to assess the overall assets and needs of the community. Based on this assessment, the partners develop a holistic plan for rebuilding the community's economic base and social infrastructure.

As an essential component of this process, the model's proponents argue, urban neighborhoods must develop consensual working partnerships with government officials and policymakers in order to leverage the resources and support necessary to achieve the community's goals. Whereas power-based organizations try to obtain influence in the public sphere by building and wielding clout, community-building organizations aim to gain local government support by presenting themselves as the legitimate representatives of the community as a whole. Emphasizing the breadth and diversity of their memberships, the organizations portray themselves as *the* voice of a unified community. And they point to the quality and technical merits of their comprehensive plans to demonstrate their legitimacy as the official policy-setting and planning bodies for their neighborhoods.

Primary Case Study of the Community-Building Model: PACT

Port Angeles Collaborating Together (PACT) is an institutional collaborative committed to the redevelopment of Chicago's Port Angeles neighborhood. PACT was created in 1993 when several local leaders, motivated by the opportunity to secure significant public resources for the neighborhood, brought together a group of local institutions and associations to develop an application for Federal Empowerment Zone designation.[5] In the process of preparing the application, the participating institutions developed a comprehensive plan for the neighborhood's redevelopment. Even though their Empowerment Zone application was ultimately unsuccessful, the participants decided to stay together to work on making their shared vision a reality.

PACT's mission is to strengthen Port Angeles' internal capacity and rebuild its economic base. The collaborative's leaders view the active involvement of all the neighborhood's institutions as a necessary prerequisite for achieving these goals. Thus, PACT's members include a wide array of institutions and organizations from within the neighborhood—social service agencies, community development organizations, businesses, hospitals, banks, block clubs, schools, and churches. More than eighty institutions are linked into PACT's network, with about thirty actively involved on an ongoing basis. As stated in PACT's comprehensive plan, "Successful community development relies on mobilizing the strengths of all players in a community. The traditional approach to revitalization of directing resources and services to externally defined problems has never adequately served our communities. The community building process must be driven from the inside, and leadership and control of planning and development efforts must be based within our neighborhoods."[6]

In order to accomplish this goal, PACT developed a comprehensive community plan based on a systematic assessment of the neighborhood's strengths and problems. The plan includes a wide array of programs and services designed to restore the community's overall heath and vitality while addressing residents' complex needs. "We have a holistic approach to solving the problems," one of PACT's organizers explained. "We really began to look at all the corners of a person's life to try to address the issues." At its core, the plan emphasizes the importance of connecting residents—and the community as a whole—to the mainstream economy. As PACT's president put it, "Economic development has to be a focus . . . [creating] more businesses and more bank loans and creating a thought in people that they want to be businessmen in the community."

While PACT's comprehensive strategies aim to address all the neighborhood's issues and problems, so far the organization's primary focus has been on issues relating to jobs and housing. Recent initiatives include an effort to acquire vacant lots throughout the neighborhood to use for affordable housing; an initiative to bring new retail and commercial establishments into the neighborhood; a program to assist local residents to become homeowners; and a youth mentoring and job training program. In all of these endeavors, PACT has developed strong partnerships with local government agencies as well as the private sector to provide the resources and support necessary to make the program a success.

Like the Port Angeles neighborhood itself, PACT's membership is predominately Latino, but it also includes a number of white and African American participants. PACT's active participants tend to be the staff and directors of its member institutions and thus are primarily middle-class professionals; the institutions themselves represent a wide spectrum of economic and social groups within the neighborhood.

PACT is funded through private foundations as well as government contracts and grants. It has five full-time staff who work with the collaborative's members to facilitate the planning and implementation of the partnership's projects.

Secondary Case Study of the Community-Building Model: CO-OP

The Central Orland Organizing Partnership (CO-OP) is a collaborative of several dozen institutions in Portland's Central Orland neighborhood. The partnership was founded in 1996 when a group of nine institutions joined together to apply for a State of Oregon grant for a comprehensive initiative to build the neighborhood's service infrastructure and social support networks. The application was successful, and the institutions built a formal collaborative structure to guide their joint project. Two years later, when the grant expired, the nine original members merged with another existing network of institutions to create a large, informal collaborative that includes a wide range of local stakeholders—social service agencies, community development corporations, residents' associations, schools, businesses, and local government agencies.

CO-OP's mission is to strengthen the health and vitality of the Central Orland neighborhood. Like PACT, CO-OP's members believe that to build a strong, self-sufficient community, the neighborhood's problems must be dealt with holistically. As explained in the partnership's publicity materials, CO-OP's mission is "to create an innovative mix of prevention-focused programs and support services to meet people where they are with the goal of increasing self-sufficiency. . . . The work of CO-OP strives toward comprehensiveness, weaving the strands of human services, community organizing, and community economic development together in service of individuals, families, and the neighborhood."

In order to achieve this vision, CO-OP brings together the neighborhood's stakeholders with partners from local government to, in the words of one participant, "provid[e] comprehensive wrap-around services, addressing the psychological, social, and economic needs of the community, and working together inter-agency to do that." By facilitating the development of joint ventures and a shared vision among these partners, CO-OP aims to maximize the community's existing assets and institutional resources. As one member explained, "We've gotten many players who wouldn't have even spoken to each other working together to try to address the needs of the community."

These collaborative projects include the development of a continuum of services designed to help residents secure living wage jobs; a neighbor-to-neighbor mentor program to assist former welfare recipients in entering the job market; a program to enable local residents to start their own home day-care programs; and a personal development program for teenage girls.

CO-OP's funding comes primarily from grants and contracts from state, county, and city government. In addition, many of the collaborative's programs and initiatives receive private foundation funding. CO-OP has one full-time staff person whose role is to coordinate the partnership and oversee project implementation.

THE CIVIC MODEL

Whereas the community-building model focuses on restoring the neighborhood's social and economic vitality, the civic model focuses on protecting the neighborhood's public order.[7] Civic organizations attribute the problems in urban neighborhoods to a breakdown of the traditional mechanisms for maintaining neighborhood stability and control. This breakdown, which is characterized by an absence of shared behavioral norms and ineffective monitoring of the neighborhood's public spaces, creates an atmosphere in which disorder thrives.

The model's proponents assert that in order to resolve this situation, residents must work together to reestablish the neighborhood's formal and informal mechanisms of social control. Blaming the decline of the neighborhood's *informal* social order on the disintegration of traditional neighborly relationships, civic organizations work to provide residents with opportunities to network and get to know their neighbors. The organizations sponsor informal gatherings and unstructured meetings where residents can share news and information, voice concerns, and develop strategies for tackling local problems. These strategies typically involve the use of organized peer pressure and hands-on voluntary activities to shore up the neighborhood's public order.

In addition to facilitating the development of informal social order in the neighborhood, civic organizations also work to mobilize the city's *formal* social control mechanisms—the police and the city services system—to address specific problems. Viewing city government as a technical and administrative apparatus that operates according to bureaucratic rules and procedures, the members try to access government services by working through officially designated channels. Participants monitor the neighborhood's streets and public spaces on an ongoing basis, submitting information and complaints about specific problems to the appropriate liaisons within particular city agencies and departments. By acting as the city's eyes and ears, they work to eliminate the signs of instability and disorder in the neighborhood.

Primary Case Study of the Civic Model: CAN

The Cranston Association of Neighbors (CAN) brings together the people who live, work, and own property in Chicago's Cranston neighborhood. CAN was founded in the late 1980s by a group of landlords and homeowners concerned about protecting their property values and quality of life in the face of increasing problems with crime and disrepair in the neighborhood. Over the years, the organization has continued to operate primarily as an association for property owners, though a few tenants and low-income residents also participate. CAN's mission, in the words of one participant, is "getting better city services, making the neighborhood safer. Our vision is improving the condition of properties in [the] neighborhood. Our mission is eliminating problems associated with landlords who don't screen their tenants and allow their property to be used for criminal purposes. . . . Everyone wants more police service, everybody wants the drug dealing to stop, everyone wants the buildings to be better."

In order to achieve its mission, the organization plays several inter-related roles in the neighborhood. First, CAN provides a forum for local residents and owners to meet and get to know one another. Every three months the organization holds an open meeting at the neighborhood's fieldhouse where residents and owners can connect with their neighbors and peers on an informal basis.

In addition to this relationship-building function, CAN offers participants a chance to meet with representatives from the city services system to share information about local problems and get updated on issues affecting the neighborhood. "One of the goals of the organization," CAN's president explained, "[is] to bring information in. So that people know what's going on, and so that we can get together and exchange information, whether it's where there are problems or what's happening in the community. Get the alderman's office in to report. Get various other organizations in. So that we know what's going on."

These exchanges usually center around issues of safety, the maintenance of public spaces, and municipal services. For example, in recent years, CAN has worked with the city's Department of Streets and Sanitation to address problems with potholes, missing street signs, and abandoned vehicles and buildings; it has worked with the Park District to improve the cleanliness and appearance of the neighborhood's parks and greenspaces; and it has helped the Building Department to monitor problem buildings and enforce city codes.

Beyond its efforts to get the city to respond to local problems, CAN enables neighbors to work together on an ad-hoc basis to address small problems affecting the neighborhood's appearance and quality of life. As one member explained, "We do a little bit with the beautification projects, you know, the tree planting, flower plantings in the corners, and clean up days— we have a couple of clean up days a year. People get out and they do things like painting the light poles and the sign posts that get scratched." Similarly, CAN's members try to improve the conditions of the neighborhood's apartment buildings and commercial areas by pressuring local landlords and business owners to abide by shared standards of conduct for building maintenance, tenant screening, and safety.

Unlike most of the other organizations in this study, CAN has no paid staff and no external funding. The members pass around a coffee can at each meeting to raise money for refreshments, photocopies, and other miscellaneous expenses. CAN has about thirty active members, though a core group of about five people do most of the behind-the-scenes work necessary to keep the organization running. Although the Cranston neighborhood is one of the most diverse in the city, CAN's membership is primarily white and middle class. However, the organization has recently begun to attract a growing number of African American property owners into its membership ranks.

Secondary Case Study of the Civic Model: CAPS

The Chicago Alternative Policing Strategy (CAPS) was founded in 1993 by the City of Chicago as part of its commitment to community-oriented policing. In order to facilitate communication between residents and police, the city created 279 new community organizations, one in every police beat in the city. Designed to strengthen the role of neighborhood residents in the police's crime-fighting efforts, the organizations provide a forum for residents and police to work in partnership to solve local problems.

My examination of the CAPS program focused on the CAPS organization located in the Cranston neighborhood. Considered by independent evaluators to be one of the best CAPS organizations in the city, Cranston CAPS has about thirty active participants, and a core group of about fifteen long-time members. Like CAN, the organization's participants tend to be both white and African American and include a disproportionate number of middle-class property owners compared to the overall demographics of the neighborhood.

The CAPS program's mission is to bring together residents, police, and other city service agencies to solve local problems affecting residents' safety and quality of life. As described in the city's publicity materials, CAPS "is a community-oriented philosophy of policing and crime prevention. With CAPS, the police, community and other government agencies work together to identify and solve neighborhood crime and disorder problems."

CAPS holds monthly meetings in which residents, police, and representatives from other city service agencies come together to share information and discuss problems and concerns. The meetings are widely publicized and are open to all residents of the beat. A local resident facilitates the meetings, and the police provide logistical and organizational support. CAPS encourages residents to serve as the police's "eyes and ears" in the neighborhood—monitoring local crime and safety problems on a day to day basis and then reporting their observations to the participating officers at the neighborhood's monthly meetings. This process keeps the police informed about residents' priorities and concerns, and it gives residents an opportunity to learn about how the city services system can be used to solve their specific problems.

In addition to these monthly information-sharing meetings, CAPS occasionally sponsors community activities such as safety marches and clean-ups. These activities are designed to strengthen the neighborhood's informal mechanisms of social control while building collegial relationships between residents and police.

All of the issues that the Cranston CAPS organization works on are directly related to public safety and crime. In recent years, the group has focused its attention on the problems of youth loitering, drug dealing, badly maintained apartment buildings, apartment buildings with problem tenants, irresponsible business owners, gang violence, public drinking, and issues related to traffic and parking.

THE WOMEN-CENTERED MODEL

The women-centered model of organizing extends women's traditional caretaking roles into broader community action to address the needs of children and families.[8] Building on traditions of "activist mothering" (Naples 1998) and "public homeplaces" (Belenky, Bond, and Weinstock 1997), the model challenges the traditional separation between the public and private spheres. Because the issues affecting families are typically defined as domestic problems to be addressed in the private sphere, the model's proponents argue, low-income women and their children are left to deal with their problems in isolation, without external support or public solutions. Similarly, even though women have historically played a central role in building communities, they have largely been excluded from formal leadership roles. As a result, the public and private institutions that serve families' needs—social services, schools, housing—frequently fail to take into account the unique interests and conditions of the families themselves when they design their services.

Proponents of the women-centered model suggest that if we are interested in building communities that are supportive of families' needs, then we must reconceptualize private household problems as public issues with public solutions. Women-centered organizations focus their work on issues associated with women's traditional maternal and domestic responsibilities—child care, parenting, housing, family safety, and education. Arguing that low-income women must be given the opportunity to develop a vision for their communities, as well as the public and private support to achieve this vision, the organizations nurture the development of women's collective leadership and voice within their neighborhoods. Because women have always worked behind the scenes to build stronger communities, the model's proponents suggest that if we support women's roles as active creators of public solutions, the entire community will benefit.

In order to achieve these goals, the women-centered model emphasizes the importance of creating safe, nurturing spaces where women can gather, build their leadership, and support one another's development. Building on the principles and techniques (though not necessarily the substantive objectives) of the women's movement, as well as traditions of women's communal support networks in communities of color, the organizations create small, intimate teams that operate more like support groups than formal organizations. Emphasizing that women cannot lead effectively if they are forced to deny their own needs, these teams combine a dual focus on individual growth and development with collective action for community change. "For community leadership to be real, women leaders have to get their own lives in order. Making your personal life fit with your desire to serve your community is often a problem. Women have to consider both what they want for themselves and what they want in the community" (National Congress of Neighborhood Women 1993: 149). Through personal sharing, careful listening, and ongoing relationship-building, the members of women-centered teams support one another at a personal level while working collectively to develop hands-on projects and initiatives to achieve their community vision.

Once the neighborhood's women have developed their own vision for the community, women-centered organizations work to build supportive partnerships between these women and public and private institutions and organizations that can help them to achieve their goals. These partnerships are rooted in face-to-face interpersonal relationships between the team's members and the staff and administrators of the partner entities. Through the creation of collaborative programs and services with these entities, the women-centered organizations strengthen the community's capacity to address local families' problems and needs.

Primary Case Study of the Women-Centered Model: PILOT

Parents in Leadership and Organizing Together (PILOT) was founded in 1994 by a group of veteran Chicago organizers interested in making community organizing more "family focused." Frustrated by the inability of traditional organizing models to address the particular needs of women and children, PILOT's founders adopted an approach that focuses on bringing low-income families into the public sphere to solve problems related to family life.

PILOT's mission, in the words of its director, is "to strengthen the voice of parents in communities in order to create and build more family friendly, family supportive communities." In order to accomplish this mission, PILOT reaches out to low-income parents—primarily mothers—in the places where they naturally gather—public schools, day care centers, and youth programs. In order to engage these parents in public action, PILOT begins by giving them the tools and support they need to address their personal problems. As one of the organization's founders explained, "I was trained if somebody was wrestling with learning English or wrestling with they desperately needed a job or their kid was in a gang, whatever, you know we pretty much told them to go home and get their life together and come back. We didn't want to be messing with them, and we just cut off that whole level. . . . [But at PILOT] we try to take a much more holistic approach, and so we start out our [leadership] training with personal goals."

With the support of a small team of other parents, participants work on their personal goals and development. In the process, the participants not only gain important problem-solving skills, they also discover the public dimensions of their private troubles. One of PILOT's founders explained, "Every mom thinks not finding a safe place for my kid after school so I can go back to work is *my* problem. And that's sort of the message they get from many sources. But when they're sitting around talking about how that's *my* problem, my ten year old is being recruited by the gang, and then some other mom and some other mom says it, the question [becomes] how to move your personal and family goals as a group."

Once they discover that many of their personal troubles are common problems that may have public solutions, the parents begin to work on tackling their shared goals through community action. Through partnerships with local institutions and agencies, the parent teams create hands-on, resident-driven programs and services to address their needs. In recent years, the parent teams' campaigns have included the development of parent patrols at local schools to keep children safe; creating community centers in the schools to provide adult education and English classes; coordinating community social events and family activity nights; and the development of parent rooms and parent volunteer opportunities within the schools.

Most of PILOT's participants are low-income African American and Latina mothers from several different neighborhoods around the city. Each participant is connected to a small team of three to fifteen parents within her school or institution. In addition, PILOT brings together parent teams from around the city to work on joint events and projects on an ad hoc basis.

PILOT is funded by local and national foundations and government grants. The organization has three full-time organizers as well as a number of community-based partner organizations that provide additional staff support to local projects. PILOT's organizers serve as coordinators of the leadership development and team building process, and they help to facilitate participants' engagement in community-level action.

Secondary Case Study of the Women-Centered Model: TLC

The Templeton Leadership Circle (TLC) is a women's community development organization dedicated to improving the quality of life for families in Portland's Templeton neighborhood. The organization was founded in 1989 by a diverse group of low-income and professional women concerned about the lack of affordable housing for women and families in the community. Some members had experienced affordable housing problems first hand, while others had become committed to the issue through their jobs as case workers, social service providers, and realtors. All agreed that the city lacked effective programs and services to meet the particular needs of low-income families, especially female-headed households.

TLC's founders believed that by fostering the development of women's voices and leadership, they would be able to build a more livable, family-oriented community. As explained in the organization's publicity materials, "Many neighborhood women have been involved in some form of community development all their lives due to their concern for their families and homes. At the heart of the Templeton Leadership Circle's work is a belief that the way to improve a neighborhood is through enhancing and expanding this participation of local women in community development by giving them the support they need to develop into neighborhood leaders."

To achieve this vision, TLC created a leadership support model drawing on techniques from the women's movement and the twelve-step movement— interpersonal sharing, relationship-building, and structured conversations. Through these techniques, TLC developed a core group of local women leaders who began working together to tackle the neighborhood's housing-related problems. Drawing on the input and vision of the neighborhood's residents, plus the support of external partners and institutions, the women worked to rehabilitate several distressed apartment complexes in the neighborhood to create affordable rental housing. Designed to meet the unique needs of women and children, the housing includes play spaces for children, on-site day care, family gardens, and places where parents can gather.

In addition to its affordable housing work, TLC coordinates a variety of other resident-controlled community development projects in the neighborhood— foot patrols; community social events such as annual festivals, children's carnivals, and potlucks; volunteer-run educational and recreational programs for youth; and physical revitalization projects to improve the condition and appearance of the neighborhood's buildings and public spaces.[9]

TLC's membership composition reflects the diversity of the Templeton neighborhood. The organization has a core leadership of about twenty-five active members, with an equal mix of African Americans and whites, and a wide range of economic backgrounds and ages. Although the organization doesn't exclude men from participation, almost all of TLC's members and leaders are women.

Like PILOT, TLC's funding base comes from both private foundations and local government grants and contracts. TLC supplements this external funding with money raised through membership dues and fundraising drives. The organization has a small organizing staff, with two organizers plus several other staff members who focus on the technical aspects of the group's housing development work.

TLC is affiliated with the National Congress of Neighborhood Women (NW), a national network of neighborhood-based women's community development organizations. NW provides TLC's members with training, support, and techniques for leadership development, team building, and meeting facilitation.

THE TRANSFORMATIVE MODEL

The transformative model is often presented by academics as a more radical alternative to power-based organizing (e.g. Stoecker 1994; Fisher and

Kling 1990).[10] The model's core precept is that the problems in urban neighborhoods are symptoms of broader systemic injustices. Like the power-based model, the transformative model's theory of change emphasizes urban residents' lack of power within the public sphere. But while proponents of the power-based model assert that the political system basically works as long as residents are sufficiently organized to participate in it, the transformative model's proponents believe the system itself is at the core of the problem. Arguing that society's dominant institutions are designed to promote and protect the interests of a powerful elite, the model's proponents suggest that these institutions are fundamentally disempowering of low-income and working-class urban residents.

In contrast to the power-based model's conception of the public sphere as a pluralist system in which residents can battle it out with other interest groups for a piece of the pie, proponents of the transformative model believe that power operates in much more subtle ways that make this conception of the public sphere unrealistic. They argue that unequal power relations permeate all aspects of society—our culture, our educational system, the media, our political system—creating a self-reinforcing web of inequality. The way the public sphere is structured—even our perceptions of our own interests—are all shaped by the interests of those in power. Thus, proponents argue, long before interest groups even enter the political arena, the public decision-making process is shaped, both directly and indirectly, by our society's underlying power dynamics.

Given this theoretical framework, the model's proponents argue that urban problems can be solved only through a radical restructuring of dominant political, social, and economic institutions. Gary Delgado, founder of the Center for Third World Organizing, contrasts this approach with the traditional power-based agenda[11]: "As community organizers what are we trying to do? Are we trying to change the size of the negotiating table, add a chair or two, or saw it up and see that everyone gets a fair piece? Or, are we saying, 'Wait a minute, the table is in a room, the room is in a house, and the house occupies a particular space in relation to the city, country, planet, and universe?' " (Delgado 1998: 18).

In order to create systemic change, the model's proponents argue, community organizing needs to challenge society's taken-for-granted ideological frameworks and introduce new conceptual categories for making sense of lived experience. Transformative organizations use popular education and reflection to foster the development of critical consciousness among urban residents and to develop an alternative vision for society. Viewing their work within the context of an overarching social justice movement, the organizations aim to build the ideological foundations within the neighborhood for the development of a broad-based movement for change. And they aim to engage residents in direct action to achieve their alternative vision within the community.

Primary Case Study of the Transformative Model: JAG

The Justice Action Group (JAG) is an organization of tenants and progressive activists in Chicago's Dalton neighborhood. Founded in 1973, JAG works to address injustice within the local community while simultaneously building a long-term foundation for broader systemic change. JAG's leaders view the organization's work as part of an ongoing effort to build a broad-based social justice movement in the United States: "We lack a strong progressive movement on the national level," writes the organization's president. "Those of us who are active in local communities are left with the responsibility for generating a vision and charting a course for change that can lay the foundation for a more just and sustainable society."

In order to accomplish this mission, JAG has focused most of its recent work on challenging the dominant political and economic paradigms guiding urban development in Chicago. As JAG's director explained, "The vision we're trying to create in Dalton is something where market forces are not the principal determining factor of what happens or doesn't happen in the neighborhood, and that the community should be able to challenge those and create structures of some kind . . . that check those forces." Given the taken-for-granted status of the dominant paradigms, much of JAG's work focuses on building residents' critical thinking skills through popular education and reflection. "What we're trying to do is to first try to get a core group of leadership that at least has the chance to think through what some of those issues are and what they mean locally," JAG's director explained. "People, I think, for the most part, have a very clear gut sense of there's something wrong here. But without having the chance to process that and figure out what really happens in the real world under certain standard policy prescriptions, then they're not equipped to say 'no, this really is a problem' and look for something different."

In addition to engaging residents in popular education and reflection, JAG organizes residents to take on local issues through direct action campaigns. JAG's staff and leaders knock on doors in low-income apartment buildings throughout the neighborhood to help the tenants organize for better treatment by their landlords. And the organization frequently works with groups of tenants and small-business owners at risk of being displaced by condo conversions, corporate development projects, or government-sponsored revitalization initiatives.

In recent years, JAG's campaigns have included an effort to fight gentrification by creating an alternative platform for local development; a battle with the alderman and private developers to prevent the conversion of several affordable apartment buildings into condominiums; a campaign to save a local small-business incubator from being torn down to make room for a firehouse; a fight to save a neighborhood job training center from displacement by a major grocery store chain; and an effort to impose greater resident control over the redevelopment of a major commercial artery in the neighborhood.

JAG's funding comes primarily from small local and national foundations. The organization's budget is smaller than most of the other organizations in this study; thus it has only one full time staff member who serves as both the director and the lead organizer. JAG also has a core of about thirty active leaders who do much of the behind-the-scenes work to keep the organization running, as well as about 250 dues-paying members who attend major meetings and events. These members include a diverse mix of both low-income and middle class residents. The low-income participants are primarily African American and Latina, while the middle class participants tend to be white progressive activists.

Secondary Case Study of the Transformative Model: CREO

The Center for Reflection, Education, and Organizing (CREO[12]) provides popular education and literacy training to recent Latino immigrants in several Chicago neighborhoods. The organization was founded in 1972 by a group of priests, educators, and activists involved in the Latin American solidarity movement. The group was inspired by the work of Paulo Freire, whose pedagogical theories emphasize the interconnection between education and social change. As a written account of the organization's history explains, "[Freire's] work in Brazil and Chile demonstrated that illiterate peasants could quickly learn to read and write, if the words they learned were charged with political significance and if literacy was accompanied by land reform and other improvements in economic and political conditions. In other words, adult basic education could best succeed when it was consciously a political act, the aim of which was to transform society." CREO uses popular education to develop Latino immigrants' critical consciousness with the goal of engaging them in public action for social change.

Whereas Freire worked through the medium of literacy instruction, CREO uses English as a Second Language (ESL) instruction as the vehicle for its popular education work. In the process of teaching residents basic conversational and written English, CREO's staff encourage participants to write and reflect about their experiences. The goal is to get participants to begin to critically assess their own lives and then, through discussion and analysis, to develop a deeper understanding of the social structural underpinnings of their experiences. As one of CREO's staff put it, "Literacy for us is not necessarily the skills to read the written word. . . . Literacy for us is the ability to read, [yes], but the world, not the word only. . . . We want [our participants] to read the political fabric of the community, the social construct of the neighborhood, so that they can understand it better and transform it to their satisfaction."

Once participants have reflected on their experiences, CREO's goal is to translate the residents' newly honed critical thinking skills into campaigns for social and political change. However, in practice, most of the organization's time and energy is absorbed in the popular education process itself. Despite its intentions of linking education and action in a mutually reinforcing cycle, CREO's work actually involves few community-based projects or campaigns (a dynamic that will be discussed in detail in later chapters[13]).

CREO works in various low-income and working-class Latino neighborhoods throughout the city. All of its participants and members are first-generation Latinos who get involved with the organization primarily to learn English and gain literacy skills. CREO recruits the participants from public schools, churches, and other places where recent immigrants gather. Participants are clustered in small learning circles of five to fifteen people, and CREO works with about a hundred participants at any given time.

CREO's funding comes primarily from state literacy grants as well as some private foundations. It has eight staff, both full-time and part-time, who act as facilitators of the popular education process.

TABLE 2 Models of Community Organizing

Model and Case Studies	Theory of Urban Change	Organizing the Community	Impacting the Public Sphere
Power-based model *Westridge Organization of Neighbors (WON)* *United Neighborhood Institutions of the Eastside (UNITE)*	BUILD POWER: Urban neighborhood problems stem from the community's lack of power within the political decision-making process. Solution is to build the community's clout so that its interests are better represented within the pluralist public sphere	PEOPLE'S ORGANIZATION: Build large, formal, highly disciplined "people's" organizations to fight for the community's interests in the public sphere	CONFLICT & CONFRONTATION: Use conflict and confrontation to demonstrate residents' power and pressure political and economic powerholders to concede to the community's demands
Community-building model *Port Angeles Collaborating Together (PACT)* *Central Orland Organizing Partnership (CO-OP)*	REBUILD SOCIAL FABRIC: Urban neighborhood problems stem from the deterioration of the community's social and economic infrastructure. Solution is to rebuild the community from within by mobilizing its assets and connecting it to the mainstream economy	COLLABORATIVE PARTNERSHIP: Build broad collaborative partnerships of diverse neighborhood "stakeholder" groups, including non-profits, businesses, residents' associations, and government	LEGITIMACY & COLLABORATION: Strive to influence public decision-making through consensual partnerships with government. Goal is to be recognized as the legitimate representative of the community as a whole
Civic model *Cranston Association of Neighbors (CAN)* *Chicago Alternative Policing Strategy (CAPS)*	RESTORE SOCIAL ORDER: Urban neighborhood problems stem from social disorder and instability within the community. Solution is to restore and maintain the neighborhood's stability by activating both formal and informal mechanisms of social control	INFORMAL FORUM: Create informal, unstructured forums for neighbors to meet one another, exchange information, and problem solve	ACCESSING EXISTING CHANNELS: Use official, bureaucratic channels for citizen interaction with local government to get the city services system to respond to neighborhood problems. Interact with city services personnel on an individual to individual basis

TABLE 2 Models of Community Organizing *(continued)*

Model and Case Studies	Theory of Urban Change	Organizing the Community	Impacting the Public Sphere
Women-centered model *Parents in Leadership &* *Organizing Together (PILOT)* *Templeton Leadership Circle (TLC)*	LINK PUBLIC & PRIVATE SPHERES: Urban neighborhood problems stem from the fact that the institutions at the core of community life aren't responsive to the vision and needs of women and families. Solution is to reconceptualize private household problems as public issues with collective solutions, and to build women's leadership roles within the community	SUPPORT TEAM: Create small teams modeled on a support group structure. Provide safe, nurturing spaces where residents can gather, provide mutual support, and build shared leadership	INTERPERSONAL RELATIONSHIPS: Seek to build face-to-face relationships with the staff and administrators of public institutions in order to make programs and services more responsive to the needs of families
Transformative model *Justice Action Group (JAG)* *Center for Reflection, Education* *& Organizing (CREO)*	STRUCTURAL CHANGE: Urban neighborhood problems are the symptoms of unjust economic and political institutions. Solution is to challenge the existing institutional arrangements in order to create a more equitable society	SOCIAL MOVEMENT: Develop the ideological foundations within the neighborhood for the emergence of a broad-based movement for social change	CREATING ALTERNATIVE FRAMEWORKS: View the public sphere as dominated by institutions that systematically disempower low-income residents. Seek to alter the dominant ideological frameworks and to change the terms of the public debate

PART II
ORGANIZING THE COMMUNITY

CHAPTER 3

BUILDING INDIVIDUAL CAPACITY: DEVELOPING LOCAL LEADERS

NTIL CARRIE Miller met Matt Galloway, a staff organizer for the Westridge Organization of Neighbors (WON), she had never considered getting involved in her community: "I was always brought up never to get involved—don't do anything, don't say anything. It's not your place." But over the years, Carrie, who lives in a small bungalow near the canning factory where she works, had seen the neighborhood decline. When Matt knocked on her door to talk to her about the community, she was feeling frustrated and ready to do something. "I was tired of seeing the trash in the alleys, not in the garbage cans. The rats in the alleys, the kids hanging out on the street corners. I was tired of seeing all of that and I wanted to see what I could do to be a part of it and change it."

Carrie joined WON's campaign to improve safety and city services in her neighborhood. She was feisty and articulate about the neighborhood's problems but skeptical that anything she could do would really make a difference. But after several months of formal leadership training and one-on-one mentoring, she decided that she had both the right and the power to fight for her interests: "Going through school they always told you, 'don't step out of line, do what you're told, he is an authority figure, you're just a woman, . . . you have no college education, you shut up and don't do anything.' And that is what you're taught all your life—don't do anything, don't say anything. And the training [WON] teach[es] you, the line is drawn in the sand. You've got to cross it or you're never going to get anywhere."

During her first year working with WON, Carrie became a confident, powerful leader. As Matt recounted, she not only learned to stand up to authority figures, she demanded their respect as well:

Before getting involved in our organization, you know, . . . [she] never really thought that her voice—nobody gave a shit what she had to say. But now, this woman, after being involved for a year with our organization ran negotiations with [the] Deputy [Police] Chief, one of the top police officials in the city. And we're sitting in these negotiations, the guy's half an hour late, and Carrie is chairing and she starts off by scolding him, saying "you know we all took a half day off work to be with you, and you can't even be on time. Do you not respect us?" This is someone who when she first started working with the organization, wouldn't do anything but sit at a sign-in table and sign people in as they walked in the door [to a meeting].

Transforming residents like Carrie into strong leaders is one of WON's primary goals: "I think that's the greatest strength of our organization," says Matt. "We're about developing leadership and that lasts forever. Even if Carrie Miller quits this organization or moves somewhere else, . . . it doesn't matter. The experience of being part of this organization has changed her in a better way."

The development of skilled, self-confident civic leaders who can play an active role in public life is an essential prerequisite for a strong democracy. Political theorists have long recognized the important role of voluntary organizations as schools for democracy (Tocqueville 1971; Bellah et. al. 1985; Putnam 1995, 2000), but little attention has been paid to the specific mechanisms through which the organizations fulfill this role. While academic studies consistently show a connection between organizational membership and strong citizenship skills, exactly how and why this relationship exists has been less clear. Theorists typically conclude that residents become effective leaders simply through the experience of working with others on shared goals. In reality, however, such a passive process of skill acquisition has a limited ability to build residents' capacities as public actors. As Carrie Miller's story shows, developing residents into strong leaders doesn't just happen by default; it takes an intensive process of recruitment, training, mentoring, and support.

The organizations in this study utilize a wide array of well-theorized techniques for building residents' leadership skills. Each model is characterized by a distinct set of theories about what leadership is, how to develop it, and exactly which residents are best suited to becoming leaders in the public sphere. If we are interested in strengthening democratic participation in urban neighborhoods, it is important to examine the potential contributions and limitations of these different approaches.

THE POWER-BASED MODEL OF LEADERSHIP DEVELOPMENT: BUILDING SELF-CONFIDENT RESIDENTS INTO STRONG PUBLIC ACTORS

For power-based organizations like WON, the development of strong, outspoken, publicly active leaders is a top priority. Power-based organizations work hard to identify residents who, like Carrie, may have little experience in public life, but who are energetic, articulate, and interested in taking on a leadership role in the community. The organizations invite these residents to participate in an intensive leadership development process focused on making them into strong public speakers and political strategists with a sophisticated understanding of the dynamics of power.

Intensive one-on-one relationships like the one between Matt and Carrie lie at the core of the power-based model's leadership development process. Power-based organizations draw a clear distinction between the roles of paid staff "organizers" who are typically educated, middle-class idealists from outside the community, and neighborhood "leaders"—low-income and working-class residents who get involved out of a concern for their neighborhood. The power-based organizer's primary mandate is to recruit and train local residents to become skilled community leaders. While the organizers work behind-the-scenes to provide training and support, the neighborhood leaders serve as the public voice and primary decision-makers for the organization.

The power-based model's leadership development process begins with extensive one-on-one outreach to neighborhood residents and community members. Through informal conversations about local problems and concerns like the one that initially brought Matt and Carrie together, the power-based organizers meet with hundreds of residents in an effort to identify people who can be cultivated as local leaders. In individual membership organizations like WON, this outreach process is accomplished through door-knocking: organizers systematically knock on all the doors within a specific geographic area and engage residents in half-hour conversations about their interests and concerns. For institutional membership organizations like the United Neighborhood Institutions of the Eastside (UNITE), these conversations take place in one-on-one meetings and "house meetings" held on-site with the constituents of their member institutions.

Throughout these interactions, the organizers are on the lookout for residents who fit their image of a potential leader. As Bill, one of UNITE's organizers, explained, "I'm looking for somebody that wants to be a leader. Someone who is committed to their own organization but can also see beyond that . . . with a bit of vision for what they'd like to see happen. . . . I'm not looking for people who have perfect, polished public speaking skills. I'm looking for someone with enthusiasm, energy and commitment. A lot of our one-on-ones and house meetings are sort of fishing expeditions looking for those people."

Once they have identified these potential leaders, the power-based organizers begin to develop ongoing relationships with them through weekly visits, phone calls, and one-on-one meetings. At any given time, Bill and Matt try to maintain intensive one-on-one mentoring relationships with ten to twenty emerging leaders. The organizers provide ongoing coaching and support to help the leaders hone their skills and gain increasing self-confidence.

Once power-based organizers have started mentoring a potential leader, they look for opportunities for that leader to expand her skills. Inexperienced participants are often only willing to do small tasks like staffing a sign-in table or handing out leaflets. The organizers challenge these new recruits to take on increasingly difficult roles until they are confidently engaged in levels of leadership that they may have never thought possible. As one emerging WON leader put it, "When they spot somebody who looks like they're involved, like they're not afraid, like they're going to be in it for the long haul, they'll gently start moving them into positions of chairing a small meeting or speaking somewhere, just having some kind of speaking role somewhere, so it kind of builds up confidence and gives them a feel for what's going on."

Throughout this process, the organizers work to ensure that the leaders are successful in their new roles by providing them with the necessary technical and logistical support. While neighborhood residents are expected to fulfill all the public roles in the organization, such as chairing meetings, representing the organization to the media, speaking in public, and interacting with politicians, the organizers support this work by typing meeting agendas and committee minutes, writing press releases, and briefing the leaders on essential information. One of UNITE's leaders explained,

> The organizers help leaders. They would help them plan the agenda for a meeting, but the leaders chair the meeting. It's not staff driven. I don't like to go to a meeting and see the organizers talk too much, because that means there's something wrong. The leaders should pick the issue, the organizers should ask them questions that help them clarify. The leaders should also be the ones that speak at meetings, particularly when we go to meet with people from the outside, public officials. Because, if there's nobody who's willing to speak on it, then it must not be that important if you have to have a paid organizer talk.

This process is highly effective in developing members' skills and confidence as public actors. For example, UNITE's Edna Davis didn't have much experience chairing meetings or speaking in front of large groups, and the very thought of it scared her. Bill, UNITE's organizer, saw her leadership potential and began encouraging her to take on increasingly challenging roles within the organization. With his support and guidance, Edna felt comfortable facing these new challenges:

> They praise you. They put you out on front street. They make you do things that you really didn't know you could do, but they give you the encouragement to do it, and the support and the manpower and the research. They won't let you go out there naked. They make sure you're fully dressed for the cause. If you need a shield of armor, [they] make sure you have that. Make sure you're prepared for whatever they're trying to get you to do. . . . Sometimes Bill will come to me and say, "I want you to chair this meeting," and I'm like, "uh, I don't think I can do it." He's like, "yes you can." They give you that encouragement and make you see that you do have the skills within you. They make you look at yourself and gain confidence in yourself. . . . Sometimes Bill will see potential in you that you really don't see yourself, but because he's been doing this for so long he can recognize the fact that you can do it. . . . And it's been successful, because the more you do it, the less you feel anxious about doing it.

Several months after she started working one-on-one with Bill, Edna was co-chairing the meetings for one of UNITE's issue committees. Soon she had developed enough confidence and skill to chair a large public meeting of more than a hundred people. And, at UNITE's annual convention, with Bill's encouragement and support, Edna spoke in front of an audience of almost a thousand people.

In addition to developing residents' skills as public speakers, power-based organizations train their leaders to be sophisticated political strategists. They accomplish this more advanced level of training primarily through formal workshops that provide leaders with an in-depth understanding of power, city politics, and how to intervene effectively in the public arena. UNITE and WON's leadership workshops include sessions about the differences between organizing and other forms of public action, how to identify political powerholders' self-interests, how to build and wield power, and how to negotiate successfully for political concessions. A primary goal of the trainings is to challenge people to think more pragmatically about issues of conflict and confrontation.

WON's Carrie Miller described these workshops as one of the most important parts of her development as a leader: "They try to teach you all the tactics that [the alderman] and everybody else throws at you—that you are not to step out of your place, missy, you just remember that. And they teach you to go beyond that—you are no different than me, I'm the one that put you in there, mister. And they give you that confidence of this is your community. You have to speak up and do what you have to in order to regain the community."

The organizers work closely with leaders to apply what they learn in the workshops to their on-the-ground campaigns. Prior to every community meeting or event, WON and UNITE's organizers meet with small groups of emerging leaders to prepare them for their public leadership roles. As part of this process, the organizers often conduct elaborate role-playing exercises to hone leaders' negotiating skills. They also work with leaders to carefully analyze logistical details such as how to arrange the seating at negotiating meetings in order to give the leaders more control, how to handle disruptive audience members at public events, and the choreography of public protests.

The following story told by one of WON's leaders provides a vivid illustration of this highly disciplined planning process:

> I can tell you just from one meeting we had, it's so impressive, it was the [Department] of Education meeting in Washington D.C. with Secretary Riley. We were locked in the room for about six and a half hours just getting ready for that meeting. . . . We just hammered that, role played it, went back and forth with it, did it each way we could or thought it was going to happen. Sure enough, the next day it happened just like we thought it would. . . . [Riley's] staff was ready to tear us up, because that's what everyone that we hold meetings with tries to do—tear us up, thinking that we're not prepared. . . . And we were so well organized. We were looking at each other with smiling faces, and their staff was like "wow, these guys did their job."

Another important component of power-based organizations' leadership development work involves training experienced leaders to support and mentor the organizations' newer members. For example, some of UNITE's long-time leaders told me that they try to defer to newer leaders in committee discussions: "Those of us who have been leaders for a long time, we take someone under our wing and develop them, and not be so strong out there [ourselves] all the time. To make sure they know they have that equal voice . . . just try to pull people in. . . . So they can have ownership and take it over, and then we can foster their development that way." Similarly, whenever emerging WON leaders appeared nervous or flustered in their public speaking roles, the organization's more experienced leaders stepped in with loud cheers of encouragement.

The results of the power-based organizations' intensive leadership development process are impressive. Both WON and UNITE have cadres of skilled and articulate leaders at their helms. And because of their continuous efforts to identify, recruit, and train new leaders, the organizations' leadership ranks are constantly being expanded and replenished. This process ensures the development of a broad, diverse organizational leadership base and a wide pool of potential leaders throughout the neighborhood.

For participants in this process, the experience is life-changing. For example, longtime WON leader Lizzie Snowden said that ever since her first public speaking role at a meeting on school reform, she had gotten enormous satisfaction from her twenty-plus years of involvement with the organization:

> When I found out the difference that little old me could make, and I'm sitting here with professors, the heads of the school system, and all these big shots. And all these people have B.A., M.S., Ph.D. after their name. And I graduated from Mercy High School, and these people are listening to me. What I'm saying is making an impact on these people, they care what I say and they're listening in order to achieve some kind of change. That's a pretty remarkable feeling. It's a pretty remarkable thing when you get to that point. Yeah, it gives you gratification. It fulfills a certain part of everybody's life.

Even though she first got involved in the community because she was concerned about educational opportunities for her young children, Lizzie remained actively involved in WON long after her children graduated from high school. She says that the opportunity to play a leadership role in the community gave meaning to her life that had not been there before.

The power-based model's leadership development methods are among the most effective and successful of all the models of organizing. However, the model has also been criticized for its tendency to "cream" the urban population by working with residents who already have certain baseline leadership skills. Because the leadership development process begins with a systematic effort to identify and recruit residents who demonstrate "leadership potential," power-based organizations end up working primarily with residents who are already outspoken, self-confident, and interested in taking on a leadership role in their communities. This leaves out the vast majority of low-income and working-class neighborhood residents, many of whom would never think of themselves as potential leaders and often lack the necessary self-confidence and verbal fluency to pursue a leadership role in the public sphere. While such residents can participate as "seat warmers" (as some WON members called them) at the organizations' public meetings and events, they are not drawn into public leadership roles or given the benefits of intensive one-on-one mentoring.

In most power-based organizations, this approach results in a distinctive, two-tiered membership composition. At the bottom tier are "members" who are recruited to attend public meetings, rallies, and events. These people are drawn by concern for the issues at hand, but they are not targeted as potential leaders. Instead, they serve as supporters, boosting the power and legitimacy of the organizations through their presence. Both WON and UNITE are capable of drawing hundreds of these supporters to public events. At the second tier is a much smaller cadre of skilled and experienced leaders. In organizations like WON and UNITE, this group numbers between thirty and fifty people.

Articulating the logic behind this approach, Carrie Miller argued, "You can't pull a wall flower out and make a leader if that person is terrified to speak in front of people. There's no way that will be possible. Either you've got it or you don't have it." However, critics suggest that while writing off the majority of urban residents as "wall flowers" enables the power-based groups to streamline their leadership development process, it also relegates far too many people to the sidelines of public life.

This criticism has fueled the adoption of a number of alternative approaches to leadership development within the organizing field. Among the most successful of these alternatives has been the leadership development work of women-centered organizations.

THE WOMEN-CENTERED MODEL OF LEADERSHIP DEVELOPMENT: BRINGING LOW-INCOME RESIDENTS INTO PUBLIC LIFE FOR THE FIRST TIME

When Angela Turner first met Gina Will, a community organizer for Parents In Leadership and Organizing Together (PILOT), Angela was a shy mother of three who had spent her entire adult life focused on her children's needs. At age thirty-six, Angela had been a single mother and public aid recipient for more than a decade. With limited work experience and no high school diploma, she felt qualified for little else besides being a full-time mom. When her youngest child started school, however, she suddenly found herself with time on her hands, and decided to try volunteering at her children's school.

Gina invited Angela to participate in a series of leadership development workshops being offered for parents at the school. The workshops were aimed at getting parents involved as volunteers in the classrooms, so Angela decided to give it a try. As an African American living in a predominately

Latino neighborhood, Angela had never really gotten to know her neighbors and had always felt disconnected from community life. But as she began to interact with the other parents she started to discover how much they all had in common.

Looking back, Angela describes PILOT's workshop series as the beginning of a dramatic transformation in her life. Not only did she start to build relationships within her community, she began to rethink her own sense of identity. After spending her entire adult life focused on the needs of her children, the workshops gave her an opportunity to start thinking about her own goals and needs.

> I really don't know where I would be if I hadn't went through the training. So it has had a huge, huge impact on my life. . . . Everything parents are supposed to do is supposed to revolve around their kids. . . . What was really strong for me was that . . . people were saying it was okay to think about yourself. . . . Just hearing those words. Just hearing that it was okay to think about myself for a change, that it was okay to want something for myself, really impacted me a lot.

For the first time, Angela began to develop a personal vision that went beyond her role as a mother, and she started to acquire the skills and the confidence necessary to take an active role in shaping her own future and that of her community.

In contrast to the power-based model's tendency to "cream," women-centered organizations typically focus their attention on residents who have little confidence in their own voices and little prior interest in being involved in public life. PILOT's participants usually have few connections to mainstream institutions and organizations, and in many cases rarely left their houses before getting involved. As one PILOT organizer explained, "One of the differences I think from most organizing that I've seen . . . is that we're working with very low income people, . . . the majority of whom do not see themselves as community leaders when they first come into our meetings. . . . It's a major transformation in how they see themselves and their ability to take action in the community."

PILOT draws these residents into public life by emphasizing the interconnection between personal and public issues. Facing problems like unemployment, illiteracy, domestic violence, and gang-affected children, PILOT's participants rarely see public action as an effective way to address their concerns. They tend to view their problems as personal matters with private solutions, and they struggle in isolation to deal with them. PILOT's organizers work to help participants to develop skills and tools to address these issues at a personal level, but they also encourage them to see the links between these seemingly private issues and their public dimensions.

This approach to leadership, while not explicitly feminist in content, draws on the methods and techniques developed by the women's movement of the 1960s—support groups, relationship building, and using personal sharing to explore the linkages between the personal and the political. These methods are also rooted in a long tradition of women's leadership and women-centered networks in low-income neighborhoods and communities of color.[1] And they emphasize the value of the care-giving roles that are typically associated with women. While most women-centered neighborhood organizations do not actively exclude men from participating, their approach tends to attract primarily female participants.

Because the model begins with personal growth and problem-solving, the recruitment process is designed to reach potential participants in places where they routinely gather for personal or family reasons. Most of PILOT's recruitment is through the public schools since the schools are one of the only institutions that have ongoing contact with poor and immigrant families. Working through the schools enables PILOT to recruit women who are not involved in community life by appealing to them as mothers. It also provides a mechanism for recruiting stay-at-home mothers in highly traditional marriages—mothers whose heavy domestic responsibilities and restrictive gender roles would otherwise prevent them from getting involved in community activities. Because the school is typically associated with a woman's responsibilities as a mother, even those women whose actions are tightly controlled by their husbands are usually allowed to attend PILOT meetings. As one of PILOT's organizers explained, "It's okay to go and work as a volunteer and get involved with your children's life. But I think if it was coming out of another setting, like out of a community organization or out of a settlement house, maybe it wouldn't be so received [by the husbands]. . . . At the school, they go there every day to drop off their children."

Whereas the power-based model of leadership development focuses on building the skills of individual leaders through personal one-on-one relationships with the organizer, the women-centered organizations have a more group-centered approach to leadership. One of the founders of the Templeton Leadership Circle (TLC) explained the concept of collective leadership this way:

> It was for all women to sit in a circle and have not designated leadership but shared leadership. It was an idea that worked—it inspired us, it fired us up and enabled us to be more collectively than we could ever be indi-

vidually. And the process of sitting in a circle and going around in a circle and enabling—requiring everybody, actually—to be a participant. . . . Something happens when people share what they care about, who they are, and what they'd like to see happen . . . to achieve a broader vision. And people begin to realize that leadership isn't a role designation, leadership is a function performed by this circle of people who are accepting responsibility for the group and acknowledging other people.

To create this kind of collective leadership, instead of working to develop the public speaking and negotiating skills of individual members, women-centered organizations focus on creating mutually supportive leadership teams. At the heart of this process, participants engage in inter-personal sharing and support. For example, PILOT's participants are encouraged to develop a twenty-year vision for their lives, along with a step by step plan for achieving this vision. Having a support structure within which to pursue their goals gives participants the confidence they need to pursue their dreams and enables them to tackle difficult personal challenges. In Angela's team, the participants were grappling with a variety of challenging problems—"It was things like continuing education, getting job skills. And there was things like abusive husbands, afterschool care, senior care so I can work type of issues. All that kind of stuff." Her own goal, to earn her GED, seemed overwhelming. But once she had the support and encouragement of the other parents, she not only finished the GED, she also went on to get a certificate in office administration and a full-time job. And she gained the self-confidence she needed to end an emotionally abusive relationship that was holding her back. Other parents also completed their education, some learned English, some found jobs, and some even started working toward longer term life changes, such as saving money to buy a house.

The achievement of these personal goals gives participants a new sense of confidence. "It was a real awakening for me," Angela explained. "My self-esteem was very, very low. I didn't think that I would be able to do any activities that didn't revolve around school and the kids and getting back in the house. Once I found out that I was the one in control of my life and my surroundings, then I started to take those small steps."

This sense of self efficacy, along with the strong mutual support structure that is developed within the group, enables participants to take leadership within their team and, ultimately, the broader community. When Debra Slaughter first got involved with TLC, she couldn't imagine playing a public role in her community: "I wasn't a leader. I wouldn't even talk out, speak out. Because I was married to a powerful man. . . . He was the one that was the controller, you know. And I didn't have any say so." But with the support she received from TLC's leadership team, Debra soon blossomed into a dynamic and powerful community leader:

> I said, 'I can't [speak in public]'. I almost fainted. And they said, 'we'll get up with you.' And I said, 'I never talked in front of other people. I can't do this.' They said, 'yes you can.' So when we got in the big meeting, they was holding me up. And then I got to talking, and the more I talked, I felt so empowered. . . . And I've been going with my mouth ever since. . . . So that really empowered me, being a member of the Templeton Leadership Circle. And it's changed my view of myself. I found my self worth, you know. I found out I'm a powerful woman. I have views, I have pretty good views. And I've gained a lot of skills that I didn't have before.

Debra went on to become TLC's chair, a board member for several other local organizations, a frequent speaker at citywide public gatherings, and a highly regarded leader in TLC's national network. Similarly, PILOT's members—many of whom rarely left the house before participating in PILOT's leadership workshops—have joined the boards of local community agencies, taken on leadership positions in regional and citywide parent organizations, and a few have even launched their own community-based organizations.

As one of PILOT's staff put it, "I think we've seen people who otherwise have not been touched by what poses as public life in a community, get touched by this work and really become leaders and activists. . . . People are seeing and creating small steps towards these bigger changes and are believing that community really can be built in neighborhoods where many had given up on them and they had given up on themselves." Thus, by providing personal support and emphasizing the connection between personal and public issues, the women-centered organizations gradually bring previously isolated residents into public life as confident and accomplished leaders.

Like all the models in this study, however, the women-centered model's approach to leadership development has drawn its share of criticism. Whereas the power-based model is sometimes accused of "creaming" the population in order to get more bang for its organizing buck, the women-centered model can be criticized for the opposite problem—sacrificing breadth for depth. Because the model is so focused on personal goal setting and interpersonal support, it is very staff intensive and time consuming. In addition, the emphasis on shared leadership and mutual support means that the leadership teams by definition must remain fairly small. Consequently, in contrast to the power-based organizations, which typically have memberships of several hundred and core leadership teams of up to fifty members, women-centered organizations tend to be composed of small, tightly knit cell groups. For example, PILOT is composed of ten to fifteen self-contained leadership teams, each made up of five to twenty members. TLC is composed of a single leadership team of twenty to thirty members. Critics of the model argue that while its impact on individual residents may be significant, the amount of time and work required to develop these leaders could be spent more efficiently by developing a broader leadership base through less intensive methods.

Some critics of both the women-centered and power-based models also argue that while organizations like WON and PILOT have succeeded in providing urban residents with the concrete skills necessary for active participation in public life, these skills do not offer a sufficient foundation for effective leadership. These critics suggest that in order to be truly effective leaders, urban residents must be able to analyze the systemic roots of urban problems and develop an alternative vision for society. The transformative model's approach to leadership development reflects this very different conception of how to engage residents in public life.

THE TRANSFORMATIVE MODEL OF LEADERSHIP DEVELOPMENT: CREATING CRITICAL CONSCIOUSNESS

During his fifteen years as a power-based organizer, Art Harper trained hundreds of residents to be strong public speakers and negotiators. But over time he began to question the underlying premises of his work. While his leaders had developed impressive skills, their training had not given them the tools to better understand the larger social forces at work in the neighborhood. As a result, while they were able to effectively confront political powerholders to demand "a piece of the pie," they were unable to conceptualize meaningful alternatives to prevailing social and political structures.

Art decided that in order to create sustainable long-term change in low-income urban neighborhoods, local residents need to do more than simply learn how to demand a greater share of available public services and resources. Influenced by the theories of popular educator Paulo Freire, he concluded that true leadership development requires residents to think critically about their experiences and to build alternative visions for society:

Helping people think through on a broad scale what the problems [are], and looking at real structural and broad social forces. . . . It's really easy to just stick to wanting a share of whatever somebody else happens to be doling out, and trying to get beyond that is a challenge . . . [But] the locuses of power are further and further away from the neighborhood. . . . It's got to be a continuous, active process of linking immediate threats with broader structural changes.

When he became the board chair and later the director of the Justice Action Group (JAG), Art began experimenting with a multi-step approach to leadership development designed to move participants toward a more sophisticated and critical understanding of urban issues. JAG's leadership development process begins with one-on-one outreach to residents living in low-income apartment buildings throughout the neighborhood. Much of this initial outreach focuses on getting residents organized into building-wide tenant councils to pressure their landlords for improved maintenance and security. JAG's organizers help to staff the tenant councils, in the process training residents in basic leadership skills such as how to conduct meetings and do outreach to other tenants in the building.

In contrast to the power-based and women-centered models, however, JAG's basic skills training is only a small component of its overall leadership development work, and JAG's staff do not give it nearly the amount of time and attention that the women-centered and power-based organizers do. While participants learn about the basics of community organizing and get an opportunity to take on leadership roles in their buildings, they do not get one-on-one mentoring or ongoing leadership support. JAG's organizers recognize the value of these intensive leadership development techniques, but with limited staff and a complex and multifaceted leadership development agenda, they have opted to prioritize the other aspects of their leadership program.

JAG's limited emphasis on basic skill building reflects the group's belief that learning how to be better public speakers and negotiators will not in-and-of-itself make the tenants into effective community leaders. Art explains:

> I don't think individual development is the most important part of [our approach]. It certainly is a part of it. There's a number of people that I've worked with who called saying, "my landlord won't do anything, what should I do?" and a couple of months later are out doorknocking in their building and talking about recruiting other people and organizing meetings and chairing meetings, and that kind of stuff. And I think that's been a real change. . . . [But] I think we'd like to try to get people to go beyond that as well, and to be able to change their sense of their own identity in terms of what it means to be part of this community. It's still easier [for] people [to] take a lead on something that's very immediate, but it's

another step to be able to change your sense of what is your self-interest and . . . [your] place in the world.

In JAG's view, if residents don't understand the connections between immediate issues like poor housing conditions, and broader social structural patterns like global capitalism, they will not be able to foster meaningful change in their communities. Thus, the next step in JAG's leadership development process focuses on giving tenants the skills to critically assess these larger social forces. Freire refers to this as the "demythologizing" of reality — helping people to "perceive critically *the way they exist* in the world *with which* and *in which* they find themselves; [to] come to see the world not as a static reality, but as a reality in process, in transformation" (Freire 1970: 70–71).

To develop this sort of critical consciousness, JAG engages residents in educational workshops and discussions that challenge them to rethink their commonsense understanding of everyday life. For example, the organization preceded a major strategic planning initiative with a ten-week workshop series that explored the links between local economic problems and the structures of global capitalism. One of the most popular workshops in the series overviewed Karl Marx's theory of use value and exchange value (Tucker 1978) and John Logan and Harvey Molotch's (1987) related concept of the urban growth machine[2]. Workshop participants then used these concepts as the basis for an analysis of the neighborhood's patterns of economic development.

While such workshops are mainly intended to build the critical thinking skills of the low-income residents who make up JAG's target constituency, they tend to primarily attract the participation of middle-class progressive activists who share JAG's broader social vision. These activists are committed to working on campaigns that promote the interests of the neighborhood's low-income tenants, and they strongly believe that the tenants themselves should be the ones to lead and direct these campaigns. Despite these commitments, however, the activists have ended up being the main beneficiaries of JAG's leadership development work.

The experiences of long-time activist Robert Henson illustrate this dynamic. As an avid participant in JAG's ten-week workshop series on the global economy, Robert credited JAG with providing him with "useful terminology and concepts" that enabled him to develop a more sophisticated understanding of neighborhood dynamics. "It's given me the avenue to see beyond. To work with people who are structuring a newer ideology, ... It has helped me see myself as a more effective, consequential individual. It's given greater wealth to the thoughts and images passing in my mind." Robert was particularly enthusiastic about JAG's workshop on Marx and the growth machine: "It facilitated a talking and sharing, so that individually I felt like I understand that, and as a group realizing that many of us understand this and it's not abstract and beyond our capability whatsoever. And so in a short time we're making an immense progression in grasping and understanding these abstruse economic terms."

Although Robert, like many of JAG's core members, is engaged in progressive politics in other contexts, he says that JAG is the only neighborhood-based organization that he knows of that works with residents to apply a progressive alternative worldview to their neighborhood. His involvement in the Central American solidarity movement gave him an understanding of the effects of global capitalism on international peace and justice issues, but until he joined JAG, Robert had never applied this kind of analysis to his own neighborhood. He credits JAG for bringing him together with other progressive residents to create an alternative vision for the community: "If we didn't have JAG as an organization, a place for us to gather and meet, this ideology and understanding wouldn't have an opportunity to move forward in a structurally, socially responsible way. Or even to be articulated. JAG has enabled that."

Like many middle-class activists who have benefited from JAG's popular education work, Robert has become a dedicated and outspoken member of JAG's core leadership. In contrast, JAG's leadership development process has been far less effective with its low-income tenant members. Because of the limited scope of JAG's basic skills training, most tenant participants do not develop the sophisticated public speaking and negotiating skills they would develop in a power-based organization's leadership training program. Furthermore, JAG has not been very successful at getting low-income participants to channel their concerns about their housing problems into an analysis of broader social structural dynamics. Most of JAG's low-income participants are interested in gaining the skills necessary to address their immediate problems and needs, an interest that does not necessarily translate into a commitment to engaging in JAG's long range structural change agenda.

For example, Melba Jones, a low-income tenant with several young children, got involved with JAG in response to a door-to-door organizing effort in her apartment building. With Art's support, she took a leadership role in her building, helping to form a tenant council to improve maintenance standards. In an effort to help Melba broaden her perspective, Art invited her to participate in a series of workshops related to housing policy and urban development issues and tried to get her involved as a leader in JAG's long-term campaign to transform citywide tenant rights policies. Despite some initial enthusiasm, however, once the conditions in Melba's building improved, she dropped out of the tenant council and cut off her connection to JAG. With her housing problems resolved, Melba's attention turned to other basic survival issues, such as her struggle to find a living wage job.

Because of this dynamic, JAG tends to operate as two separate groups—the low-income tenants who organize to win material improvements from their landlords, and the progressive activists who focus on developing far-reaching social change campaigns. Both sets of members regret the lack of integration within the organization. Speaking for the activist core, Robert said, "There's an intelligentsia about us, of knowledgeable, experienced people in community organizing—read, studied. And then there's a great portion of our community which is outside that. Our paths don't cross. . . . We're going to be frustrated until we can broaden our organizational base." So far, however, JAG's members have had little success in accomplishing this goal.

My research on the Center for Reflection, Education, and Organizing (CREO)—another transformative organization—offers further insights into this dynamic. Like JAG, CREO recruits its participants on an individual basis around their immediate material concerns—in this case the desire to learn English. CREO tries to use English as a Second Language (ESL) classes as a vehicle for engaging residents in a Freirian popular education process. But the participants are usually so focused on their immediate survival issues that they often are not even aware of CREO's broader agenda. Participants join CREO in order to learn English, and few seem to have any interest in engaging in critical social analysis or broader community action. As a result, while CREO has been successful in bringing about small personal transformations among the organization's participants—primarily by helping them to gain the language skills and sense of self-efficacy they need in order to take control of their lives—the organization has by and large failed to move the participants toward any kind of social structural analysis or community-based action.

One former participant, Juan Alcantar, suggested that urban residents struggling with basic survival issues can't afford to focus their energy on abstract social and political analysis. Juan came to the United States from Colombia in the 1970s not knowing any English. After surviving a harrowing experience with the immigration authorities at the border, he was depressed to find that the only job he could get was as a bus boy. His classes at CREO helped him gain the English skills he needed to get a better job; and the experience of working with American instructors who had confidence in him restored his sense of self-esteem and pride: "If I were going to use a word that is the benefit that I got from CREO, it's the confidence. . . . I felt like the lowest person in the world. But they changed me, they helped me to change all that." Even though Juan had been actively involved in radical politics in his homeland, he rejected CREO's efforts to engage participants in social structural analysis and action, and he recalls that most of CREO's participants had the same response: "They are hungry, they are probably unemployed, they have children to sustain. . . . They have the language barriers and other things. . . . These people are not interested in getting educated in the politics of the world. They want a job, they want to make a living."

Juan's analysis points to the difficulties of trying to do transformative popular education in a program that recruits its participants as individuals, based simply on their desire for concrete improvements in their material living conditions. Faced with basic survival issues, participants are understandably compelled to prioritize strategies that promise the greatest short-term benefits. In most cases, solving their own problems on an individual basis (for example, by learning English in order to get a better paying job) is far more realistic than trying to address the problems through long-term social structural change.

This doesn't mean that low-income and disenfranchised people aren't capable of developing a systemic analysis of their daily experiences or engaging in long-term struggles for social change. An examination of Paulo Freire's work with Brazilian peasants (Freire 1970, 1985) demonstrates the power of popular education to transform the consciousness of even the most oppressed populations. But Freire also emphasized that popular education must be an organic process in which, after much discussion and reflection, participants work together to develop new conceptual frameworks for making sense of their common experiences. Because JAG lacks the resources and staff time necessary to facilitate such an intensive process, it tries to move participants quickly from analysis to action by introducing externally derived ideological frameworks rather than waiting for participants to develop their own organic theories over time (Fisher and Kling 1990). While this approach streamlines the popular education process, it also tends to leave many low-income participants behind.

JAG and CREO's effectiveness in applying Freire's methods is also undermined by the highly individualistic nature of our society, particularly in large urban neighborhoods. Freire worked in small, agrarian villages whose residents were united by a shared economic fate. Since individual participants were unlikely to gain improvements in their own conditions except through broader transformations of the village's social and economic arrangements, they were better able to appreciate the importance of engaging in structural analysis and critique. In contrast, for JAG and CREO's participants, economic survival means competing as individuals for decent jobs and affordable housing within the capitalist marketplace. In the context of this individualistic struggle for survival, the linkages between individual interests and broader social structures tend to be far less tangible or straightforward. Consequently, abstract reflection and the pursuit of long-term systemic change can seem like a luxury compared to the more immediate struggle to meet basic needs.[3]

Because of this dynamic, transformative organizing is often easiest with middle-class activists who have a preexisting ideological commitment to structural analysis and who, because of their relative economic stability, can afford to focus on long-term change. This doesn't mean that low-income residents can't be effectively engaged in transformative organizing efforts. It simply means that the organizations must be able to commit the time and resources necessary for facilitating a very gradual, organic process of reflection, popular education and leadership development.

THE CIVIC MODEL: LEADERSHIP BY DEFAULT

Despite their differences, the women-centered, power-based, and transformative models of leadership development are all rooted in the assumption that the best way to foster residents' participation in public life is by engaging them in leadership development programs facilitated by trained organizers. This assumption flies in the face of the traditional image of citizenship as something that emerges naturally through the process of participating in a democratic society.

The fourth model of leadership development that I will examine, the civic model, is premised on this more passive conception of leadership development. My case studies of the civic model, the Cranston Association of Neighbors (CAN) and the Chicago Alternative Policing Strategy (CAPS), are all-volunteer groups with no formal strategies for recruiting, training, or mentoring local leaders. The leadership development that happens within these organizations takes place merely as a byproduct of residents' involvement with the group.

When Carolyn Dainton bought her first house on a quiet, tree-lined Chicago street, she expected to spend her evenings relaxing at home with her dogs. But when her boyfriend was assaulted by a group of local youth, she decided it was time to get involved in the community. One of her neighbors had told her about the local CAPS meetings, so she started attending. After the first meeting, she was hooked. She enjoyed getting to know the ins and outs of the police and city services systems, and she was glad for the opportunity to get to know her neighbors.

Carolyn had never taken a leadership role in her community, but she had good writing and computer skills from her job in the high-tech industry. Over time, she began to find ways to contribute those skills to the organization: "We were going to meetings and I was taking notes, because it's just a habit I have when I'm in meetings. . . . Then I started publishing a written report of things that were discussed and decisions that were reached. . . . That takes a considerable amount of time. And then because I was involved to that extent, I never missed a meeting because then there wouldn't be any minutes and I felt very personally responsible." Carolyn's writing skills were soon noticed by the local CAPS coordinator, and she was invited to become the editor of the city's first district-wide CAPS newsletter. She also spearheaded several letter-writing campaigns to improve conditions at a local park, eventually becoming a valued member of the park's advisory council.

As Carolyn's story demonstrates, civic organizations like CAPS provide a valuable forum for residents to contribute their skills and talents to their communities. However, while the organizations thus enable residents with existing leadership skills to become active participants in local public life, they do little to engage the vast majority of urban residents, many of whom don't see themselves as potential leaders or have the skills necessary to play such roles. Whereas the women-centered, power-based, and transformative organizations recruit their participants through intensive one-on-one outreach, civic organizations rely on far more passive methods of recruitment. CAN and CAPS publicize their meetings through small handbills and flyers that they post in buildings and businesses around the neighborhood. The organizations' existing members also engage in informal discussions with their neighbors and friends to invite them to upcoming meetings and events. This recruitment process enables both organizations to attract ten to thirty participants to most monthly meetings. However, the reliance on such informal recruitment has also limited the composition and scope of their participant base. Residents who don't see themselves as potential community leaders are unlikely to attend a community meeting simply because they have seen a public notice or flyer. And residents of all backgrounds are less likely to respond to anonymous flyers than they are to a personal invitation from somebody they trust.[4] Since CAN was founded by local property owners—a population that tends to socialize and interact primarily with others in the same economic class—most of the group's personalized outreach has been to a relatively narrow slice of the local population. Similarly, when CAPS was formed, the people who responded to its initial outreach efforts were primarily homeowners and condominium owners who then encouraged their neighbors and peers to participate. As a result, even though over eighty-five percent of the Cranston neighborhood's residents are renters, both organizations have remained dominated almost entirely by property owners.

Once involved, the civic organizations' participants are welcomed and encouraged to take on leadership roles. As one CAN member explained, "If people want to do certain duties, it's not heavily structured—if you want to take charge of this, take care of this, if you want to head this up, yes we'd love for you to do that. . . . It tries to build upon itself, giving everyone a chance to do things and be involved in whatever they want to be involved in."

For example, Tim Dale joined CAN's board after finding himself in the midst of an annual board election at the first meeting he ever attended: "It went on and on and on and all these various people who had served before were being cajoled to serve again and they were refusing. It was one of those situations where, partially out of I'd like to put this thing out of its misery, I raised my hand and said 'Oh, I'll do it. Tim Dale.' Because nobody knew who I was. It was like the first meeting [I had ever been to], I moved immediately into this board position."

While those residents with existing leadership skills may be able to take advantage of these opportunities, nothing is done to build the skills or capacities of those members who are not ready to take on leadership roles. As one longtime CAN member put it, "I wouldn't say [we] necessarily do anything to build the leadership in the aspect of any formal thing. . . . It makes it available in the aspect of why don't you come on, participate. If you'd like to be on the board, be on the board. It doesn't do it, but it makes it available to do it. . . . It's a platform, too, if you have any leadership abilities or desires, it really makes it available for that to happen." Because of this lack of leadership support, CAN and CAPS members were usually grateful to anyone who was willing and able to take on the necessary leadership roles. Shortly after joining the board, Tim became the organization's unofficial president when it became clear that he was one of the only board members with the necessary skills to perform the leadership tasks that the role required. Most members attributed his leadership qualifications to the skills and knowledge he had gained working as a lawyer at City Hall: "I think he took [the president's position] because he [had already] dealt with the people in the alderman's office, the other community groups, so he was very familiar with those other people. So a lot of the things that we need to do and people we need to talk to, he knew."

In the absence of formal leadership training, almost all of CAN's leaders were people who had gained their leadership skills from their jobs or from previous involvement in community organizations. For example, longtime member Fiona Black explained that she often volunteered to help Tim run

CAN's meetings because she had facilitation experience from her job in marketing. She said that most of the organization's leaders either owned their own businesses or had corporate jobs.

Because the civic organizations offer no formal leadership training, the CAN and CAPS participants who I interviewed said that they had not developed any new leadership skills through their involvement. Instead, participants said they had simply learned how to apply their existing skills to new settings. In addition, some leaders said they had gathered useful information about how the city services system works. For example, when I asked Carolyn what impact her involvement had had on her personally, she replied,

> I have definitely gained knowledge I didn't have before. I know so much more about the laws, how they work, how the court system works, what the housing code says, what the building code says, how you get the city to come out and inspect a bad property, how the Section 8 system works. . . . It really gives citizens a knowledge of how the police and city services work, and who you call and what their phone numbers are and what their addresses are.

In addition to gaining this kind of useful information, leaders like Carolyn said they enjoyed the experience of becoming involved in their communities. Carolyn's experiences with CAPS were so rewarding that she eventually decided to change careers so that she could focus on neighborhood safety issues in a professional capacity.

Clearly, by giving people like Carolyn and Tim a chance to utilize their skills in new settings, the civic organizations provide an opportunity for personal growth and development. However, because these leaders must already have the skills necessary for effective participation in the public sphere, the organizations provide few opportunities for anyone but the neighborhood's most socially privileged residents to get involved in leadership positions. Research on neighborhood participation rates shows that middle-class residents are far more likely than their less affluent neighbors to come into organizations already having the kinds of skills that are necessary for effective leadership in voluntary associations (Mansbridge 1983; Berry, Portney and Thomson 1993; Putnam 2000). Thus, it is not surprising that the vast majority of leaders in CAN and CAPS are educated middle-class property owners.

The civic organizations' reliance on skills gained in corporate and professional settings exacerbates this pattern. For example, business professionals who have been trained to prioritize efficiency typically prefer to complete tasks on their own rather than using the tasks as a way to develop the skills of others. As Fiona put it, "I think some people tend to—for example, they know how to get the job done, so they just do it rather than trying to bring somebody else along to learn. I've been that way most of my life. I recognize the problem. . . . We definitely have to find a way to get more people involved at all levels."

Similarly, the kinds of facilitation skills that people tend to learn in corporate settings are not very effective for trying to foster broad participation by a wide variety of residents. Fiona told me her main priority when facilitating meetings was to keep the meeting short by curtailing what she defined as annoying or uninteresting discussions. "I figure if a person's a bore I don't care if their feelings are hurt." She said that she frequently cut people off whenever she thought their comments were boring or unclear. While this approach may have served her well in the corporate world, it is not necessarily appropriate for a community meeting in which broad participation is a primary goal and where some residents are likely to be less articulate than others.

In sum, while the civic organizations provide some residents with valuable leadership opportunities, the approach tends to privilege the participation and development of middle-class, educated and professional residents who already possess strong leadership skills, while offering few opportunities for less experienced residents to become actively involved in community life. Consequently, although the civic model of leadership development may be well suited to increasing the levels of public participation within homogeneous middle class communities, it is not very appropriate for the diverse, low- and moderate-income urban neighborhoods that are the focus of my research.

THE COMMUNITY-BUILDING MODEL OF LEADERSHIP DEVELOPMENT: A "COMMUNITARIAN" APPROACH

The final approach to leadership development that I will examine in this chapter is the community-building model. Unlike any of the other organizations in my study, community-building organizations do not actively foster the individual-level leadership of neighborhood residents. Instead, the organizations promote a "communitarian" (Lichterman 1995, 1996) model of leadership that emphasizes the shared voice and collective identity of all the organization's members. This unique approach is best illustrated by the leadership dynamics at a typical community-building organization meeting.

It was a cold January evening, but the turnout at the monthly membership meeting of Port Angeles Collaborating Together (PACT) was surprisingly good. The room was filled with the energized sounds of PACT's participants—almost all of whom are the directors and professional staff of local nonprofit organizations—greeting one another and sharing neighborhood news. The group's large size and the high energy levels in the room were impressive. Earlier that week the federal government had announced its rejection of PACT's hard-fought application to make the Port Angeles neighborhood into an Empowerment Zone. Despite the bad news, the group's two charismatic leaders, chairperson Enrique Sosa, and staff director Julio Ramirez, were in high spirits. And, as was clear from the faces in the room, their mood was infectious.

Calling the meeting to order, Enrique and Julio set the tone for the evening with lively and impassioned speeches focusing on the importance of the group's continued unity and optimism. They emphasized PACT's accomplishments over the past few years, and declared that the loss of Empowerment Zone status would not dissuade the group from its mission. Then, in a burst of excitement, Enrique announced that he and Julio had decided to take the symbolic step of publicly declaring Port Angeles an "empowerment zone," despite the federal government's decision. His announcement met with wild applause and enthusiasm from the group, and within minutes the entire room had assembled together around Enrique and Julio for a previously scheduled press conference. As the two leaders made impassioned statements about the group's work, the forty-plus members who were at the meeting stood silently behind them, forming a powerful symbol of the group's unwavering solidarity and shared commitments.

In contrast to the other organizations in my study, the community building organizations did very little to develop or promote the leadership of the neighborhood's individual residents. Instead, the organizations' primary objective was to build the visibility and legitimacy of the neighborhood itself within the wider economic and political arena, and they believed that unity (and unanimity) were the best ways to achieve this objective. As one PACT member explained, "I think the mission is to let the Federal Government, the city, let everyone know that we're there, we're united and working together. United by the cause of empowering our community."

In order to create a shared identity and common voice for the neighborhood, PACT and CO-OP worked to unify the neighborhood's stakeholders around a collective vision. Because of this focus, the organizations' membership recruitment efforts focused on the neighborhood's institutions and associations—hospitals, banks, non-profits, block clubs, and community development corporations. The organizations' active participants were primarily the leaders of these institutions—their executive directors and upper level staff. As one member put it, "The Central Orland Organizing Partnership [is] really about the empowerment, in some ways, of agencies that hadn't been empowered up until this point. . . . [It's] really about agencies coordinating, it's not about individuals coordinating."[5]

This distinctive membership composition created a rather unique role for the community-building organizations' professional organizers. In contrast to the training and mentorship role played by the staff organizers operating within other models, PACT and CO-OP's organizing staff served primarily as administrators and coordinators. Because the organizations' active participants were already leaders within their own institutions, PACT and CO-OP's organizers had little need to work on developing these participants' individual leadership skills. Instead, they focused their energy on the process of building a unified voice and shared vision among their members. As Carlos, one of PACT's organizers, explained, "[A] lot of organizations want coalitions, want partnerships, but if you don't have someone to organize those coalitions, no matter how well intentioned they are, they are not going to succeed. So PACT has really [focused] on identifying the key issues and putting a point person to organize on those issues. If not to facilitate meetings, to provide technical assistance."

In many cases, PACT and CO-OP's staff also served as the primary spokespeople for the organizations. In contrast to other models, which focus on training community residents to serve as the organization's public leaders, PACT and CO-OP relied on their own professional staff and a handful of charismatic leaders to represent the group in the public arena. For example, PACT's chair and director were the primary speakers at almost every PACT meeting and served as the organization's official representatives at almost every public event. And in contrast to most of the other organizations in this study, which draw a sharp distinction between the roles of staff and leaders, PACT's members seemed to accept the predominance of these charismatic leaders as both natural and desirable.

Not surprisingly, while this approach can be very effective in strengthening the unity and visibility of the neighborhood within the public sphere, it has a limited impact on the growth and development of individual residents as public actors. Whereas members of all my other case study organizations spoke to me about the significant impact that their involvement had had on them personally, CO-OP and PACT's members talked primarily about the impact their involvement had had on their organizations and the community as a whole. Few attributed any personal benefits or leadership skill development to their involvement.

Furthermore, the community-building model tends to leave individual residents who are not already affiliated with local institutions and associations out of the organizing process altogether. While many of PACT and CO-OP's participants did reside in the neighborhood, they tended to be far more educated and skilled than the average resident of the community. Meanwhile, the vast majority of the neighborhood's residents played no meaningful role in the organizations' work.

In sum, the community-building organizations in my study did not offer an effective avenue for leadership development among individual neighborhood residents. While the organizations effectively built the leadership capacity and public voice of local institutions, they had a limited impact on individual residents' participation in local public life.

MODELS OF LEADERSHIP DEVELOPMENT: IMPLICATIONS FOR PRACTICE

If we are interested in strengthening participatory democracy in urban neighborhoods, the development of resident leadership is an essential starting point. What lessons can we draw from this chapter about the most effective ways to create an actively involved public?

Since the early American republic, democratic theorists have found that middle-class residents are far more likely to participate in voluntary organizations than their lower income neighbors (e.g. Tocqueville 1971; Berry, Portney and Thomson 1993; Putnam 2000). While they typically lament this finding, the theorists have also tended to write it off as an inevitable feature of American democracy.

My analysis in this chapter suggests an alternative conclusion: the predominance of middle-class residents in mainstream organizations is not inevitable at all, but instead is a direct product of the underlying structure of these organizations' work. Meaningful participation in the democratic process requires a range of skills and abilities that are not evenly distributed in the population because of disparities in power, economic resources, education, and social status. Meanwhile, most of the structures for democratic participation in our society operate much like the civic model—they are open forums that provide opportunities for citizens to get involved based on their own initiative. This tends to reinforce the impact of existing inequalities on patterns of participation. Residents who are lacking in verbal fluency, self-confidence, political experience, and public legitimacy are far less likely to participate in open democratic forums than their more privileged neighbors. And when they do participate, they are far less likely to be heard.

If we are interested in expanding the leadership role of low-income and working-class residents, we need to overcome these obstacles. The women-centered, transformative, and power-based models of leadership development all offer valuable tools for doing this. By working proactively to counterbalance the effects of social inequalities on residents' ability to participate effectively in public life, these models mitigate the impacts of class disparities on democratic participation rates.[6] Furthermore, each model provides a specific segment of the urban population with a distinctive set of skills, creating a complementary division of labor between the various approaches. The women-centered model develops the self-confidence and rudimentary organizing skills of the neighborhood's most disenfranchised, socially disconnected residents. The power-based model offers more advanced skill training to residents who are already relatively confident, outspoken, and open to taking on public leadership roles. And the transformative model develops experienced community activists into sophisticated critical thinkers and agents of social structural change.

How organizations can harness this complementarity, as well as the impact of these distinct approaches on other aspects of the organizing process, will be explored further in later chapters.

TABLE 3 Building Individual Capacity

Model	Population targeted for leadership development	Methods of leadership development	Specific skills and capacities that are developed
Power-based	Residents who are confident, out-spoken, interested in public involvement, and can recruit others to participate	Intensive one-on-one mentoring and support; hands-on experience; formal training workshops	Public speaking, strategy development, negotiating, understanding power dynamics, developing others' leadership
Women-centered	Low-income residents who have little connection to the mainstream community and lack confidence in their own voice	Training and support focused on personal and family goals; ongoing support by leadership team as leadership expands from personal to community issues	Skills in relationship building, support network development, and goal attainment. Focus on self-esteem and a sense of self-efficacy
Transformative	Low-income residents with no previous leadership experience (middle class progressive activists are also involved)	Limited one-on-one mentoring and support. Popular education workshops and discussions focusing on the development of critical thinking skills	Basic organizing skills. Critical thinking skills and the capacity to analyze personal experiences in terms of broader social structural patterns
Civic	Any resident who is willing to take on a leadership role and already has the necessary skills and self-confidence	No leadership training or support. Participants are encouraged to take on whatever leadership roles they are able to perform	No new skills developed. Participants can apply pre-existing administrative and facilitation skills to a community context
Community-building	Community institutions and established leaders of local groups	No leadership training. Organizers provide coordination and facilitation. Charismatic leaders create a unified voice for the group	No individual skills. Emphasis on communitarian leadership characterized by a strong, unified collective voice

CHAPTER 4

BUILDING COMMUNITY CAPACITY: NETWORKS AND SOCIAL CAPITAL

CHAPTER 3 demonstrated the importance of working to develop the capacity of individual residents to engage in public action. But creating a base of grassroots leaders is only the first step in building a community's capacity to generate change. Acting alone, even the most skilled leaders will have a limited ability to impact the public sphere. This chapter examines how community organizing groups build the community's capacity for collective action through the development of relational networks among residents.

The collective efficacy of urban neighborhoods has been the subject of much academic research and popular concern over the past decade. Emphasizing the connection between contemporary urban problems and the erosion of "social capital" among urban residents, academics have underscored the importance of informal networks as one of the primary foundations of a strong community (Putnam 2000; Sampson 1995; Wilson 1996). But while the academic and popular concern over these concepts is a relatively recent phenomenon, the concepts themselves are hardly new. In fact, although community organizers rarely refer to their work in these academic terms, building the social capital of urban communities is one of community organizing's fundamental goals.

Simply put, what the academics have "discovered" and community organizers have long understood is that interpersonal networks among residents are an essential building block for effective collective action at the community level. Robert Putnam defines social capital as the "connections among individuals—social networks and the norms of reciprocity and trustworthiness that arise from them" (2000: 19). These social connections are what enable communities to work together to address shared problems, improve community members' quality of life, resist threats to community well-being, and take advantage of opportunities as they arise. Operating as the "social glue" that enables residents to overcome the challenges of collective action, social capital helps communities to "translate aspirations into realities" (2000: 288).

Community organizing creates this "social glue" by bringing residents together, fostering relationships among them, and building formal organizational structures to link them together. The specific methods that organizers use to develop these networks—and the kinds of networks they ultimately create—vary significantly depending on which model of organizing they adhere to. This chapter explores the implications of these different approaches for the development of social capital and collective efficacy in urban neighborhoods.

The social science literature on networks and social capital provides some useful analytical frameworks for understanding the distinctions between the case study organizations' approaches to network building. The most important distinction in network types is that between "bonding" and "bridging" networks (Putnam 2000). *Bonding* networks involve dense linkages among relatively small numbers of people. Each member of a bonding network typically knows every other member, and these relationships often overlap into multiple dimensions of the members' lives—like the members of a small town who attend church together, work in the same factory, know one another's families, and shop at the same stores. Because of the bonding networks' closely intertwined, multi-stranded links, these networks tend to be exclusive and insular, as epitomized by the intense bonds of an extended family or tightly knit social clique.

In contrast, *bridging* networks are composed of single-stranded ties that loosely connect large numbers of individuals. The relationships within these networks are generally less intimate or intense than those of the bonding networks—like the acquaintanceship between two neighbors who take the same bus each morning but may not even know each other's names. And in contrast to the bonding networks' densely interwoven ties, members of bridging networks are typically linked to one another through indirect ties—such as the ties connecting one neighbor to the CEO of a local company who plays squash with the husband of the neighbor he chats with every morning at the bus stop. Because they are made up of less intimate ties, bridging networks can link far greater numbers of people than the bonding networks. As a result, whereas bonding networks tend to be insular, bridging networks are more expansive—they connect people across different social groups or localities.

In addition to these distinctions in network *form*, there are also significant variations in the *substance* of the social bonds that tie a network's members together. The substance of the relationships within a network are primarily a function of the specific commitments that motivate the network's members to join and remain in the network. These commitments can generally be categorized according to whether they are (a) instrumental; (b) affective; and/or (c) normative in nature (Kanter 1972; Lawler and Yoon 1996). Residents who get involved in community networks for *instrumental* reasons are motivated by the expectation of tangible, material benefits; they remain connected to the networks on the basis of a cost-benefit analysis of whether continued involvement will enable them to fulfill their individual needs. In contrast, networks that are based on *affective* ties are rooted in each member's personal and emotional attachment to others in the group. Finally, networks that are based on *normative* ties arise from a shared sense of obligation to uphold specific overarching values or principles. People who participate in networks for normative reasons are committed to a common abstract mission or ideology.

Participation in voluntary organizations is typically motivated by one or more of these three types of commitment. For example, Marilyn is a member of her local grocery store's preferred buyer club for *instrumental* reasons because her membership enables her to save money on her groceries. If her membership no longer provided financial benefits, or if she found another preferred buyer club with even greater savings, she would most likely terminate her membership in the club. In contrast, she is a committed participant in a local women's support group for *affective* reasons, based on her close friendships and emotional ties with the other members. Whether she remains a member of this network does not depend on whether she gains immediate material benefits from her membership but rather on the personal bonds and mutual affection she shares with the other members. Finally, her membership in the local chapter of a national animal rights group is based on normative commitments—she believes as a matter of principle that all living beings should be treated with respect. She will continue to participate in the group even if she gains nothing from it personally, because she is committed to the organization's values and principles.

These distinctions in both the form (bonding or bridging) and substance (instrumental, affective, or normative) of a network's ties can have significant implications for the collective capacity of the networks' members. This chapter explores the effectiveness of the case study organizations' networks in achieving the following outcomes—all of which are essential to the development of a neighborhood's collective efficacy:

- *Sense of collective identity:* In the process of developing relationships with others, residents come to recognize their connection to a "community" beyond their own household. This sense of collective identity makes community action possible by enabling residents to perceive their shared fate.

- *Mutual support:* By building relationships of reciprocity and trust among residents (and, in some cases, institutions), social networks enable residents (and/ or institutions) to assist one another in achieving their individual goals.

- *Cooperative action:* Social networks also enable residents (and/or institutions) to work together on group goals—shared objectives that could not be achieved by individuals acting on their own.

- *Expanded scope:* By connecting residents to people, resources, organizations or institutions outside of their own community or social group, social networks can expand residents' capacity beyond what they could achieve simply by working together as a group.

Each model of community organizing entails a distinctive approach to capacity building that shapes the form and substance of the social networks it creates. In the following sections, I analyze the *substance* of the case study organizations' networks by examining the specific types of commitments that motivate the organizations' members to be involved. Then I analyze each network's *form* by examining the composition of the organizations' memberships and the nature of the relationships among these networks' members. Finally, I examine the impact of each organization's distinctive networks on its ability to achieve the outcomes listed above.

THE CIVIC MODEL: CREATING BONDING NETWORKS BASED ON INSTRUMENTAL AND AFFECTIVE TIES

The civic organizations' approach to network building results in the creation of bonding networks based on a combination of both instrumental and affective ties. These networks bring together small groups of relatively homogeneous residents into tight-knit cliques. Through their connections to other network members, the residents develop a sense of collective identity that enables them to engage in mutual support and cooperative action with their immediate neighbors. However, the networks' small size and homogeneity also foster an insularity and exclusivity that can significantly constrain the community's problem-solving capacity.

The Form and Substance of the Civic Organizations' Networks

Because civic organizations don't do active outreach or recruitment of new members, most of the residents who participated in CAN and CAPS came to their first meeting for instrumental reasons. Hearing about the organizations through word-of-mouth or flyers, these residents were motivated to get involved because they had a specific problem they hoped to solve. For example, when I asked long-time CAPS member Darrin Snow why he joined the organization, he told this story:

> I was walking down the street and I felt something go by my head, and it was a chunk of metal about the size of a baseball. I heard footsteps behind me and I went and picked up the piece of metal. . . . My first instinct was to turn around and throw it back, but I didn't because there were four guys, and I couldn't really prove that they had thrown it. So I put it in my pocket, I went home. . . . But that's pretty much what got me thinking how can I get involved to stop . . . this kind of thing happening. . . . So we just started showing up, going to [CAPS] meetings.

Like Darrin, many residents came to CAPS meetings in order to report specific incidents of crime. Others got involved in an effort to solve problems with drug houses and loitering or to gather information about how to deal with graffiti, garbage, or other nuisances around their blocks. Similarly, many of the landlords who participated in CAN started attending meetings because they worried that the neighborhood's lack of stability would undermine their ability to attract and retain "decent" tenants.

While CAN and CAPS each attracted several dozen participants to their monthly meetings, most of these residents never became part of any ongoing community networks; once their problems were solved (or once they realized the problems couldn't be solved by the organization) most residents stopped participating. As one CAPS member explained, "A lot of people come and it's the only CAPS meeting they attend. They have a specific problem they want to talk about, they talk about it, it gets dealt with, and then we'll never see them again because their problem is fixed."

The small core of participants who do continue their involvement with the organizations past one or two initial meetings tend to be property owners—landlords, homeowners, and condo owners—whose material interests are directly related to the neighborhood's long-term stability. By building relationships with other responsible owners and working with one another on an ongoing basis, they hope to strengthen the neighborhood's social order over the long term. "There's people next door or just across the street that may have been here for years and don't even say hi to each other," one landlord explained. "If you have drug dealing or things like that or gang activity, . . . you have to get [people] together to get those problems solved. . . . I'd like to see it where it's a friendlier neighborhood and people know each other and people can count on each other when problems arise."

While their initial involvement with the organization is typically motivated by self-interest, in the process of meeting and working together month after month, these core members develop personal relationships with one another that go beyond simply an instrumental motivation. For many participants, these relationships are the primary reason why they continue to participate in the organization over the long haul. As one CAN member explained, "Part of the reason why I stay involved is because of the great people that I've met through the organization. And the people in my neighborhood who really make it my home. That's a big part of the reason."

The affective nature of the ties among CAN and CAPS' long-time participants were evident in the ways they interacted at the organizations' meetings. The discussions before and after most CAN and CAPS meetings were filled with informal, neighborly exchanges of the kind that typically take place over backyard fences. Participants talked about their home repair projects, their gardens, problems with their tenants, and complaints about their neighbors. CAN's committee meetings were frequently held at a local restaurant where participants mixed their business talk with animated storytelling and neighborhood gossip.

The experiences of CAN's president, Tim Dale, illustrate the combination of instrumental and affective ties at the heart of the civic organizations' networks. When Tim bought his first condo, he was anxious to make the surrounding neighborhood a safe and pleasant place to raise his family. After hearing about CAN for several months from some of his neighbors, he attended a meeting. Over the next four years, he developed relationships with many of CAN's core participants—relationships that he cited as the primary reason why he stayed involved with the organization.

> We provide kind of a forum for people in the neighborhood to come and get together and get to meet each other, which doesn't really happen naturally that much in the city of Chicago in the '90s. And that's been very positive for me from a personal perspective, because without CAN, I know the people in my building, maybe know the people next door, but I don't know that I'd know anyone else in this neighborhood. And because of CAN, when I walk around with my son or something to go to the park, I mean, very, very often I will see somebody on the street that I know and be able to strike up a conversation, kind of in the same way that my parents would relate in the suburb where they knew a lot of people.

Through this combination of instrumental and affective ties, CAN and CAPS built strong, bonding networks in the Cranston neighborhood. Because of the organizations' lack of extensive membership recruitment and the fact that many participants never became ongoing members of the group, these bonding networks tended to remain relatively small—both CAN and CAPS' core memberships averaged about 10–15 members. And because the participants that stayed involved with the organizations over the long haul tended to be primarily homeowners and landlords, these bonding networks were relatively homogeneous in their demographic composition.

Impact of the Civic Organizations' Networks

These bonding networks fostered a strong *sense of collective identity* and shared fate among CAN and CAPS' members. As Tim put it, "You're a different type of person if you know your neighbors than if you're just kind of living in your own world, or isolated. It [has] change[d] me. It makes me a little less of the, like now I'm going to go to work, now I cocoon at home type of approach that I think has become pretty prevalent in our society."

While this sense of group belonging enabled residents like Tim to overcome their social isolation, it didn't necessarily give them a feeling of connection to the neighborhood as a whole. Because most of CAN and CAPS' participants were property owners, the organizations' members defined the parameters of their "group" quite narrowly. Assuming that the commitments and motivations of tenants and low-income residents were different from their own, CAN and CAPS participants didn't perceive these residents as part of their community of shared fate. As Tim explained, "The people that come to the meetings tend to own condos, own property, own some of the two- or three-flats in the neighborhood, because they're the ones who have the biggest stake in it and are the most concerned. . . . If [tenants are] really concerned about things, [they] can move much more easily. That would be [their] response, instead of devoting a lot of hours to a community group."

The shared sense of group identity among CAN and CAPS' core members enabled them to work together on cooperative activities of various kinds. First, because of their strong neighborly ties with one another, CAN and CAPS members frequently engaged in *mutual support* around each other's individual goals. As one longtime CAN member explained, "The core membership . . . understand that for a neighborhood to function, there has to be the give and take of it. And there has to be the looking out for [people] beyond your immediate household. And if that is freely given by you, hopefully it gets returned to you, if it ever comes up." This mutual support revolved primarily around the kinds of instrumental concerns that brought the organizations' participants together in the first place. CAN's members frequently kept an eye on each other's homes and rental properties, calling the police at any sign of suspicious activity and reporting their observations to one other. Many shared advice on property maintenance and repair; some even exchanged clippings from their yards. Similarly, participants often gave each other advice and information on how to deal with problem tenants in their buildings or how to get rid of abandoned vehicles on their streets.

In addition to providing mutual support to help network members with their own individual issues and problems, the civic organizations' bonding networks also provided a basis for network members to engage in *cooperative action* to achieve shared group goals. For example, in an effort to reclaim the neighborhood's public spaces away from drug dealers and gang members, CAN members organized regular safety walks in the neighborhood. The organization's members were motivated to participate in the walks partly because of their instrumental desire to make the neighborhood safer, but also because of their affective relationships with one another. The walks, which took place at night and on weekends, served as a fun social activity for many of the participants, who enjoyed strolling the neighborhood while chatting and sharing gossip with their neighbors. Walking the streets on their own, the participants would have had little impact on the neighborhood's safety. But by drawing on their network, CAN members were able to establish a visible presence of "law-abiding residents" in the neighborhood's public areas.

By fostering collective action among their members, the civic organizations strengthened residents' capacity to address the neighborhood's problems and achieve their goals. However, the denseness and homogeneity of these networks limited their overall impact on the community's problem-solving capacity. While dense ties among small groups of residents can enhance the sense of community and social cohesion among network members, they can also cause greater isolation from other groups.[1] The civic organizations weren't formally connected to any other institutions or resources outside the neighborhood and rarely worked in cooperation with anybody outside their own membership. Even though property owners made up only 15 percent of the Cranston neighborhood's population, CAN and CAPS' core members made little effort to reach out to the neighborhood's other social groups. Similarly, although the organizations were connected to the police and the city services system, these connections were limited primarily to information sharing and did not involve any shift in the agencies' officially proscribed role in the neighborhood. As a result, beyond providing a forum for local property owners to work in cooperation with one another and the city services bureaucracy, the civic organizations did not significantly increase their members' access to external resources for solving problems.

This tendency toward insularity limited the civic organizations' ability to solve problems affecting more than just their own insular networks. For example, CAN spent several years fighting a local "slumlord"—Rudy Atti—who owned a number of poorly maintained apartment buildings. Calling his buildings a blight on the neighborhood, CAN's members claimed that Atti was contributing to a decline in property values and damaging the neighborhood's reputation. They tried desperately to get Atti to clean up his act, but with little success. At the same time, Atti's tenants had been working for months to get him to improve the living conditions in his buildings. But because CAN's participants viewed the tenants as having interests very different from their own, they never tried to reach out and work with them. The tenants could have served as valuable allies, using their financial leverage as rent payers to hold Atti accountable. Instead, CAN's members defined the tenants as part of the problem, in the process limiting their own ability to achieve their goals.

CAN finally succeeded in its campaign against Atti, but only because another organization from outside the neighborhood reached out and offered its support. Atti owned buildings in several other Chicago neighborhoods, and when a community organization in one of these areas heard about CAN's fight, they suggested joining forces. CAN had never been involved in this kind of a strategic alliance, and the connection significantly expanded the organization's capacity. The other organization had access to resources, leadership, sophisticated strategies, and media relations that CAN didn't, enabling the coalition to eventually win the campaign. Once the campaign ended, however, CAN did not make any effort to sustain the partnership or to create similar relationships with other organizations. Without such connections, its capacity for effective problem-solving action in the community was severely limited.

CAN's exclusivity not only reduced the organization's effectiveness, it also exacerbated tensions and divisions within the neighborhood. CAN eventually "solved" the Atti problem by getting his creditors to seize his buildings, in the process evicting all of his tenants. This "victory" left the tenants homeless, permanently reduced the number of low-cost housing units in the neighborhood, and ultimately placed a substantial burden on other organizations in the neighborhood to find adequate accommodations for the hundreds of low-income families CAN had helped displace. Many of Atti's tenants were unable to find affordable housing in the same neighborhood and ultimately had to move to other parts of the city, a process which further disrupted their social support structures and imposed even greater instability on their lives. CAN's actions angered the neighborhood's low-income residents and produced lasting tensions with tenants rights organizations in the city.

In sum, civic organizations create bonding networks characterized by a combination of instrumental and affective ties. These networks promote mutual support and a basis for joint action among the neighborhood's property owners. At the same time, however, the networks' insularity and homogeneity limit their contribution to the community's overall collective efficacy and may even exacerbate social tensions within the neighborhood.

THE WOMEN-CENTERED MODEL: CREATING BONDING (AND BRIDGING) NETWORKS BASED ON AFFECTIVE TIES

Women-centered organizations also create small, primarily bonding networks, but with very different characteristics and outcomes. The women-centered networks are rooted in affective commitments but, unlike the civic organizations' neighborly ties, these bonds are intense, intimate, and deeply personal in nature. And, in contrast to the civic organizations' highly insular networks, the women-centered organizations work to build bridges between their closely bonded teams and external communities and institutions.

The Form and Substance of the Women-Centered Organizations' Networks

As discussed in chapter 3, one of the characteristic features of the women-centered model is its emphasis on the interconnection between residents' personal lives and emotional well-being and effective action in the public sphere. Organizations like PILOT and TLC bring residents together into small, supportive teams infused with the principles of personal sharing, careful listening, and relationship-building. The organizations' members spend a significant portion of each meeting updating each other on their personal lives, talking about their problems and dreams, and providing one another with advice and support around these issues. Both PILOT and TLC also sponsored informal social events where members could share in each other's lives and build a sense of community together. As one of TLC's founders explained, "We came together a lot around food, potlucks, and people telling their stories and sort of the relief of connecting. . . . I think one of the nice things was that we got to know people personally. . . . We connected with each other's kids, and stuff like that."

This sharing and support creates intense emotional bonds among the members—*affective* ties that produce a strong sense of commitment to the group. These ties tend to be both dense and multi-stranded—every member typically knows every other member, and their relationships often extend into multiple areas of their lives. For example, members of PILOT's parent teams frequently visited each other's homes, took care of one another's children, and engaged in their daily rounds together. Since it would be hard to build such intimate connections within a large group, the women-centered networks tend to remain quite small. The PILOT parent teams ranged in size from three to twenty members, and TLC's active membership hovered between fifteen and thirty.

The distinctive nature of the women-centered organizations' networks is illustrated by the experiences of PILOT member Rosario Inez. When Rosario first got involved with the PILOT team at her school, she was a young mother struggling to raise two sons. Like many PILOT participants, most of her family and support networks were still in Mexico, and Rosario felt alone and exhausted. She started attending PILOT's parent team meetings and one year later had become part of a closely knit group of mothers: "They're my family now. I call them regularly and we get together to support each other. . . . We were all running in different directions, but now we're united."

Now, every morning after dropping off her children at school, Rosario heads to the parent room in the school basement to share stories, get advice, and socialize with the other mothers. These gatherings are often the highlight of her day. By the time she arrives, several of the mothers have usually started a coffee pot perking and are busy cooking oatmeal and making toast for the group. While the food is being prepared, Rosario chats with clusters of mothers gathered in different corners of the room. They share stories about their husbands and children and updates on their personal struggles with their jobs, their health, and their families. Rosario appreciates the support she gets from her teammates as she deals with the challenges of her job—a job that she found through her connections within the parent team. And she values the opportunity to talk to other working mothers about the difficulties of juggling her new job with her family obligations.

Eventually Rosario gathers with the other mothers around a large table to eat breakfast over boisterous conversation and story-telling. After a few minutes, she must leave to go to work. She walks to work with one of the other team members, and once the work day is over, they frequently return to the school to help out at the after-school community center that Rosario and her teammates helped to create.

As Rosario's experience illustrates, the close friendships and interpersonal support among the women-centered organizations' members create strong *bonding* networks among small groups of neighbors. However, in stark contrast to the civic organizations' insularity, the women-centered organizations also work to build *bridging* networks to connect these dense teams with other external supports. PILOT and TLC's teams developed collaborative working relationships with public institutions, businesses, resident associations, and nonprofit organizations in their neighborhoods. PILOT also organized social events and work groups that brought together parent teams from neighborhoods across the city, in the process building relationships across geographic, racial, and cultural lines. In addition, both PILOT and TLC were members of national networks of women-centered organizations that brought together women from all over the country to share their stories, learn from each other's experiences, and provide one another with support.

Impact of the Women-Centered Organizations' Networks

PILOT and TLC's combination of bonding and bridging networks had a distinctive impact on the community's overall capacity for collective action. Like the civic organizations' networks, the relationships among the women-centered organizations' members gave them a *sense of collective identity*. By bringing residents together to talk about their personal goals and private troubles, the organizations enabled them to discover their connections to others. As one participant explained,

> My life before [PILOT] was very boring, very sad, because I [was] here in this country for five or six years and I didn't do anything. I stayed in my house and cleaned my house, watching TV, and only [leaving to] go to the school [to drop off] my son. And when I come back, that's it. . . . When I started on this program, I felt that my life was changing, because I know other persons, I can speak with other persons, and they have the same troubles, the same problems as me.

The experience of discovering commonalities with other women and developing relationships with those women helped PILOT and TLC's members to feel like part of a community. This sense of collective identity encompassed primarily the teams themselves, but PILOT and TLC's bridging networks also broadened participants' sense of belonging beyond the narrow confines of these small groups. For example, many of PILOT's participants said the opportunity to build relationships with parent teams from other parts of the city made them feel connected to communities they had previously felt very isolated from. As one mother who lives in a 99 percent African American neighborhood put it, "A lot of times, our percentile of mixed cultures is so small here you probably can't find a number for it as far as white, Hispanics, or Asians. We just see basically our own in the living setting. . . . A lot of times we have a tendency to be a little clone by ourselves. I think coming together is something I really appreciate."

This sense of collective identity fostered a spirit of *mutual support* among the participants. But unlike the mutual support in the civic organizations—which focused primarily on the kinds of instrumental, property-related concerns that brought the organizations' members together in the first place—the women-centered organizations' members supported each other at an extremely personal level. Members shared their aspirations and goals and provided each other with advice, moral support, and logistical help in achieving these goals. For example, when the husband of one of the PILOT team members got injured, forcing her to overcome her fear of driving, her team rallied around her. Two of the women on her team babysat her children while a third taught her how to drive. And the entire team provided her with encouragement throughout the ordeal. Likewise, when several members of another PILOT parent team discovered that they were all struggling with health and weight problems, they started their own aerobics class to help each other stay motivated and on task. Led by two of the group's members, the class met several times a week in the school gym, and the personal ties among the participants created an almost perfect attendance record.

In addition to providing a basis for mutual support, the women-centered organizations' bonding networks also enabled participants to engage in *cooperative action* toward shared goals. For instance, TLC's members were all concerned about the lack of affordable housing for low-income families in the neighborhood. Acting as individuals there was little they could do to increase the available housing supply. But the relationships among the members enabled them to take on a labor-intensive hands-on rehab project that involved hundreds of hours of cooperative effort. The project required extensive manual labor as well as time-consuming meetings and administrative work. The affective ties among the group's members kept them committed and enthusiastic throughout the process, and the project resulted in the creation of four new units of affordable housing for families.

By creating bridging networks to link their closely bonded teams with external supports, the women-centered organizations further *expanded the scope* of what their members could accomplish. PILOT and TLC's relationships with neighborhood institutions, public and private agencies, and local businesses gave their members access to resources, expertise, and information that were not otherwise available to the group. For example, when TLC's members decided to take on a second housing renovation project that was significantly more ambitious than their first, they knew they wouldn't be able to accomplish the project on their own. They worked to build face-to-face relationships with the lending officers at several local banks and the staff from several city bureaus. Through these relationships, they secured seed money for the project as well as valuable technical support. In addition, TLC expanded its capacity for volunteer labor by forging partnerships with local businesses and congregations who provided volunteers for several work parties. Through these and other partnerships, TLC's members significantly expanded their capacity to address the community's needs.

Although PILOT and TLC's combination of bonding and bridging ties enabled them to overcome many of the limitations of the civic organizations' more insular bonding networks, their approach involved some tensions that made the combination hard to sustain. As their links to outside partners increased, it became harder and harder for PILOT and TLC to balance the time-consuming process of maintaining their intimate interpersonal relationships with the new demands created by these external connections. The two organizations dealt with this dilemma in very different ways. PILOT's parent teams minimized the tension by focusing most of their energy on maintaining their bonding networks, often at the expense of any efforts to build broader bridging networks. While some of PILOT's organizers were frustrated by the limitations this imposed on the participants' overall collective capacity, they also recognized the inevitability of this choice. As one put it, "[Because] we're starting with the personal stuff, it's a very slow process. . . . Because we're very focused on the parent action team, it's not like the first thing we do is to rush out and talk to other groups. . . . On the other hand, we want the parents to establish relationships with social service agencies that can help them. . . . We like to see those linkages being built."

In contrast, in order to expand its capacity as a housing developer, TLC aggressively pursued the creation of greater and greater numbers of external ties with public agencies, banks, social service agencies, and other nonprofits. Over time, the complex demands of these relationships made it difficult to retain the original group's close, intimate bonds. The organization's meetings became dominated by complex business decisions, and the members spent less and less of their time on mutual support (a process that will be discussed further in chapter 5). Eventually, the organization lost its close-knit, affective connections and began to operate more like a professional community development agency, a transition that many members described as TLC's shift from a "family" to an "organization." TLC's experience suggests that while women-centered organizations can develop extensive bridging networks, this increased capacity often comes at the expense of the affectively bonded group.

In sum, the women-centered organizations' bonding networks create a sense of collective identity among small groups of residents, building a strong foundation for collective action. The relationships among the groups' members provide a basis for mutual support, enabling participants to accomplish their individual goals and respond to personal crises more effectively. And the networks enable community members to work cooperatively on joint projects to achieve their shared goals. To a certain extent, the women-centered organizations also expand residents' problem-solving capacity by forming bridges between these closely bonded networks and external actors and institutions. However, because of the tensions between the networks' bonding and bridging functions, the extent to which the women-centered organizations can sustain this expanded capacity is somewhat limited.

THE COMMUNITY-BUILDING MODEL: CREATING BRIDGING NETWORKS BASED ON NORMATIVE TIES

Whereas the civic and women-centered organizations create primarily bonding networks among small groups of residents, the community-building organizations create bridging networks among large numbers of institutions. The organizations work to build a shared vision of the common good among diverse neighborhood stakeholders. As a result, in contrast to the affective and instrumental ties discussed so far, the members of community building networks tend to be connected by normative ties.

The Form and Substance of the Community-Building Organizations' Networks

As discussed in chapter 3, one of the community-building organizations' primary goals is to unify the neighborhood's stakeholders around a shared vision for the community. This means bringing together organizations that have traditionally been in competition with one another, or on opposing sides in neighborhood struggles, around their common commitment to the community's overall well-being. PACT's membership, for example, includes nonprofit organizations that have traditionally engaged in turf battles over funding and clientele, and organizations—such as banks, social service agencies, and homeowners' associations—whose interests vis-à-vis the neighborhood have historically clashed. Despite their differences, because each of these institutions has a "stake" in the Port Angeles community, PACT invited them to work together to restore the community's social and economic fabric. By appealing to their common interest in having Port Angeles become a healthy, self-reliant community, PACT's leaders convinced the institutions to set aside their own agendas to work on developing a comprehensive plan for the neighborhood.

In the process of developing this plan, the institutions forged a shared vision of the "common good" for the neighborhood that superseded their individual interests. As one PACT member explained, "They've been able to put this coalition of people together, agencies together—agencies with different agendas and different politics and different ideas—and bring them all together to agree on [a plan for] Port Angeles." The agencies' commitment to this vision provided the social glue that held them together. Thus, PACT created *normative* ties among large numbers of institutions, based on their shared belief in the importance of strengthening the "community" as a whole.

In contrast to the small, bonding networks created by the civic and women-centered organizations, PACT's *bridging* network brought together more than eighty diverse institutions from within the neighborhood. Similarly, while the civic and women-centered organizations built networks that were dense and multi-stranded, the connections between most of the community-building networks' members were loose and indirect. Other than their shared involvement in planning meetings and their common connections to PACT's organizing staff, many of the networks' members didn't know one another. Their relationships focused primarily on their shared commitment to PACT's comprehensive plan and did not generally extend into other aspects of their lives.[2]

The experience of PACT member Daniel Solano illustrates the unique characteristics of the community-building organizations' networks. Prior to PACT's emergence, the Port Angeles neighborhood had half a dozen social service and economic development agencies all working independently to attract businesses to the neighborhood, provide residents with job training, and connect their clients with living wage employment. As the assistant director of a local job training and placement agency, Daniel felt frustrated by the isolation among these various organizations, but he also knew that unless he was willing to compete with the other groups, his agency wouldn't be able to secure enough funding to survive. Because most of the agencies received government funding based on the number of residents they placed directly in jobs, they had a strong incentive not to work together. When one agency had access to a job opening but no qualified applicants, even if another agency had a client who would be a good fit for the job, the agencies rarely collaborated to make the match. Daniel explained, "If we refer someone to another agency we get no credit. . . . You don't want the jealously and the secrecy, but the contracts force you to for survival."

As a participant in PACT's comprehensive planning process, Daniel got to know the staff and directors of dozens of organizations from around the neighborhood—including many of the organizations he had traditionally been in competition with. In the process of developing a common vision for the community, PACT's members all agreed that if they were going to strengthen Port Angeles' overall health and vitality, lowering the neighborhood's unemployment rate was essential. In the past, the lack of coordination among the area's employment and training agencies would have created significant obstacles to achieving this goal. But their shared commitment to PACT's broader vision gave the agencies an incentive to work together to try and resolve this ongoing dilemma. "We're all aiming in the same direction and with the same purpose," Daniel explained. "Everyone has the vision and the same goal. . . . We listen to each other's views and we sit there and toss it back and forth. And then you try to put the wisdom of all the people working with PACT and do what's best for everyone, and especially the community." After several months of discussion and planning, the group designed a computerized job placement system that would protect each agency's funding while maximizing the community's ability to successfully place local residents in jobs.

Impact of the Community-Building Organizations' Networks

The community building organizations' bridging networks have a significant impact on their neighborhoods' collective capacity. By bringing together such a diverse array of institutions around a common vision, PACT and CO-OP developed a *sense of collective identity* among institutions representing a wide range of social groups and institutional niches. As Daniel put it, "When you work at your job on a daily basis, you basically just see what's around you. You go out and you handle certain specific tasks. But working with PACT, you're able to hear the concerns of other organizations. . . . So it kind of like lets you see the whole picture." In the process of working together, PACT's participants developed a greater understanding of one another's interests and perspectives. "Everyone's connected. So bankers know what residents want. Residents know what the bankers want, [what the] businesses want," explained one PACT member. Through this process, participants came to see themselves as members of a broadly defined community composed of a wide range of institutions and social groups.

While the community-building organizations' networks fostered a sense of collective identity that was far more expansive and wide-reaching than that of the civic and women-centered organizations, these networks did little to build a sense of connection among the neighborhood's individual residents. Even though most of PACT and CO-OP's member institutions claimed to represent a base of residents either through their clientele or their membership ranks, PACT and CO-OP spent relatively little time trying to build connections within this grassroots base. Consequently, the organizations' networks were limited primarily to the staff and directors of the member organizations and did little to build a sense of collective identity among the rest of the neighborhood's residents.

The institutional basis of the community organizations' networks also shaped the specific nature of their collective activities. Whereas the civic and women-centered networks created a foundation for *mutual support* among individual residents, the community-building networks enabled the neighborhood's institutions to support one another in achieving their respective missions. For example, CO-OP's members kept each other informed about available funding opportunities and wrote letters of support for each other's grant proposals. Similarly, by drawing on the relationships they had with other complementary agencies within the network, CO-OP's member agencies were able to serve their own clients more effectively. As one CO-OP member explained, "We've got enough of an identity to get to know each other and build relationships. So when I refer [my clients to another organization], I'm not referring to a nameless organization outside this area, but I'm referring to a person. It's a very relationship-based community, and if I can create some image of the person they're going to see and what will happen there, I can make a bridge that will be easier than if I'm saying 'Go across town to this office.' "

In addition to facilitating mutual support among agencies, the community-building networks enabled the member institutions to engage in *cooperative action* toward their shared goals. In order to achieve their collective vision of the common good, the member institutions had no choice but to work collaboratively. After all, implementing a comprehensive community plan is not something that any single organization can accomplish on its own. Working together enabled the institutions to leverage the neighborhood's assets and resources in innovative ways in order to develop new programs and services.

Building the trust necessary to make institutional collaboration possible, however, also involves significant challenges. As Daniel's story demonstrates, getting institutions to risk their professional reputations and institutional resources to work in cooperation with one another on joint projects is a high-stakes undertaking. In order to make these cooperative ventures successful, PACT and CO-OP frequently relied on formal agreements to protect the participating institutions from undue risk. For example, CO-OP worked with a lawyer specializing in collaboration to create a contractual agreement to distribute the responsibilities and benefits of joint projects equitably among the partners. The agreement addressed potential free rider problems by requiring all members to commit a certain number of hours per month to partnership meetings and activities. And it included specific rules of engagement designed to enforce mutual accountability and minimize the risks involved with high-stakes collaborative activities like joint fundraising. The agreement stipulated that if a participating organization did not adequately meet its obligations to the collaborative, the other partners would have the right to revoke its membership.

This contractual agreement enabled CO-OP's members to take risks that would have been impossible without such guaranteed protections. For example, CO-OP's members worked together to streamline their institutional budgets and spending patterns based on their collective assessment of the value of each institution's programs for the neighborhood as a whole. And when the community was faced with an overall reduction in government funding, the members went one step further—working together to prioritize specific line items from each agency's budget and making drastic cuts to all but the most essential programs. As CO-OP's coordinator explained, "We literally took all our budgets and laid them on the table, which is something I've never heard of being done before. But each of us opened our books and said 'This is where we're spending our money.' And agencies were realistic about what they really needed, and they cut a lot."

In addition, CO-OP's contractual agreement enabled its member agencies to embark on several innovative collaborative programs that no single agency could have developed on its own. For example, in order to increase the capacity of the neighborhood's only jobs skills training center, CO-OP built partnerships between a social service agency that agreed to provide job seekers with access to a free van service, a mental health agency that provided free counseling to those on the job market, and a local women's organization that provided a phone message service and clothing bank with interview clothing.

While CO-OP's formal collaborative agreement made it possible for the member institutions to participate in such high-stakes ventures without excessive risk, the agreement ultimately ended up constraining the network's flexibility and scope. Participants will usually only buy into a contractual agreement that they have been involved in creating. This makes it difficult to incorporate new members into the partnership without jeopardizing the high levels of trust and mutual accountability among the original participants. When CO-OP merged with a similar institution-based network in the same neighborhood, the dramatic change in its membership base undermined the validity of the group's original partnership agreement. The new partnership included dozens of new members who had not been involved in creating the formal agreement and thus refused to abide by it. The resulting hostilities and mutual distrust made cooperation impossible. As one member put it, "They destroyed two reasonably cohesive groups and ended up with one amorphous mess. . . . They created total chaos . . . some sort of multi-headed hydra. Just a disaster." Thus, while contractual agreements can help institutional members overcome the dilemmas of collective action, they can also make it difficult for community-building networks to adapt to changes in their membership composition.

In addition to fostering cooperative action among a wide array of local institutions, PACT and CO-OP also *expanded the scope* of these institutions' collective capacity by linking the institutions to external resources and supports. For example, in its efforts to strengthen the local neighborhood economy, PACT developed relationships with several national corporations and a Puerto Rican grocery store chain. It also worked in partnership with a local university to analyze the economic feasibility of several potential urban development projects. Similarly, in its attempt to secure control over vacant land in the neighborhood, PACT developed relationships with Chicago's mayor, Department of Planning and Development, and Department of Housing. And in order to boost local residents' access to mortgages and small business loans, PACT established ties to several national banks and lending institutions. Through these and other external connections, PACT significantly expanded the community's ability to develop programs and services to address residents' needs.

In sum, the community-building organizations create large bridging networks that bring together a diverse array of stakeholder institutions based on shared normative commitments. These networks provide a basis for mutual support among the institutions, enabling them to achieve their individual goals more effectively. They also enable the organizations to produce collaborative projects to better address the community's needs. And they expand the community's ability to solve its own problems by linking the neighborhood's institutions with external resources and support. However, while the networks' breadth and size provide a significant boost to the community's capacity, they are not very effective at building direct connections among the neighborhood's individual residents, and their reliance on formal partnership agreements can make them less flexible than most resident-based networks.

THE POWER-BASED MODEL: CREATING BRIDGING NETWORKS BASED ON INSTRUMENTAL TIES

Like the community-building organizations, the power-based organizations create large bridging networks. However, whereas the community-building organizations' networks are based in a normative commitment to an overarching vision for the community, power-based networks are rooted in *instrumental* commitments—the members get involved to the extent that they can reap concrete individual benefits from their participation. By linking together hundreds of residents both locally and nationally, the power-based organizations' networks enable their participants to effectively address their individual self-interests through large-scale collective action.

The Form and Substance of the Power-Based Organizations' Networks

Proponents of the power-based model view residents as rational actors who make decisions about whether to get involved in community organizations based on an implicit cost-benefit analysis about whether it is in their immediate self-interest to do so. Thus, power-based organizers try to recruit residents into their organizations by convincing them that by joining with other residents they'll be able to solve their immediate problems. When WON's organizers doorknock in the community, they ask residents to identify their greatest frustrations and concerns regarding the neighborhood. Then they invite the residents to join with their neighbors to work together on finding a solution to the specific problems they identified.

If residents' interests cannot be resolved at a neighborhood level, WON connects its members with other residents around the city—and in some cases around the nation—who are trying to tackle similar problems in their own communities. In addition to participating in several ad hoc citywide coalitions relating to specific issue campaigns, WON is a member of National People's Action, a loose coalition of more than 300 grassroots groups from 38 states. NPA's members join the coalition not because they share an overarching vision for society or strong interpersonal relationships, but because their individual participants have the same instrumental goals. Through NPA, groups of residents from around the country who have been independently working on similar issues and problems in their own neighborhoods come together to push for changes at the national level that will help them to better achieve their local agendas.[3]

The experiences of WON member Janice Aspen illustrate the unique nature of the power-based organizations' networks. As a recently divorced single mother, Janice was concerned about whether she would be able to offer her young son the kind of life she had always envisioned for him. The only neighborhood she could afford to live in certainly didn't seem like an ideal place to raise a child. Among other concerns, she worried constantly about her son's safety: "I know our community has a lot of gangs—I haven't really seen any of them or dealt with them, but that's what I've been hearing. And I have a son that's three years old, and I do not have the money to move into a better neighborhood."

Not knowing any of her neighbors, Janice dealt with her worries by keeping a vigilant watch over her son and staying inside as much as possible. Then Matt, WON's organizer, knocked on her door. Arguing that the only way to change neighborhood problems is through people power, Matt encouraged her to get involved with a group of neighbors from the immediate area who were working to address the neighborhood's gang problem. He suggested that if she joined forces with these other residents, together they might have enough power to get something done. Several weeks later, Janice participated in a public meeting with more than 200 other local residents to demand that the police respond to the neighborhood's gang problem more forcefully. Faced with such a large group, the commander agreed to commit additional manpower to address their concerns.

With her concerns about safety somewhat assuaged, Janice turned her attention to other aspects of the neighborhood that had long worried her. As her son approached school age, she had become concerned about the poor quality of the neighborhood's schools and the community's lack of educational resources. When Matt told her that other residents had expressed an interest in getting a better public library for the area, she decided to join the fight: "I know kids have assignments which require resources from the library, and [the local libraries] don't have [the books]. So to me that's a main concern. I have a child that's going to need to have access to books in a library very soon, and they probably won't be there—because I have needed things from the library and I have [had to go] to a much farther one. . . . I don't think that's fair." This new campaign put Janice in contact with a large group of residents from around the area. She recognized some of them from the anti-gang campaign, but many of the faces were new and unfamiliar. As she explained, many of the people who she had worked with on the first campaign had no reason to be involved in this one: "I really care about our library . . . but other people don't have kids. Other people have a computer at home, they have no need for a library. So obviously they don't care about that, but they might care about the gang that's at the corner of their house. So I think everybody has a different vision of what they want to accomplish in the neighborhood."

As Janice's experience demonstrates, because WON's networks are based on the specific overlapping self-interests of the participants, the relationships among the network's members tend to be more single-stranded and impersonal than those that characterize the civic and women-centered organizations. Individual participants may develop friendships with other residents that they meet through the organization, but on the whole WON's members do not have strong relationships with one another outside the context of specific campaigns. And because residents join the power-based networks in order to achieve their individual goals, the networks' individual membership composition is likely to change each time the organizations resolve one campaign and take on another.[4] As one WON member explained, "The people in the neighborhood, they're only going to get involved on issues they [care about]. A lot of people, as soon as . . . that problem is solved, . . . they just slowly drop out. . . . You're always going to have a turnover in leadership—you're going to have people coming in and going."

Despite this frequent turnover, by focusing their campaigns on problems of concern to large numbers of residents, both WON and UNITE were able to build extensive networks of several hundred residents around each campaign.[5] And because of the networks' instrumental basis, the organizations adapted easily to changes in their membership base. As long as WON's organizers were able to keep developing campaigns based on the self-interests of the majority of the neighborhood's residents, the organization's overall numbers remained relatively stable, even when the specific composition of its membership fluctuated. For example, over a period of less than ten years, WON's neighborhood changed from a white ethnic enclave into a predominately Latino neighborhood. Thus, whereas WON once built its membership through campaigns that tapped into residents' fears of racial turnover in the neighborhood, now its organizers mobilize residents based on their shared desire to improve their access to public services. As a result, even though the specific composition of the organization's membership has changed dramatically, the organization's size and the power of its networks have remained relatively constant.[6]

Impact of the Power-Based Organizations' Networks

The power-based organizations' networks have a substantial impact on the neighborhood's collective efficacy. Through their participation in power-based campaigns, residents develop a *sense of collective identity* with other residents around the neighborhood who share their interests and concerns. This collective identity doesn't necessarily provide the kind of feel-good sense of belonging that's created by the women-centered bonding networks, but it does give residents a sense of being part of something bigger than themselves. "When one person tries to make a difference by themselves, it hardly ever works," Janice explained. "[But] when they get a big group of people together, it makes me feel like, you know what, we're not alone. Even if it's just ten or twenty people, a lot of people care about this."

Like the civic and women-centered networks, this sense of collective identity enabled residents to engage in *mutual support*; but because the relationships among the power-based networks' members were primarily impersonal and single-stranded, this mutual support tended to focus narrowly around the members' shared instrumental goals. For example, when a participant in WON's anti-gang campaign was threatened by a group of local youths throwing rocks at his house, over a dozen WON members mobilized to help him build a fence around his property. Many of the members who came to help didn't even know the man personally, but they felt it was important to show the gangs that WON's members support and protect their own. Describing a similar incident in which WON's president had a pile of dead rats placed on his front porch, one member explained,

> People from all blocks went to his house that evening and were all out on his lawn showing a message of support for that community, show them hey we're here, we're all supporting him. And you get that support—you need support, you've got people, maybe not on your block, people from around you, people from other regions that work with us that will be there to support you. You're not alone. So we have that support within the organization. They need us, we'll be there.

Implicit in this ethic of mutual support is the assumption that if individual WON members aren't given the support they need to help them stand up to intimidation, the group's clout in the neighborhood could be undermined.

More importantly, the power-based organizations enabled large groups of residents to engage in *cooperative action* to achieve their shared goals. By helping residents to band together around shared self-interests, WON and UNITE gave residents far greater influence over the public sphere than they would have had as individuals acting alone. Many residents in Janice's neighborhood, for example, were concerned that the overcrowding in the local elementary school was affecting the quality of their children's education. WON brought these residents together to develop a coordinated strategy for addressing the issue, but after several meetings the parents realized that if they were going to have an impact on the issue, they needed to get a commitment of funding from the Chicago School Board. Given the School Board's citywide scope, they decided they would be more effective in securing this funding if they teamed up with parents from other schools with similar concerns. WON's organizer connected them to parents from four other schools in WON's geographic area that were also facing overcrowding problems. Working together, this united front of almost 400 parents was able to secure a commitment from the School Board to resolve the overcrowding problems at each of the five schools.

In addition to building residents' collective capacity to address shared problems, the power-based organizations further *expanded the scope* of this capacity by linking local residents to networks of residents and institutions outside of the neighborhood. When the School Board insisted that without more federal funding for school construction, the city simply didn't have the capacity to build any new schools, a delegation of parents from WON's five schools traveled to Washington D.C. to participate in National People's Action's annual gathering. Dozens of other community groups around the country who were experiencing similar problems with school overcrowding also sent delegations of parents to the gathering, and together this coalition descended upon the Capitol to demand more federal funding for each of their schools. Working with a thousand other angry parents, WON's leaders successfully negotiated an agreement with the Secretary of Education that resulted in an influx of funding for school construction. WON then negotiated with the Chicago School Board to ensure that this funding was targeted to each of the five schools whose parents had spearheaded the campaign. Given that much of the political decision-making about public resources takes place at the state or national level, the ability to tap into these kinds of extra-local networks significantly increases local residents' ability to achieve their goals.

In sum, the power-based organizations create large bridging networks based on instrumental ties. By enabling residents to band together to build a power base within the neighborhood and beyond, these networks significantly increase the community's ability to address local problems through public action within the political sphere.

THE TRANSFORMATIVE MODEL: CREATING BONDING AND BRIDGING NETWORKS BASED ON NORMATIVE TIES

In contrast to the community-building and power-based organizations, the transformative organizations create *both* bonding *and* bridging networks rooted in *normative* ties. The organizations build intense relationships among small groups of residents who share common ideological commitments. Through their involvement with the organizations, these residents also become connected to groups of activists and organizations outside the immediate neighborhood who share their ideological vision. While these networks often include organizations from all over the world, they tend to be less organized than the power-based or community-building organizations' bridging networks, and thus have less of an impact on residents' overall capacity to create change.

The Form and Substance of the Transformative Organizations' Networks

In contrast to the instrumental motivations that connect the power-based organizations' members to one another, the transformative organizations' members are motivated by their commitment to a set of abstract principles and ideals. Most of JAG's long-term members got involved with the organization because they were searching for ways to live out their political values and philosophical beliefs. Many were already involved in activist work at a city or national level and were looking for ways to get involved in their neighborhoods. In almost all cases their involvement was rooted in ideological commitments that shaped all aspects of their lives—their other political activities, their lifestyles, their friendship networks, and their career choices. Thus their participation in JAG and the relationships they built with other JAG members were part of a multifaceted, all-encompassing worldview.

The totalizing nature of these commitments and their rejection of mainstream values and beliefs limited the number of residents who were likely to get involved with JAG's network. JAG's staff and leaders tried to broaden the organization's core membership beyond this small group of progressive activists, but with limited success. As discussed in chapter 3, JAG tried to use popular education to build a commitment among the neighborhood's low-income tenants to the organization's long-term ideological agenda, but because of the organization's limited capacity, these efforts were largely unsuccessful. As a result, while JAG was able to engage the neighborhood's low-income residents in specific campaigns around their immediate housing-related needs, for the most part they did not become members of JAG's ongoing networks. Instead, JAG's networks were dominated by a small group of fifteen to thirty progressive activists whose worldviews were already compatible with JAG's ideological agenda.

The story of long-time JAG member Hannah Stern illustrates the unique nature of the organization's network. When Hannah got involved with JAG, she was already a veteran social activist who had participated in dozens of progressive movements and organizations for more than twenty years. Her activist experience had revolved primarily around national and international issues, but in the early 1990s she became increasingly concerned about the problems affecting her community. She found out about the work that JAG was doing on these issues through two existing members whom she knew through her connections to other citywide progressive organizations:

> At some point about six or seven years ago, housing struck me as an important issue and I heard about a housing committee meeting and wanted to find out more about it, have some voice in it, see what I could do. I had avoided getting into a community organization because I was more interested in national and international issues and didn't want to tie myself down to something. I guess I'm just not as anxious to make close attachments in my neighborhood . . . but the issues pulled at me. . . .

[and] I think it's an important thing to fight for your values where you are.

Hannah became an active participant in JAG's work, integrating her commitments to the organization with her ongoing involvement in other progressive causes.

Hannah also worked on an ongoing basis to connect JAG's participants with the other social justice organizations she was a part of. She frequently passed out flyers and made announcements at JAG's meetings for rallies and events sponsored by a range of other progressive organizations throughout the city. And she kept JAG's members up-to-date on a variety of local and national political issues by forwarding them the e-mails she received from several social justice list-serves. She also tried to incorporate participants from other progressive organizations into JAG's work. Through Hannah's connections, members of the Green Party, the New Party, and several other ideologically compatible groups became active JAG members. And for those local activists who weren't interested in becoming ongoing participants, Hannah held house meetings to educate them about neighborhood issues and update them on JAG's most recent campaigns.

With many of its members doing similar informal bridging work, JAG developed loose connections to several dozen like-minded organizations. These connections included not only local and national groups, but also groups around the world rooted in similar normative commitments. For example, one JAG member spent six months visiting and participating in social justice organizations in Asia and Australia. He sent weekly e-mails to JAG's members to introduce them to the organizations and to reflect on the parallels between local neighborhood dynamics and the struggles faced by peasants in India, activists in Australia, and urban workers in Thailand. Another JAG member visited Spain's Mondragon community—an extensive worker controlled cooperative—to explore the lessons local residents could glean about sustainable development from this international example. Thus, through the informal "bridging" work of its members, JAG developed a distinctive network structure that combined bonding networks at the local level with bridging networks at a citywide, national, and global level.

Impact of the Transformative Organizations' Networks

JAG's multilayered networks had a distinctive impact on the neighborhood's collective efficacy. First, the networks created a distinctive *sense of collective identity* among JAG's core members. Many of these residents were

used to feeling marginalized within the broader society because of their political beliefs. Through their involvement with JAG, they felt a sense of belonging, not to the community as a whole, but to a smaller "community" of
like-minded activists within the neighborhood. In addition, the organization's informal ties to social justice groups outside of the neighborhood
helped residents to feel connected—in a structural sense—to residents
around the city and around the world.

The transformative organizations' networks also provided a basis for *mutual support* among the members. Given the nature of their normative ties,
this support usually revolved around participants' activist commitments. For
example, JAG's members often sold each other tickets to fundraising events
sponsored by other progressive organizations, and they frequently recruited
JAG members to attend these organizations' rallies and events. In addition,
JAG as a whole engaged in mutual support with some of the other organizations that were part of its loose bridging networks. When these other organizations held workshops or protests, JAG often brought a handful of members
to the event in support and solidarity with the other group. And these organizations often returned the favor for JAG's events.

The networks also enabled residents to engage in *cooperative action* to
achieve their shared goals. For example, when JAG's members learned
about a plan to transform one of the neighborhood's commercial strips into
high-end housing and retail, they mobilized their network to oppose the initiative. A handful of dedicated JAG members worked several hours a week
over a number of months to conduct an ongoing survey of shoppers in the
commercial area to find out their priorities for local development. Then one
of JAG's members compiled the survey data into a series of sophisticated
graphs and charts. Meanwhile, other members worked together to analyze
the development plan in light of the survey results. Finally, when all the research was complete, the members organized a community meeting to present the results of their analysis. The meeting was attended by dozens of
neighborhood residents as well as representatives from other like-minded organizations throughout the city. Through their efforts, JAG's members were
able to generate significant public discussion and debate about the proposed
development plan, ultimately preventing the plan from being adopted.

In addition to building residents' capacity for cooperative action, JAG
built extra-local bridging networks in an effort to *expand the scope* of residents' capacity to effect change. Because the organization saw its work
within the context of a broader social justice movement, its members viewed
the creation of such linkages as an essential component of the organization's
mission. However, while JAG successfully built informal connections to a
wide range of different kinds of organizations—a labor organization, a gay

rights organization, several churches, a voting rights organization, local progressive think-tanks, and several international solidarity organizations—these relationships didn't have a very significant impact on JAG's overall capacity. Because of JAG's limited size and the ambitious nature of its goals, it was not very successful at mobilizing these relationships into effective, coordinated action.

JAG helped to form several citywide coalitions of organizations with similar political orientations and worldviews, but the coalitions usually had so few members and so little capacity that they operated more like study groups than action organizations. For instance, JAG worked with a coalition of tenants' rights organizations, public education advocacy groups, and neighborhood organizations to develop a "Community Bill of Rights" for the city. Their platform covered a broad range of principles, each of which on its own would have been extremely challenging to achieve, especially at a citywide level: "(1) Nobody should be priced out of their own neighborhood; (2) communities should be able to determine their future; (3) elected representatives [should be] truly accountable to the people." With only a handful of participants and no resources to speak of, the coalition spent most of its energy researching and fine-tuning its platform. After several months of unsuccessfully trying to get other groups to sign onto its agenda, the group eventually disbanded. Without broad-based support, it had become increasingly clear that there was nothing more the members could do to move their agenda forward. Thus, JAG's networks provided a basis for intellectual exchange and solidarity with other organizations sharing similar values, but unlike the power-based and community-building organizations' bridging networks, they did not represent an effective basis for shared action.

There were a few notable exceptions to this pattern. For example, when a local landlord who also owned a popular gay nightclub refused to concede to the demands of an organized group of his tenants, JAG teamed up with a citywide progressive gay rights organization to step up the pressure. After JAG's core members, the tenants, and the gay rights organization held weekly protests in front of the landlord's club, he finally agreed to negotiate with the tenants. Successes such as this demonstrate the potential impact of broader extra-local networks, but again, for the most part the limited capacity of JAG's networks made this kind of success more the exception than the rule.

In sum, JAG built local bonding networks as well as extra-local bridging networks based on normative ties. These networks helped participants to feel part of a small community of like-minded people within the neighborhood. And they provided a basis for participants to support one another's political and activist commitments. The networks also enabled residents to engage in cooperative action to address their shared goals, both at a local level and, to a limited extent, in the larger public sphere. And, while these networks did not significantly increase the community's ability to solve local problems, they did expand participants' connection to social justice struggles around the world.

CONCLUSION: BUILDING COMMUNITY CAPACITY—IMPLICATIONS OF DIFFERENT APPROACHES

Each model of community organizing entails a distinctive approach to capacity building that shapes the form and substance of the social networks it creates. The strengths and limitations of these network types can best be assessed in relation to the four levels of potential outcomes that were highlighted in the chapter's introduction:

- *Sense of collective identity*: In the process of developing relationships with others, residents come to recognize their connection to a "community" beyond their own household. This sense of collective identity makes community action possible by enabling residents to perceive their shared fate.
- *Mutual support*: By building relationships of reciprocity and trust among residents (and, in some cases, institutions), social networks enable residents (or institutions) to assist one another in achieving their individual goals.
- *Cooperative action*: Social networks also enable residents (or institutions) to work together on group goals—shared objectives that could not be achieved by individuals acting on their own.
- *Expanded scope*: By connecting residents to people, resources, organizations or institutions outside of their own community or social group, social networks can expand residents' capacity beyond what they could achieve simply by working together as a group.

Each organization succeeded in achieving some of these outcomes but was less effective at achieving others.

The civic organizations created bonding networks rooted in instrumental and affective ties. These networks were most effective at building a basis for mutual support and group cooperation among groups of relatively homogeneous participants. But the networks' insularity and small size made them unable to significantly expand the community's ability to solve problems. And their homogeneity actually exacerbated social divisions and a tendency towards parochialism within the neighborhood.

The women-centered organizations also built bonding networks rooted in affective ties; but they worked to connect these networks with external institutions and supports. The women-centered organizations' networks were most effective at building a basis for extensive mutual support and cooperative action among small groups of residents. The organizations' partnerships with external institutions also helped to expand the community's ability to solve problems. But, ultimately, the tensions between the bonding and bridging components of the women-centered organizations' networks made this combination difficult to sustain.

In contrast, the community-building organizations built bridging networks linking diverse stakeholder groups throughout the neighborhood based on normative commitments. These networks provided a foundation for local organizations and institutions to engage in mutual support and collaborative projects. In addition, the networks linked these institutions to an array of external resources and supports that significantly increased the community's ability to address its problems. However, while these institutional connections strengthened the community's problem-solving capacity, they did little to build linkages among the neighborhood's individual residents.

The power-based organizations built bridging networks connecting residents at the local, citywide, and national level based on instrumental ties. The networks provided a limited basis for mutual support around shared interests. More importantly, they enabled residents to engage in cooperative action to achieve their shared interests. And by connecting residents to hundreds, and in some cases thousands, of other residents with similar concerns, the networks dramatically increased the community's ability to solve problems through public action in the political sphere.

The transformative organizations created local bonding networks and extra-local bridging networks based on normative (ideological) ties. These networks helped residents to feel part of a small community of activists within the neighborhood and enabled residents to provide one another with mutual support around their activist commitments. The networks also enabled residents to engage in cooperative action at the local level around their shared goals. And although the organizations' bridging networks did not significantly expand the community's ability to solve its problems, they provided a basis for solidarity and exchange among organizations sharing similar values.

The next chapter explores another feature essential to overall community capacity-building—developing the community's ability to make collective decisions about neighborhood priorities and goals.

TABLE 4 Building Community Capacity

Model	Network form	Substance of ties	Impact on community capacity
Civic	Small, dense bonding networks	Combination of instrumental and affective (based on self-interest and neighborly relations)	Mutual support around instrumental interests. Cooperative action among a small, homogeneous group. Insularity limits the networks' impact on the neighborhood's overall capacity to solve problems
Women-centered	Small, dense bonding networks with some bridging as well	Affective (based on intimate friendships)	Mutual support around personal goals. Cooperative action around shared goals. Some expansion of community's capacity, but tensions between bonding and bridging networks
Community-building	Large, loose bridging networks	Normative (based on shared collective vision)	Mutual support around institutions' individual missions. Cooperative action to achieve the group's collective vision. Expansion of community's capacity by connecting neighborhood to external resources
Power-based	Large, loose bridging networks	Instrumental (based on self-interest)	Limited mutual support around overlapping interests. Cooperative action to achieve shared interests. Significant expansion of community's ability to solve problems through public action in the political sphere
Transformative	Small, dense bonding networks plus bridging interests	Normative (based on shared ideology)	Mutual support around activist interests. Cooperative action around shared goals. Limited expansion of community's overall capacity, but creates an expanded worldview

CHAPTER 5

BUILDING A COMMUNITY
GOVERNANCE STRUCTURE

CHAPTER 4 demonstrated how community organizing develops the social infrastructure to enable urban residents to engage in collective
action. In order to exercise this capacity, community members must
be able to make collective decisions about their goals. To facilitate this
process, community organizing groups build democratic governance structures at the local level. By providing mechanisms for community members
to deliberate about their common affairs, these structures enable participants to make shared decisions about community priorities. In addition, by
fostering popular participation in community decision-making, these structures create microcosms of genuine democracy at the neighborhood level.

Community governance structures can vary significantly depending on
the specific conceptions of democracy that underlie their formation. A good
starting point for understanding these differences is the distinction between
"adversary" and "unitary" democracy (Mansbridge 1983). *Adversary* democracy, which forms the basis of our society's dominant political institutions, is
premised on the assumption that the members of a community have varying, and often conflicting, interests. In contrast, *unitary* democracy pre-
sumes that a community's members naturally have, or can develop, common interests.

Whether an organization espouses a unitary or adversary conception of
democracy has significant implications for its formal structures of governance, the distribution of power and authority within the organization, its
methods of discussion and deliberation, and its decision-making rules.
Decision-making processes within *adversary* democracies are designed to
"weigh and come to terms with conflicting selfish interests rather than trying
to reconcile them or to make them subordinate to a larger common good"
(Mansbridge 1983: 16). Thus, adversary democracies typically use a system of
elected representation and majority voting.

Organizations that espouse a *unitary* conception of democracy rely on a
more consensus-oriented approach to decision-making. The specific mechanisms and procedures that they utilize in order to achieve consensus vary,

however, depending on their conception of the basis of the community's shared interests. For example, organizations that take it for granted that the members of a community naturally share the same interests try to reach consensus through unstructured discussion without formal decision-making rules or procedures. In contrast, organizations that believe community members can *develop* shared interests through mutual empathy utilize a highly structured face-to-face process of discussion and deliberation. Other organizations attempt to reconcile community members' divergent interests through the identification of a "correct" solution to the community's problems—a "common good" that can be identified through solid reasoning and analysis. Thus, within the broad category of "unitary" democracy, lies a continuum of potential governance structures.

This chapter examines the case study organizations' approaches to deliberation and decision-making, beginning with an analysis of the power-based model—the only model in my study that espouses an adversary approach to democracy. Power-based organizations aim to create neighborhood governance structures that protect each participant's individual interests while mediating among these interests to produce collective decisions that are recognized as legitimate by all participants. As a result, they build formal, hierarchically structured organizations based on elected representation and the vote.

All the other models in the study can be broadly defined as unitary democracies, but the specific features of their governance structures vary significantly according to how they conceptualize the nature of participants' shared interests. Civic organizations assume community residents should be able to make decisions about neighborhood priorities without conflict or disagreement. Consequently, the organizations operate as unstructured forums with no formal mechanisms for mediating among different interests and no decision-making rules.

In contrast, community-building organizations assume that while multiple community stakeholders may have conflicting individual interests, they can and should subordinate those interests for the sake of the community's common good. The emphasis of decision-making within such organizations is on finding the correct solution to the community's problems. As a result, community-building organizations tend to relegate decision-making authority to a small group of community experts and charismatic leaders.

Women-centered organizations, on the other hand, operate on the belief that community members can *develop* shared interests by listening to one another and building empathetic relationships. Consequently, the organizations make decisions through a face-to-face consensus-building process in which all participants are given an equal opportunity to speak so that everyone's voice is included and all perspectives are reflected in the final decision.

Transformative organizations believe that although their constituents may have differing subjective perceptions of their own interests, they nonetheless all share the same fundamental "objective" interests. The organizations encourage extensive deliberation and debate as a way for residents to develop a more accurate understanding of the structural patterns underlying their common experiences. But because effective decision-making requires a sophisticated understanding of the structural dimensions of residents' interests, final decisions are often relegated to a small group of leaders.

In order to evaluate the relative merits of these different approaches, I will analyze the case study organizations' experiences along four principal dimensions, all of which are important elements of effective democratic governance:

(a) promoting individual participation, inclusion, and equal voice;
(b) promoting genuine deliberation over important community issues;
(c) producing decisions efficiently;
(d) producing decisions that further the organization's strategic objectives for the community in the wider public sphere.

Due to the differences in their formal structures, methods of discussion and deliberation, and decision-making rules, the case study organizations had varying levels of success in achieving these objectives. In most cases, the prioritization of one or two resulted in an inability to effectively achieve the remaining objectives. The organizations utilized a variety of strategies to deal with these tensions and trade-offs.

THE POWER-BASED MODEL: PROTECTING INDIVIDUAL INTERESTS THROUGH REPRESENTATIVE STRUCTURES AND THE VOTE

Espousing a traditional, adversary conception of democracy, power-based organizations create what is, in essence, a microcosm of the American government system at the neighborhood level. Proponents of the power-based model believe that decisions about the neighborhood's priorities should be determined by the community's residents, based on their subjectively defined interests. But power-based organizations also assume that every community is composed of competing interests and that conflicts among these interests are natural and inevitable. Because all residents do not share the same interests, power-based organizations create formal decision-making structures that mediate among these interests in order to determine the will of the majority. These governance structures are essentially the same as those used by our established political institutions—elected representation, majority voting, a centralized system of checks and balances, and relatively autonomous localized decision-making bodies that are accountable to higher-level leadership.

The following description of a typical meeting of the United Neighborhood Institutions of the Eastside (UNITE) illustrates the dynamics of this highly structured, somewhat bureaucratic approach to community governance:[1]

After fighting through rush hour traffic at the end of a long day, I was one of the last to arrive at UNITE's quarterly Action Council meeting. As I rushed into the large church basement where the meeting was being held, a voice behind me demanded to know "which organization are you with?" I turned to face a sign-in table stacked with agendas and handouts, and staffed by UNITE's office administrator. With her hands poised over a large filing box filled with carefully labeled envelopes, she again asked me to identify my organizational affiliation. When I explained I was just a visitor, she allowed me to sign in and be on my way.

When the next participant arrived, I saw that the envelopes were filled with brightly colored voting cards labeled "yes," "no," and "maybe." Each of UNITE's member organizations is entitled to bring one to three delegates to the Action Council meetings (the specific number of delegates depends on the organization's size). Prior to each Action Council meeting, the member organizations decide how their delegates will vote on the key policy issues on the meeting's agenda. The voting cards enable the delegates to represent their organization's position during the Action Council voting process.

The meeting began at seven p.m. sharp, with the loud bang of a gavel against a wooden podium. The participants sat in a circle, behind long tables displaying printed placards that identified each participant's organizational affiliation. As participants scrambled to take their seats, Myrna, UNITE's vice-president, welcomed everyone. After one of UNITE's board members read a brief inspirational poem, Myrna asked the participants to go around the table, introduce themselves, and give a three-word answer to the question "why UNITE?" The participants moved quickly through the exercise, giving answers like "strength in numbers," "do justice," and "for the people." When Wanda, an elderly public housing resident, tried to use the go-round as an opportunity to start complaining about the neighborhood's problems, Myrna listened politely for a few seconds and then cut her off by leading the group in a brief round of applause. Wanda was momentarily confused, but remained quiet for the rest of the introductions.

After the introductions, Myrna asked Laverne, UNITE's membership

chair, to formally introduce the group's newest institutional members. As Lav-
erne introduced the delegates from a local tenant's association and senior citi-
zen advocacy group, the Council members applauded warmly and welcomed
them.

Next Robert, another UNITE board member, led the group in an evaluation of UNITE's convention, held two months earlier. The evaluation included
an opportunity for open feedback (all of which was recorded on large sheets of
butcher paper) as well as a more structured go-round in which the delegates
were asked to account for their institution's success or failure in recruiting participants to this event.

Then Myrna called for a representative from each of UNITE's Strategy
Teams to report on their team's work. The representatives took turns at the
lectern delivering brief prepared statements on the Strategy Teams' recent accomplishments and campaigns and upcoming meetings and events. After each
team had reported, Myrna asked the newest Strategy Team subcommittee—a
youth-police relations group led by teenagers—to present their proposal to the
Council. The team handed out an outline of the committee's mission and
plans, and then Raul, one of the committee's leaders, began the group's presentation: "We presented our strategy plan to the Youth and Families Strategy
Team and they voted 'aye'. We're presenting it to you now so you support it
and hopefully join us." Along with three other youth leaders, Raul talked
through the committee's mission and plan. Myrna asked if the Council members were ready to vote on the committee's proposal, and one of UNITE's
newest staff members asked if they could have questions and discussion first.
Myrna explained that according to Robert's Rules of Order, you have to call
the motion before discussing it. She asked for a motion to approve the committee's proposal, and then opened the floor to questions and discussion.

After several minutes, the questions had been exhausted, and Myrna called
for a vote. Each delegate quietly held up a "yes" or "no" voting card, and
within moments the vote had been tallied and a decision reached. Myrna announced the tally—thirty-four yes votes and one abstention—and declared
"the motion passes" to loud applause.

Myrna pointed out that the meeting was running four minutes behind
schedule and warned that they would need to move quickly through the rest of
the agenda in order to make up the time. She introduced Angie, a representative from United Power, the regional coalition of which UNITE is a member.
Myrna explained that it was time for UNITE to renew its annual membership
dues to United Power. With a dues obligation of $15,000, the Action Council
would need to make a formal decision about whether to renew.

Angie made a brief presentation about United Power's work and explained
the value of membership. After several members asked Angie for more informa-

tion about specific aspects of United Power's work, a few members stated their position on the issue. Mike, a relatively new UNITE member, said "I'm in favor, but my concern is I'd feel nervous after two years and $30,000 if there wasn't something we could point to that we did." He asked if there was enough money for the $15,000 dues in UNITE's budget, and UNITE's director explained that there was, but it would mean having one less staff person. Next, the director of one of UNITE's largest nonprofit members asserted "if UNITE doesn't join, my organization will have to join independently. It gives us an important chance to get our issues on the table here and in the suburbs."

Myrna asked if there were any more questions or comments. There weren't, so she suggested they move on. She explained that in order to make a decision, they would first need to take a vote on whether each delegate was ready to take a position on the issue on behalf of his or her organization. She explained that because of the magnitude of the decision, she wanted to make sure that the member organizations had had an opportunity to take a position on the issue prior to the meeting. Myrna articulated a motion and the delegates raised their cards. With twenty-two yes votes and six no, Myrna said they could go ahead and vote on the membership dues.

Without any further discussion or debate, Myrna made another motion, and the delegates once more raised their cards. The six delegates who had voted no on the previous motion abstained, and the final vote was eleven abstentions and twenty-one yeses. Shortly thereafter, Myrna made a motion to adjourn, and the meeting ended, about two minutes later than planned.[2]

Efficient, Fair, and Legitimate Decision-making

One of the clearest benefits of the power-based organizations' highly structured approach to democratic governance is that it is an efficient and effective way to reach decisions. In adversary democracies, decisions are made by weighing individual interests in an impersonal, quantitative manner. As the example demonstrates, even though UNITE's Action Council meetings require dozens of delegates, representing more than sixty organizations, to make decisions on a variety of important and potentially contentious issues each month, the meetings begin and end on time, and clear decisions are almost always reached. Using Robert's Rules of Order (Robert 1990), the meeting chair introduces the issue, opens the floor up to questions and a brief discussion, and then the members vote by holding up the appropriate card. The cards are counted, and whichever response is in the majority determines the outcome of the vote. Members typically do not discuss or respond to the votes of other members or become emotionally engaged in the process. Instead, the individual interests of each member are aggregated, and a final decision is reached.

Given the importance of the vote within our national electoral process, participants tend to view majority voting as synonymous with democracy and thus as a valid mechanism for resolving differences of opinion. This makes the outcomes of these decisions highly legitimate with the members. As a result, they are unlikely to challenge the result of a vote or engage in interpersonal conflict in response to their disagreements with other members. And because voting creates the perception that each individual's interests have been taken into consideration, the members generally view this method of decision-making as egalitarian and fair.

In addition to the vote, the power-based organizations' use of formal representative structures furthers the efficiency and legitimacy of their decision-making. With more than sixty institutional members, each representing potentially hundreds of individual members, UNITE's use of delegates streamlines the decision-making process, while assuring members that their voices have been included. Through the delegate system, the interests of all the members are, to some extent, protected within the voting process because each delegate is accountable to his or her institution. As UNITE's director explained, "The thing about having an institutional structure, or at least the theory, is that if I come to a meeting I'm representing my church congregation and I've discussed the issue of welfare and immigration reform [for example] with my church congregation, and therefore I'm representing what my congregation feels about the issue." Thus, even though each congregation member isn't present at the decision-making table, the reliance on formally accountable delegates assures each member that his or her interests were included in the decision-making process.

Even those power-based organizations like WON that have individual members rather than an institutional membership base utilize elected representation to maximize the efficiency and legitimacy of decisions. WON's board is composed of two representatives from each of its neighborhood affiliates. The board members are expected to represent the interests of their own neighborhoods in all organizational decision-making.

Equality of Access Versus Equality of Influence

Although voting is often viewed as the fairest and most democratic basis for decision-making, the formal equality of the vote can actually conceal real inequalities of influence within the organization. While the actual vote may allow each member a voice in the final outcome, it obscures the very different levels of political skill a member can bring to bear on the decision-making process. As Mansbridge points out, "Opening up the doors to participation in a direct, face-to-face democracy does not guarantee equal participation, let alone equal power. . . . At the moment of a vote, each individual 'counts for one and none for more than one' but this is not true in the many moments before, between, and after votes" (1983: 100–109). Differences in verbal fluency, education, confidence, and levels of involvement significantly shape participants' influence over the positions the members take when the vote finally happens.

In UNITE's meetings, people who were charismatic and articulate or had high levels of social status—such as pastors and the directors of non-profit agencies—often played a dominant role in discussions; in contrast, low-income participants and recent immigrants were typically much less vocal and less influential. In interviews, several of UNITE's members mentioned a concern with this pattern. As one put it,

> I think that sometimes people don't have as much of a voice because we forget about cultural issues. . . . There are a lot of people, things have to be quiet and there has to be a pause before they're willing to jump in. I think sometimes we forget—we take on this [attitude] like if they feel it's important they'll speak up, they'll jump in. Some people need a much longer conversational pause than others. So I think sometimes people get bowled over by those of us with stronger personalities, shall we say, on the board or the strategy teams. . . . I think it's arrogant to say they'll have to snap out of it, you're an American now, or you're at the table now. It's a very white male way that we run some meetings.

UNITE's continued reliance on Robert's Rules of Order (Robert 1990) exacerbated this problem. The system of Robert's Rules is so formal and complex that it often intimidates inexperienced participants from speaking at all (Stout 1997). Participants who are not comfortable with these rules may not get heard because they don't know the proper procedures or the appropriate time or format for raising their concerns.

While patterns of unequal influence are by no means limited to the power-based model, the use of majority voting obscures these patterns through the veneer of formal equality. Furthermore, relying on the vote to arbitrate among divergent interests deletes the minority's opinions from the final decision. While the disagreement of the minority may be recorded, the substance of their disagreement is typically not incorporated into the final outcome. For example, even though one-third of the delegates present at the UNITE meeting described above did not vote in favor of renewing the organization's annual dues to United Power, because those delegates were in the minority, their views were ultimately ignored. While they had the opportunity to vote or to abstain from voting, they were not asked to articulate the reason for their abstention, and their views were not reflected in any substantive way in the final decision. Instead of working to make sure that all viewpoints were expressed during the discussion period, which might have enabled the group to reconcile conflicting perspectives before the vote, Myrna simply used the vote itself as the arbiter of these disagreements.

As part of this dynamic, the losing members in a majority vote may respond by exiting the organization altogether rather than work on something that they don't agree with or don't see as a priority. This pattern is most pronounced in individual membership organizations like WON. For example, when a group of WON members and several co-sponsoring organizations were planning a candidate's forum, a disagreement arose regarding the event's date. Some participants felt the original date should be rescheduled to accommodate the alderman's agenda, while others advocated keeping the original date. Rather than debate the issue in an effort to reach agreement, participants took a vote. Those wanting to accommodate the alderman were outnumbered, and Matt, WON's organizer, told them that if they would prefer to withdraw from working on the forum altogether given the outcome of the vote, there would be no hard feelings. The losers caucused in the hallway, decided to withdraw, and left the meeting.

WON's participants took this incident in stride and didn't seem particularly surprised or upset. Matt closed the incident by saying matter-of-factly, "Everyone was able to speak and we took a vote and the majority said [to keep the forum on] the eleventh. . . . This is a democracy and we voted. We have to make those hard decisions." Speaking about the incident later, one of the members on the winning side of the vote explained, "The majority's going to rule. And if you don't like it, you don't feel like doing it, you don't have to come with us. But the majority of the people there feel like this is what they want to do. . . . If you don't want to come and participate in this, fine. I'm not going to hold it against you that you don't come, because it has to be in you to do it." Although membership attrition is an inevitable reality of community organizing, the use of the vote as the arbiter of disagreements is likely to exacerbate the attrition of participants whose views aren't consistent with those of the majority.

In sum, while the use of the vote enables power-based organizations to maximize the efficiency of their decisions while preserving a level of formal equality, it frequently undermines genuinely egalitarian deliberation about the issues. By permitting the substance of the opposition's concerns to be ignored, the vote may also leave a portion of the group without a real voice.

Whether or not members who feel excluded decide to exit the organization, this dynamic threatens the central democratic values of inclusion and equality of voice.

Subtle Manipulation

The ideal of one-person, one-vote can also create a dilemma for power-based organizers at the strategic planning and implementation phase of decision-making. In a one-person, one-vote system, the organization places the formal equality of individual members above the knowledge or expertise of specific members or staff. This is not a problem when the decisions at hand involve the identification of members' interests or the selection of community priorities. These kinds of decisions simply require community members to articulate their individual interests which are then aggregated to determine the group's priorities.

However, once the community's interests and priorities have been defined, the organization must select strategies and campaigns to address these issues. Given the reality that in most community-based organizations not all the members will be equally knowledgeable about the complex dynamics underlying the neighborhood's problems or have the same degree of organizing experience, the use of majority voting at this stage in the decision-making process frequently puts the organization at risk of choosing suboptimal strategies. This is particularly likely to be the case in small committee meetings and strategy sessions where individual participants are directly engaged in making decisions.

Because the selection of ineffective strategies is likely to undermine the organization's ability to successfully fight for the community's interests in the wider public sphere, this dynamic can be problematic for power-based organizations. Power-based organizers try to resolve this dilemma over the long term through the process of leadership development. In the short term, they often resort to using subtle manipulation to guide less experienced participants to make the "right" strategic decisions.

The extent of this manipulation varies depending on the knowledge and experience of the participants. WON's organizers rely on manipulation more frequently than UNITE's organizers because most of UNITE's active participants are the professional staff of the organization's member institutions and thus are fairly politically sophisticated.[3] In contrast, at most of WON's committee meetings, a significant proportion of the participants are new and inexperienced residents who, in the words of one leader, "come to these meetings . . . looking for someone to tell them what to do. They're not coming with an agenda or a thought. They have a problem. They want to know how to solve it." The organizers deal with these members by carefully steering discussions and decision-making in a very specific direction.

This steering process was a standard component of almost every WON meeting I attended and was used by every WON organizer I observed. The basic techniques were even outlined in training manuals produced by WON's national network, demonstrating the extent to which this manipulation is an institutionalized part of the network's approach (e.g. see Trapp 1976b: 12). The process works as follows: Prior to every community meeting, WON's organizers meet as a staff to brainstorm about the next steps in each of WON's campaigns. Then each organizer meets one on one with several core leaders to brainstorm about the campaign's next steps, all the while subtly selling the leaders on the ideas developed at the staff meeting. By the time these core leaders meet together to plan the committee meeting, they have already bought into the organizer's basic agenda. They then work with the organizer to figure out how they can sell the idea to the rest of the members at the committee meeting.

At the committee meeting, the organizer facilitates the discussion, leading participants to believe that they are fully responsible for selecting the strategies and that no decisions have yet been made. As the organizer leads the group in a "brainstorming" session, the core leaders introduce their strategic planning proposals and the organizer carefully guides the discussion so that the participants are persuaded that they have developed and endorsed this proposal. The organizers accomplish this feat through a strategic method of facilitation: they ask participants a question, solicit a response from one or two people, and then repeat the response back, as if paraphrasing and synthesizing the participants' ideas. In this "paraphrasing," the organizers may alter the participants' original ideas to fit with the desired outcome. This question, answer, and paraphrase routine continues until the participants have "decided" on the right strategic plan.

To illustrate, in a meeting of WON's Anti-Gang Task Force, John, WON's safety organizer, wanted to move participants away from their inclination to write letters in order to get them to focus on more confrontational strategies. WON's staff had already scheduled a large community meeting to apply public pressure on the police commander and local landlords, and John wanted the Task Force members to buy into this strategy. At the beginning of the meeting, several participants blamed the area's problems on irresponsible landlords, so John asked the group what they could do about these landlords. One woman immediately suggested that they tell the landlords' tenants to attach complaint letters to their rent checks. John nodded, replying, "yeah, we need to tell the landlords there's a problem. So why don't we invite the landlords to a meeting to let them know there's a problem?" His intonation suggested that he was taking this idea directly from the woman's response. Another woman shouted, "the landlords don't even care so it's a waste of time." John smoothly responded to her, saying "so does that make sense, to invite problem landlords to a meeting?" Not waiting for a response (and thus creating the impression that everyone had already agreed with him), John said "But if they don't show up, what should we do?" Maria, a core leader who had participated in an earlier planning meeting said "go to his house and let his neighbors know." John responded by asking the group, "is this a good idea?" Several women complained that the landlords were irresponsible and didn't care, and one insisted that she was in danger of retaliation if she tried to go against the landlords. John focused only on the last woman's comments. He turned to her, saying, "what's the difference between you calling and us here?" She thought for a moment and then said "strength in numbers." From there, without further discussion, John moved the group on to planning out the strategy they had just "developed." His process of moving things forward was so skillful that nobody seemed to realize (or care) that none of them had actually created or verbally endorsed the plan.

WON's organizers talked openly about the manipulative aspects of their organizing, but they argued that this manipulation is precisely what enables residents to develop effective organizing strategies and gain victories in the public arena. They pointed out that if they didn't guide the decision-making, they would be relying on inexperienced participants to shape the organization's strategies, rather than building on the combined experience of the organization's professional staff and long-time leaders.

In most cases, participants didn't appear to recognize or be concerned that they were being led. The organization's decisions about community priorities *were*, after all, genuinely based on residents' articulation of their interests. And because important decisions were made through majority vote, members typically felt that their opinions were receiving equal weight in the strategic decision-making process. Thus, through this process, the power-based organizations were able to achieve many of the benefits of formal democracy while manipulating certain decisions in order to make the organization more effective in the public arena.

This trade-off may be justifiable, but it often sacrifices meaningful community participation in discussions about how best to solve the community's problems. Simply giving participants the opportunity to vote when they have not been given the opportunity to really deliberate about different strategic options may fulfill the adversary model's formal definition of democracy, but it is democratic only at a superficial level. Using manipulation to move participants to a predetermined viewpoint is more consistent with authoritarianism than democracy (Pratkanis and Turner 1996), and limits the extent to which residents can truly become effective participants in the democratic process.

In sum, through a highly structured process based on formal representation and the vote, power-based organizations are able to mediate among the interests of large numbers of people efficiently and decisively. Because of the legitimacy of majority voting within our society, this process produces decisions that are generally viewed as fair and equitable by all involved. However, the organizations' reliance on the simple aggregation of votes often undermines genuine inclusion of all members' voices and obscures the opposition of the minority. Furthermore, in order to resolve the tension between formal equality and expertise, power-based organizers often resort to manipulation of the decision-making process.

THE CIVIC MODEL: DEMOCRACY AS AN OPEN FORUM

In contrast to the power-based organizations' adversary approach to democracy, civic organizations espouse a unitary conception of democracy. CAN and CAPS' leaders assumed that all members of a community automatically share certain interests, and that as long as their meetings focused around these universal concerns, participants should be able to reach decisions about neighborhood priorities without significant conflict or disagreement. Consequently, instead of creating formal governance structures, the organizations operated as open forums where residents could share their ideas in an ad hoc, unstructured manner. Not anticipating the need for mediation among conflicting opinions, the organizations didn't create any mechanisms for identifying residents' interests, selecting community priorities, or developing problem-solving strategies. Instead, they assumed that these decisions would emerge naturally through informal discussion.

While this unstructured approach to decision-making may be well suited to small, homogeneous communities, it can be somewhat unrealistic in diverse urban neighborhoods like the ones at the heart of this study. Without any mechanisms for mediating among different interests, it is extremely difficult to reach unified decisions about neighborhood priorities. Furthermore, without a structure for dealing with conflict, the mere expression of divergent interests can undermine the stability of an organization. CAN and CAPS attempted to resolve this dilemma by avoiding any issues that might provoke controversy among participants and, when necessary, by avoiding decision-making altogether.

These dynamics, which were evident in my observations of more than thirty CAN and CAPS meetings, are illustrated in the following description of a typical CAPS meeting:

Despite the pleasant weather—or perhaps because of it—there was already a sizable crowd at the Cranston area CAPS meeting by the time I arrived. As I looked for an empty seat, I was greeted cheerily by Rita, a local homeowner whom I had interviewed earlier that month. I settled into the seat beside her as she filled me in on the details of a gang-related shooting that had taken place the day before, all the while cursing the warm weather and the increased violence it always seems to bring.

Eventually, Darrin, the neighborhood's volunteer CAPS coordinator, called the meeting to order, and the friendly banter died down. After explaining the purpose of the meeting, he asked us to briefly introduce ourselves. We were seated in semi-circular rows facing a head table, and as we quickly went up and down the rows, the meeting's thirty or so participants called out their names and addresses. Along the side of the room sat a line of police officers, most still in uniform. They introduced themselves after the residents, quickly calling out their last names and shift assignments.

After a series of brief announcements, Darrin launched into the substance of the meeting, asking participants to report on problem spots in the neighborhood from the previous month. Barnie, an entrepreneur who owned several apartment buildings in the area, was the first to take the floor. He described some suspicious activity he had recently observed at one of the buildings on his street, and Darrin asked him a few questions for clarification. But before the discussion could go any further, a loud voice cut through the room. "Can we discuss the shootings on my block?"

A tall man who had come to the meeting with three of his neighbors stood up to get the group's attention: "Why are there so many shootings? The police must have some intelligence on these guys. These guys aren't invisible. I know you need so many [undercover drug] buys before you take a [drug dealer] down. But if you arrest someone and [then] every time he's back on the street you keep [arresting him], I [would] think through attrition there would be less and less people [selling drugs]. I'm sure that's naïve because I'm not a police officer, but I'd like to be enlightened on it. . . . How come these people aren't being taken down?"

Before anyone could respond, the man's neighbor jumped in with his own explanation: "The biggest problem in our community is the ACLU. We passed the anti-loitering law[4] and the ACLU continues to fight it. We've spent a lot of taxpayer money fighting for that law. Until the police can stop and search these people, we've got nothing we can do." His comment met with nodding heads and a brief verbal agreement from several of the police officers. Explain-

ing that the anti-loitering ordinance was in the process of being reviewed by the courts, Darrin said "that's a little beyond the scope of what we can discuss here." Turning to the police, he asked, "In the meantime, with the laws the way they are, what are the strategies we've been working on?"

One of the officers stood up to assure the group that the police were indeed doing their job—"We've made some great arrests with big numbers and pounds and kilos." He described the locations where the police had been targeting their operations, telling the two men "that answers a lot of your concerns." But before the men could respond, Sandra, a homeowner who was a regular participant at these meetings shifted the tone of the discussion, asking the officers "how can we help you?" The officers started talking about what residents could do to assist them with surveillance. Before they could get very far, Doug, a local landlord, interrupted. "If they're dealing drugs on private property, the landlord can be arrested, correct?" His question was drowned out by a young woman who stood up to ask the police to explain which gangs were involved in the neighborhood's recent shootings. As one of the officers began to explain the dynamics of the current gang wars, Clarice, another CAPS regular, interrupted—"I'd like to know how to identify a dangerous situation— insignia clothing or something." An officer briefly described the local gangs' colors and said he would bring an informational flyer.

Clarice started to ask a follow-up question, but at this point, a woman who had been trying to speak for over fifteen minutes stood up and, with Darrin's help, finally got the group's attention. She started talking about her problems with a local gang, insisting that the police from neighboring districts needed to work together more effectively. One of the officers immediately interrupted her to say, "we do work together," and another officer told her they had two parked police cars monitoring the area near her house. Then, before the woman could respond, a man stood up and started complaining about how the police had responded to a particular incident on his block the previous week. He began by talking about how one of the officers had slapped one of his neighbors and harassed some of the youth on his street. Nobody responded, so he went on to describe a recent incident in which the police had shown up half an hour late in response to his call about a gang shooting.

His story came out in bits and pieces, and was continually interrupted by the police and other participants, who insisted on giving him unsolicited advice before they had heard the whole story. Nobody responded to his allegations of police abuse, instead focusing on his complaints about police response times. Their suggestions all focused on what he should have done differently in his initial 911 call. The man kept pointing out that he had done all the things people were suggesting, and maintained that the problem was with the police, not him.

After several minutes, Sandra interrupted, talking over him in order to get the floor: "What can you do if there's evidence of child abuse?" The sergeant gave her a phone number to call and explained the city's official response process. She got a chance to ask one additional question before she was interrupted by another participant asking about a shooting that had taken place the previous month. . . .

The civic model's conception of democracy as an open forum fits with many of our commonsense notions of what community-level democracy should be. While the adversary model of elected representation and one-person, one-vote reflects most Americans' assumptions about how large-scale democratic governance structures need to operate, most of us assume that participation at the community-level should be far less structured and formal. When democratic decision-making entails face-to-face discussions and deliberations, we tend to believe that the more open and unstructured the organization is, the more democratic it will be.

My examination of the interactions at the civic organizations' meetings suggests that this assumption is significantly flawed. In fact, formal governance structures are just as important for democracy at the community level as they are at the state or national level. This doesn't necessarily mean that community organizations need to use the hierarchical structures that characterize the power-based model, but simply leaving residents to identify priorities and make decisions without any clear process or decision-making rules is problematic.

Lack of Genuine Deliberation

The civic organizations' lack of formal structure and decision-making rules results in meetings that are often chaotic and disorganized. CAPS' monthly meetings provide residents with an opportunity to raise their concerns regarding neighborhood safety and to hear updates from the police. However, the meetings do not include any process for making sure each resident's voice is heard or for mediating among the concerns that are raised. In the absence of facilitation, the meetings operate primarily as venting sessions rather than as opportunities for meaningful deliberation or decision-making. Participants compete for the opportunity to get their problems heard by interrupting each other, talking over one another, and engaging in side conversations. Hypothetically, this lack of structure means that everyone has an equal opportunity to speak. But in reality, the loudest and most aggressive members are the only ones who regularly get the floor. And even those who get a chance to state their concerns aren't necessarily listened to.

Not only do the civic organizations' meetings fail to give all residents an opportunity to express their concerns, they also don't provide any mechanisms for discussing or resolving of the concerns that *are* raised at the meetings. Without a structure for mediating among different interests, the only way to maintain the semblance of organizational stability is to avoid any issues that are likely to bring out disagreements among the participants. Consequently, the civic organizations focus their energy on least-common-denominator issues that are assumed to be of universal concern to all the organization's members. For example, at the time of my research the Cranston neighborhood was wracked by controversy over several issues that would determine the long-term future of the neighborhood. These issues included the rapid gentrification of what had once been one of the most diverse and affordable areas in Chicago, the local alderman's recent shift from an independent voice in city council to a faithful member of the mayor's political machine, and allegations by some residents of police brutality and corruption. Fearing that such issues would create conflict among the groups' members, CAN and CAPS participants consciously avoided discussing them. As CAN's president explained,

> Other groups [in the neighborhood] are involved in controversial things that our organization is not; it would not be appropriate for us to be involved in those issues. . . . [If a controversial issue was raised at a meeting], my concern would be, look, we're never going to reach agreement on this issue, are we going to hold a debate? Because you only have an hour and a half to talk about it. Is this really the appropriate time to hold a debate on that? . . . Something like that hasn't come up very much. There seems to be a sense of what's appropriate to bring up and what is not[5].

The only time that active facilitation was used at CAN and CAPS meetings was to steer the conversation away from these kinds of controversial issues. When newcomers to the meetings raised issues that were seen as controversial, the groups' core members would quickly intervene. In some cases this entailed a deliberate effort to change the subject. In other cases, core members defused potentially controversial issues by translating them into technical problems (Eliasoph 1998).

Both of these techniques are illustrated in the vignette at the beginning of this section. When a participant accused the police of harassing his neighbors, nobody at the meeting responded to his allegations. And when he complained about police response times, Darrin and other core members turned his complaints into a technical issue by suggesting that he had not followed the proper procedures when placing his 911 call. They barraged him with unsolicited advice and suggestions about how to contact the police:

> "You should have asked to talk to a supervisor. The assignments are prioritized downtown and the officers don't pick which calls to respond to. Next time ask to talk to a supervisor." "Sometimes you need to call 911 back and say 'no, I need to speak to a supervisor.'" "Don't call the station. They don't dispatch them from the station. 911 goes specifically to a specific place. 911 is the answer. You have to insist to see a supervisor and they have to dispatch one."

Even after the man angrily pointed out that he had followed all of these procedures, the police officers and core participants continued to respond to his allegations of police neglect and incompetence by framing the problem in technical terms. One officer tried to end the conversation by pointing out that "there are 250 officers about to graduate from the police academy, so that should solve the problem." Another, using the tone one would use with a child, said "sometimes the police *are* there, but you just can't see them." Once the group had finished giving all the advice it could muster on how to call 911, the man was interrupted by another core member who shifted the conversation to a completely different topic.

Lack of Priority Setting

By refusing to take positions on important matters, the civic organizations made it impossible for participants to establish collective priorities for the community. As CAN's president explained,

> We don't make decisions, we don't take positions. . . . If the decision is going to cause controversy and disagreement, it's not going to be made. We're just not going to deal with that issue, for better or for worse. . . . I don't want to go to something where I'm going to fight with somebody all the time, and always picking up my toys and going home. Because I think that's what people would do. Suddenly you wouldn't have any organization, because there would be enough issues that would divide people that the whole thing would just split apart, you know.

As a result, when I asked one longtime CAN leader about the organization's vision for the neighborhood, she said, "[The members] have never really had a true discussion on what type of neighborhood we really want. Because certain people know how certain people feel, so they just do not bring it out in the open. Now, many of us will discuss it among ourselves, but not in an open meeting. Not as an organization. Since I've been there, and I've been there a long time."

Even with relatively uncontroversial issues, when priorities had to be identified, the organizations resorted to an unstructured process that rarely resulted in formal decisions being reached. For example, each month CAPS participants were supposed to identify the neighborhood's top three crime priorities for the police. Instead of utilizing a formal decision-making process for selecting these priorities, participants seemed to assume that the unstructured sharing of complaints *was* the prioritization process. Most CAPS meetings ended without the formal designation of specific priorities, leaving it to the police and the CAPS facilitator to try and distill the priorities from the discussion. In interviews, many participants said that having a more formal decision-making process to identify community priorities was unnecessary; since everybody who wanted to speak had an opportunity to voice their complaints, the community's priorities should be obvious to anybody listening to the meeting. As one member explained, "We all agree on which problems should take the three priorities—the cops and citizens. It's a mutual decision. . . . We don't have any arguments generally about it. It's pretty obvious which situations are the worst."

The problem with this approach, of course, is that it is likely to privilege the interests of the group's most vocal members. For the most part, the residents who were able to dominate the floor during the meeting were also the ones whose problems were ultimately perceived as being priorities. Furthermore, by leaving it up to the police and CAPS facilitator to interpret which issues were the greatest priorities, CAPS participants put a considerable amount of power in the hands of these leaders. This was particularly problematic since none of these leaders was elected by the membership or accountable to the participants in any formal way.

The Myth of Structurelessness

Organizations that embrace the notion of democracy as an open, unstructured forum tend to eschew formal leadership. Neither CAN nor CAPS had a formal process for selecting the group's chairperson, but both groups had members who played these roles. As the groups' top leaders, these individuals (in this case both men) had a considerable amount of discretionary power over the organizations' agendas and priorities. Most members, however, told me they had no idea how these men had gained their leadership roles. In interviews, the men revealed that they had acquired their positions through informal, behind-the-scenes processes that most members weren't even aware of. Darrin became the CAPS coordinator when the previous co-ordinator decided to quit and called him in desperation to ask him to take over. Tim became CAN's "president" simply because nobody else was willing to run the meetings and do the necessary administrative work.

Jo Freeman (1973) points out that when the mechanisms for choosing a group's leaders aren't clear and don't involve the genuine participation of all the members, the leaders will not be accountable to the group as a whole: "As long as the structure of the group is informal, the rules of how decisions are made are known only to a few and awareness of power is curtailed to those who know the rules. . . . [If the group] continues to deliberately not select who shall exercise power, it does not thereby abolish power. All it does is abdicate the right to demand that those who do exercise power and influence be responsible for it" (1973: 151–52, 160). In other words, in much the same way that CAPS' lack of facilitation and meeting structure enabled the most vocal members to dominate meetings, the lack of formal leadership enabled a few individuals to have disproportionate control over the organizations' agendas and priorities.

In sum, the civic organizations' open, unstructured forums did little to foster genuine deliberation and inclusive decision-making on community issues. Simply providing people with a space to come together and share ideas and concerns proved to be an ineffective way to create a democratic community governance structure. The organizations' efforts to maintain the ideal of a unitary democracy while providing no mechanisms for mediating among conflicting interests resulted in an avoidance of controversy, a focus on neutral, least-common-denominator issues, and in some cases an avoidance of decision-making altogether. In addition, the lack of formal structures for making decisions and selecting leaders enabled a handful of individuals to control the organizations' agendas, without meaningful accountability to the group.

THE COMMUNITY-BUILDING MODEL: CREATING A UNIFIED VISION OF THE COMMON GOOD

In contrast to the civic organizations' assumptions about residents' universal interests, community-building organizations view the urban neighborhood as a diverse but interdependent organism in which groups with competing and conflicting interests must learn to work together. They believe that in order to create a healthy neighborhood, all the community's stakeholders must unite around a common vision that transcends individual interests and reflects a broader common good. Even if these stakeholders have conflicting individual interests, community-building organizations believe that they can and should subordinate these interests to the broader goal of creating a strong community.

In order to achieve this objective, the community-building organizations utilize a formal governance process designed to build unity and broad consensus around shared neighborhood goals. Whereas the power-based organizations mediate among conflicting interests through a mechanical process in which the "right" answer is defined by the calculation of votes, the community-building organizations believe that the neighborhood's priorities can be determined objectively, based on expert knowledge and sound collective reasoning.

It was time for PACT's January meeting to begin, but nobody seemed to be paying much attention to the clock. As people arrived, they circulated around the room, networking and exchanging news. The chairs were arranged around long tables positioned in a large rectangle, but few people were sitting. Thick photocopied packets of information were stacked on the sign-in table, and those participants who weren't socializing thumbed through these handouts while they waited for the meeting to begin.

Eventually Enrique, PACT's chair, called out a welcome and encouraged everyone to take their seats. He asked the participants to introduce themselves, and we went slowly around the room as each member shared his or her name and organizational affiliation. Several people used this as an opportunity to make brief announcements or say a few words about their organization's work. There were more than forty participants—the professional staff of PACT's member institutions, the local alderman and his staff, and a handful of newcomers.

After the introductions, Enrique launched into an energetic pep talk. "Empowerment Zone[6] designations were announced this week, and we did not receive one. But I don't want to see any frowns. The same day that we found out about that, we found out that Port Angeles will likely be a Redevelopment Area[7] (applause). If we had never applied to be an Empowerment Zone and we found out we were a Redevelopment Area, we would be celebrating. It would be PACT's biggest accomplishment to date. At the same time, we should have been an Empowerment Zone. Our application was one of the best, and it was probably the most community driven. HUD[8] didn't value what we value to be important. . . . They don't have to give us Empowerment Zone designation, because the application wasn't for them. It was our plan and it was for us, and we can move forward on it. I would like to present a motion . . . let's proclaim ourselves an 'empowerment zone.' "

Turning to the alderman, Enrique said, "The media's going to be here any minute. Not to put you on the spot, Alderman, but it would be powerful to have you there and supporting this designation." The alderman nodded slightly and said "fine" softly. Turning back to the members, Enrique contin-ued, "This is your meeting. I'd like to open the floor and see what people think. We have a plan and shouldn't let it go. I'd like to designate ourselves and do it nationally."

As soon as Enrique finished, Rita, one of PACT's core leaders, stood up and proposed a motion to declare themselves an empowerment zone. The motion was quickly seconded. A moment later, Julio, PACT's director, stood up and made an impassioned and forceful statement in support of the motion. "We put together the most comprehensive plan. I've never seen a plan like this put together, and I've been working in the community a long time. One reason why we should declare ourselves an empowerment zone, we met with HUD and they said they couldn't believe it—a group of young Latino professionals with a solid idea to address the problems in our community. . . . Let's tell the national government that if they don't recognize the tremendous plan that this community with its own sweat did—. You are the experts, you know what the community needs, not them. We are challenging the federal government and saying we are powerful. . . . Let's stick together."

Julio sat down again and Enrique asked if there were any other comments. One member made a brief statement about the importance of moving forward. As soon as he was done, Enrique pointed to a cluster of reporters and camera-men huddled by the entryway. "The media is here to take our statement based on our vote. Are there any other comments?" The motion was repeated, and there was a brief and unanimous verbal vote to approve it. Enrique an-nounced, "we'll take ten minutes from the meeting to make a statement to the press. We ask people to stand here behind the table while we make the state-ment." Within seconds, almost everyone in the room (minus a handful of new-comers) stood and arranged themselves behind Enrique, Julio, Rita, and a few other core leaders, forming an impressive phalanx. Julio and Enrique made lengthy statements to the press about their decision, while the rest of the membership stood solemnly behind them, demonstrating their unity to the cameras.

Once the reporters had finished their questions, Enrique asked the partici-pants to return to their seats. He asked, "Do you all feel good about this?" but before anyone could respond, he said "good" and moved on with the agenda, turning to Julio for a report on next steps. Julio explained that he had devel-oped an outline of the projects from the Empowerment Zone application which the group could begin working on without official Empowerment Zone status. He referred people to one of the handouts, and went over it in great de-tail, explaining all the pieces of his proposal. After he had spoken uninter-rupted for about twenty minutes, Enrique opened up the discussion to the floor "to see if there are pieces we missed that are important to you."

Mark, the president of one of the neighborhood's block clubs, made a brief statement emphasizing the importance of focusing on homeownership rather than rental housing in any plan for the neighborhood. His comments angered Roberto, the director of CASA, a local affordable housing organization, who quickly responded back, "I know there is opposition in this group to affordable housing, but instead of attacking us, let's sit down and talk about it." His manner was clearly defensive, and he looked directly at Mark in a hostile way as he spoke. Then he accused Mark of sending letters to public officials condemning CASA's most recent rental housing project.

Enrique tried to defuse the situation, saying "this is not the place for this. But I need to address what you said because you said in this group there's opposition to affordable housing, and I've never heard that." Julio added "for the record, PACT has never stated we're against rental housing. But the community needs to be consulted and we need to make sure that's done first. This is not the place to discuss the issue, but we have never said we're against affordable rental housing."

Mark was clearly angry, but tried to remain calm. "This is not the forum for this issue," he said. "We are here to be united on the Port Angeles plan. I've told you never to accuse us of being against poor people. We are against your proposal to put a fifty-three unit building on Delaney Street because we feel economic development is more appropriate in that location. . . . We support affordable housing, when it is done correctly. I don't come here to slam you or have you slander me. We support the people in this community."

At this point Enrique turned to Julio, who made an impassioned plea for continued unity: "We need to realize what's best. Not with anger but with clear vision. . . . This forum is for us to develop plans for the community. We respect the block club's decision. Developers need to consult with people who live in this area before going forward with plans. We can mediate some of these differences. I don't oppose CASA's project, but if the community doesn't support it, we don't do it. But we can work together to resolve things. We need to become partners here and agree to disagree."

Enrique asked if anyone else had comments on the plan that Julio had presented. A few people asked questions for clarification about some of the components. The meeting ended with PACT's staff organizer making a pitch for an upcoming community meeting, encouraging all of PACT's member institutions to recruit their members and constituents to attend: "We need to show the people in your organizations that you're part of a larger picture. Everyone in this community working together to make a positive change. We're keeping our community ours—this is a key phrase. We're asking you to commit to bring the people you serve and work with. We want the input of the community in terms of where we should go." Enrique briefly went around the table asking the par-

ticipants to make a verbal commitment to turn out their members, and then adjourned the meeting.

Whereas the first step of decision-making for the power-based organizations consists of individual members (or member institutions) determining their positions vis-à-vis a particular issue, the first step of decision-making in community-building organizations involves the analysis of the issue by community experts. PACT's director and staff have considerable discretion in guiding organizational decision-making based on their professional knowledge and technical expertise. Each staff member leads one of five issue committees, composed of the professional staff of the member agencies that have expertise in that particular issue area. These committees are responsible for analyzing the community's needs in relation to specific issues, and designing strategies and solutions to present to the larger group. For instance, PACT's housing committee—which is staffed by PACT's housing organizer and composed of the staff of two community development corporations, a citywide tenants' rights organization, a representative from the local HUD office, and a citywide green space organization—was responsible for developing a plan for revitalizing the neighborhood's housing stock.

When issues arise that are outside the purview of the issue committees, such as the question of how to respond to the federal government's rejection of PACT's Empowerment Zone proposal, PACT's staff will typically make the necessary decisions, often in consultation with PACT's chair (who, in this case, is also a former staff member.) Similarly, day-to-day decisions about PACT's programs and campaigns are usually handled by the staff since they are seen as having more familiarity with the organization's strategies than the members. PACT's director and staff seemed very comfortable making critical decisions for the rest of the group, and they often attributed the organization's successes to their own leadership.

Once PACT's experts have made decisions about the issues at hand, they bring these decisions to PACT's governance body. As illustrated in the vignette, the organization's governance meetings typically revolve around the presentation of proposals by the staff to the membership for their endorsement. The staff's presentations are usually followed by impassioned speeches by Julio, Enrique, and one or two other charismatic leaders in support of the proposals. Then, after giving participants a brief opportunity to comment or ask questions, these leaders ask for a quick verbal vote of approval. In some cases, as in the vignette, they take the membership's approval for granted and simply move on to the next item on the agenda.

Because of the community-building organizations' emphasis on unity and consensus, the membership's endorsement of the staff's recommendations is typically unanimous. Mansbridge (1983) suggests that this pattern is common in unitary democracies where decisions are seen as embodying a correct solution and the members have agreed to subordinate their interests to a common good. In such situations, members will often rely on a small group of leaders who are seen as knowledgeable and competent decision-makers to make most of the group's decisions. PACT's committee members and staff were seen as professionals who could best understand the issues and develop appropriate solutions that would contribute to the common good. In turn, PACT's charismatic leaders were trusted to understand the broad, intertwined needs of the community as a whole and help the membership focus on the common good. As a result, the proposals made by the expert committees and staff and endorsed by the organization's charismatic leaders were typically accepted as legitimate and worthy of support by PACT's members.

As discussed in chapter 3, this process creates limited opportunities for direct participation by the members in the actual process of discussion and deliberation. While individual participants are encouraged to ask questions or make statements about a proposal, there is rarely any debate. This pattern is similar to what Lichterman (1995, 1996) found in his study of environmental organizations with a strong emphasis on communal loyalty. In contrast to groups that emphasize the protection of individual interests, groups that prioritize communal loyalty and the common good are usually dominated by the opinions of a few key leaders so that when decisions must be made, the organization is able to speak with one voice.

Making this model of democratic decision-making work is not a simple task. Community-building organizations need to be able to convince dozens of stakeholders to set aside their individual and institutional interests in favor of the community's common good. Because community-building organizations are typically large and extremely diverse, common methods of consensus building—such as lengthy face-to-face discussions among all participants—are generally not feasible.[9] Instead, organizations like PACT must develop alternative methods for building member unity.

Building Unity Through Symbolism and Rhetoric

PACT's success in building member unity can be attributed in part to its leaders' effective use of symbolism and rhetoric to forge a sense of common identity among the members. During observations of more than thirty PACT meetings, I recognized a repeated, almost ritualistic, pattern of speech-making and story-telling by PACT's core staff and leadership. The speeches focused on two intertwined themes: Port Angeles' cultural identity as a Puerto Rican neighborhood and the threat posed by gentrification.

PACT's staff and leaders mobilized a strong Puerto Rican identity within the partnership. For example, Julio and Enrique frequently talked about how the Puerto Rican community had been overlooked and maligned in the past, but that now that they were united they could be ignored no longer. Even though not all of PACT's participants are of Puerto Rican heritage, and the organization openly welcomes the participation of other ethnic and cultural groups, the sense of common cultural identity gave PACT's members a certain shared strength and passion that I did not see in any of the other groups I observed.

This sense of unity was further strengthened by PACT members' shared perception of the threat of gentrification. Port Angeles is located adjacent to several of Chicago's most rapidly gentrifying neighborhoods, and has already begun to feel the effects of market pressures. Whereas most neighborhoods become divided over gentrification along class lines, PACT's leaders framed gentrification as an ethnic issue. In meeting after meeting, participants told of how their families had been displaced from one neighborhood to the next since arriving in Chicago:

> I started out on the south side. . . . In the early '50s, they were going to open Whitney Young [School], so we were asked back then to move. . . . I remember going to grammar school and then all of a sudden we had to move. And then we had to move, and all of a sudden in the '50s, we were on Ogden and Ontario. . . . And then we had to move from there. It's like a trend following us. First we're on the south, and then we're by the lake, and then we started moving this way. So how long before we have to move out of here?

Whenever PACT's leaders talked about the threat of gentrification, they depicted it as the next step in this historic pattern of displacement—white developers pushing the Puerto Rican community once more from its home. A frequent symbol of gentrification used in PACT's leaders' speeches and statements was Bob Babcock, a rich white developer who had bought more than a hundred vacant lots in Port Angeles for a pittance and had left them to deteriorate while he waited for the market to turn. Confronted by this image, PACT's leaders passionately declared in meeting after meeting that it was time for the Puerto Rican community to take its last stand. As Enrique frequently put it, "what we're saying is we're not going to let go of this community."

By attaching ethnic significance to the threat of gentrification, PACT successfully convinced its members of the importance of putting aside their individual interests for the sake of the community as a whole. By depicting gentrification as a battle against the displacement of the Puerto Rican community, PACT was able to unify stakeholder groups around a common threat and shared goals, enabling them to overcome divisions that might have torn other organizations apart. This is exemplified by the quick resolution of the argument between Mark and Roberto during the meeting recounted in the opening vignette. After their brief flare-up, both acknowledged the need to put aside their differences for the sake of remaining unified behind PACT's overall vision for the community. In neighborhoods facing gentrification, homeowners' associations and affordable housing agencies typically are in conflict with one another, but by focusing on the shared fate of the entire Puerto Rican community, the two groups were able to cooperate.

PACT's members' prioritization of the common good was reflected in their use of the phrase "agreeing to disagree"—a term that was used repeatedly throughout meetings and in my interviews. PACT did not avoid the expression of conflicting individual interests, but emphasized the importance of putting aside these conflicts for the sake of unity. After giving people like Mark and Roberto a chance to express their views, PACT's leaders would remind them of the importance of working together, encouraging them to agree to disagree in order to focus on their shared support for the group's comprehensive plan for the neighborhood.

The Limits of a Common Good

PACT's ability to create neighborhood unity around the group's shared priorities is impressive. But is a "common good" really possible in urban neighborhoods, or do all community issues entail trade-offs among different groups' interests?

Unlike majority voting, which is a strictly mechanistic process of decision-making, a governance process that is focused on maintaining adherence to a common good cannot be value neutral. Whatever frameworks shape a community-building organization's definition of the common good, these frameworks are likely to be rooted in specific commitments or value systems that favor certain interests and priorities over others.

For example, in the battle between Mark's block-club and Roberto's affordable housing agency over the building of the Delaney Street housing project, PACT's leaders stressed that the dispute needed to be resolved in a way that served the needs of the community as a whole. In the weeks following their dispute, it became clear that PACT's leaders' conception of the community's interests was shaped by their belief that homeownership is the best way to stabilize an urban neighborhood. The Delaney Street issue impacted a wide range of community members, including the homeowners in Mark's block club, residents in need of affordable rental housing, and the staff and board of CASA. But because of their desire to support homeownership, PACT's leaders implicitly defined the block club's interests as a more legitimate reflection of the community's broader interests than those of the other affected groups.

Despite the rhetoric of agreeing to disagree and working for the common good, in this and many other situations PACT's decisions did not necessarily serve the interests of all portions of the population equally. In today's urban context, genuine "win-win" solutions are extremely rare. Almost every issue involves inevitable trade-offs between different interests and priorities. Consequently, certain members of the community will usually have to sacrifice more than others in the service of the "common good." The community-building model's rhetoric obscures this reality.

Lack of Resident Participation

The potential for bias in defining the "common good" is exacerbated by the lack of meaningful resident participation in PACT's governance structure. The emphasis on building unanimity around technically correct solutions largely excludes individual residents of the neighborhood from the community-building model's decision-making process. In order to identify residents' interests and needs, groups like PACT gather residents' input through surveys, research, and an occasional community meeting. But residents have little role in the more important process of prioritizing among the community's diverse interests and developing strategies to address these priorities. PACT's leaders insist that their meetings are open to all, and that they want more resident involvement. At the same time, most of these meetings are held during the work day, in private offices, and with agendas and discussion styles that presuppose significant technical information about the topics at hand.

PACT's members defend the organization by pointing out that although most of the active participants are the paid staff of member institutions, they are also community residents. But while PACT's participants may *live* in the neighborhood, their middle-class incomes and professional backgrounds distinguish them from the vast majority of Port Angeles' residents. And because they participate in PACT as representatives of the institutions where they work, their decisions are likely to be shaped more by the institutions' priorities than by their own interests as residents. The few non-staff residents who do participate in PACT's meetings are primarily the leaders of homeowners' organizations. While this population is often the easiest to recruit and involve, it also represents a small percentage of the economically diverse population that PACT claims to represent.

The limited opportunity for direct resident involvement in community-building organizations' decision-making is not surprising. After all, groups like PACT are focused on developing comprehensive plans that address all of the neighborhood's needs. Because residents often "approach the neighborhood as isolated individuals, or know little about the neighborhood as a planning unit" (Checkoway 1985: 477), it is difficult to effectively involve them in comprehensive planning without first doing extensive leadership development (which, as chapter 3 demonstrates, was not a central priority for the community-building organizations in this study). Community-building organizations are best equipped to gather residents' input through surveys and research studies rather than through their substantive involvement in organizational decision-making.

The consequence of this is that while the residents provide the raw data about their interests and needs, the data is assessed and processed by a small group of professionals using pre-conceived frameworks for making sense of the information and deciding on an action plan. Without an opportunity to represent their own interests at the decision-making table, the neighborhood's diverse populations and conflicting interest groups are unable to engage in a dialogue that would yield a true consensus on the issues. Instead, the consensus that is developed through this process involves only a select group of community leaders and professionals and is based on a conception of the common good that necessarily favors some interests and priorities over others.

In sum, the community-building approach to neighborhood governance builds consensus among diverse stakeholder groups by developing a shared vision of the common good. Because the common good is presented as a technically correct solution to the neighborhood's problems, the community-building organizations tend to rely on small groups of community experts to make most of their decisions. In order to build the unity necessary for this approach to work, organizations like PACT focus on developing a sense of shared culture or common opposition to an external threat. This approach successfully brings together groups that might otherwise be in conflict, enabling the community to produce comprehensive plans that are widely accepted as legitimate. However, the approach involves minimal resident participation in the governance process and, despite the rhetoric of the "common good," may not address all interests equally.

THE WOMEN-CENTERED MODEL: UNITARY DEMOCRACY BASED ON FACE-TO-FACE CONSENSUS

Women-centered organizations also espouse a unitary approach to democracy, but their consensus-building techniques are far more inclusive than those of the community-building organizations. Whereas community-building organizations seek to subordinate participants' individual interests to a greater good, women-centered organizations believe that through discussion and sharing participants can develop the same interests. In order to build consensus, the organizations foster the development of mutual empathy through face-to-face listening. As a result, the women-centered organizations operate more like friendship groups or families than formal organizations. Emphasis is placed on making sure every participant's voice is heard, and that all members' needs are incorporated into the group process. As one of the Templeton Leadership Circle's founders explained,

> Somewhere along the way what's good for the group has to be internalized as that's what's good for me, and how can I support that vision that's not my vision but a collective vision. And how can I give up my idea of how it should be [in order] to support this other person over here who I love in her vision of how it should be. It's a hard thing to sustain, and it takes a lot of work, a lot of being together. . . . Only when people honestly are committed to the group because they're really committed to it . . . because of the process, because of the support, because of the camaraderie and shared vision and passion, [will it work].

Face-to-face consensus decision-making is a difficult, time-consuming process. It requires participants to share their views with one another, to try to empathize with other participants, and to come to decisions that respect the diversity of interests in the group. In order to make this process work, the women-centered organizations pay close attention to the micro-processes of interaction in meetings. They carefully structure their meetings and use specific facilitation tools to enable participants to relate effectively at this level. These mechanisms are illustrated in the following description of a typical Templeton Leadership Circle meeting.

Thirteen members of the Templeton Leadership Circle's board sat together around a small rectangular table to make one of the most important decisions in the organization's history. The agenda for the evening's meeting focused on whether the organization should take on a new project far more ambitious than any it had attempted before. The project would involve purchasing, rehabilitating, and managing a large apartment building that had historically been the center of much of the drug and gang activity in the neighborhood. Despite the magnitude of the decision, TLC's members were calm and relaxed, trusting in the group's consensus process to generate the best decision for the group.

The meeting began with a hearty welcome from Debra, TLC's chair, a warm, grandmotherly woman who ran TLC's monthly meetings as skillfully and as lovingly as she handled her own family. Debra began by asking one of the members to read a posted list of groundrules to remind the group of their agreements. Carla volunteered, carefully reading each item on the list and then pausing to explain the purpose of each one: "Speak from your own experience. . . . No put downs of self or others. . . . Equal time for all. . . . No interruptions or cross-talk. . . ."

After Carla reviewed the groundrules, Debra invited the group to begin the process of individual check-ins. One by one, each member briefly introduced herself and then shared a few words about how she was doing, updating the group on her personal life and the events of the week. Once each member had spoken, Debra thanked everyone for sharing and then turned to the evening's agenda, the Prospect Park apartment building. First Susan, TLC's director, briefly reviewed the parameters of the decision they would need to make: The forty-two unit Prospect Park building was being sold at a sheriff's auction, and the city had invited TLC to bid on the project. Given the fact that TLC's only previous housing development experience was with a four-plex, taking on this project would be a significant leap and a definite challenge.

Next Mary, a local realtor and TLC board member, described the condition of the building, reviewed the building's ownership history, and explained its current status. During her ten-minute talk, she carefully explained all the relevant technical aspects of the decision: what it meant that the property was in receivership, the level of debt on the property, how to calculate whether the project would pencil out financially, and the risks the project would entail.

After Mary had reviewed the technical aspects of the decision, Regina, a longtime board member, described the ramifications of the project for the community. Whereas Mary had spoken from her experience as a realtor in the area, Regina spoke from her experience as a resident in the neighborhood. She described the apartment building's history, its current problems with gangs and drugs, and about how angry and frustrated the community had been with two previous failed efforts by for-profit developers to rehab the building.

Once Mary and Regina had given their perspectives on the project, Debra led the group in a go-round to determine each member's feelings about the issue. She encouraged everyone to speak from her own experience and to share whatever thoughts and opinions she had. When several members demurred, shyly pointing out that they didn't really know a lot about housing develop-

ment, Debra warmly encouraged them to say what they thought, emphasizing that "everyone's an expert here."

As the go-round progressed, it became clear that while many of the members were excited about the prospect of taking on such an important project, they also had significant concerns. Some shared their fears that this project was too ambitious for TLC; others worried that once they completed the rehab, the property would be too difficult to manage; still others feared that TLC would fall into debt and would have to fold. Despite these worries, many members pointed out that if TLC didn't take on this project, nobody would, and the neighborhood would suffer.

Once each member had a chance to speak, it was clear that a group consensus had not yet emerged. Debra asked the group to do another go-round, now that they had heard each member's views, in order to try to reach a decision. By the time the second go-round was complete, Debra said it sounded like everyone was in agreement: TLC should move forward with the project. She asked if this was correct and was greeted with enthusiastic nods from around the circle.

Only one member, Shana, didn't join in the excitement, and as she sat with a worried look on her face, Debra asked her to share her reservations. Explaining that she still feared the project would be too ambitious for the group, Shana said she didn't feel like she could fully endorse the decision. Everyone listened quietly to her concerns, and talked about how they might address some of her issues in their planning for the project. Once all her concerns had been put on the table, Debra asked if she could live with the group's decision even if she didn't wholeheartedly endorse it. Shana said she could, and the other members thanked her for her honesty and support. There was enthusiastic applause as Debra announced that a consensus had been reached.

The meeting was ready to wrap up. TLC's director announced that the Property Development Committee would need to work on constructing an offer for the property. The meeting closed with "appreciations," a ritual in which, one-by-one, each member turned to the woman on her left and told her something she appreciated about her contributions to the meeting.

Women-centered organizations use highly structured processes for discussions and decision-making in order to ensure that all the group's members participate fully and equally. Proponents of the women-centered model believe that unstructured meetings are disempowering for all but the most confident and articulate participants. In particular, they feel that women, the poor, and people of color tend to be silenced by the unstructured, free-for-all atmosphere that is such a common feature of many "democratic" community organizations. But in contrast to the power-based organizations, which emphasize the importance of creating a highly structured organizational form, the women-centered organizations focus on structuring the microprocesses of interpersonal interactions. It is at this level that the women-centered organizations believe the greatest disparities in power and voice tend to occur. Veteran community organizer Linda Stout (1996) explains,

> Many middle-class people are comfortable with theoretical, impersonal discussion in which people just jump in when they want to speak. . . . For low-income people (many of whom are women), the approach is unfamiliar, and many do not feel comfortable about entering the discussion. Similarly, in many groups, a lack of explicit structure means that only those people who feel comfortable talking (usually people with privilege) will do so. It's not that low-income people have nothing to say, we just feel that we don't have a way in. . . . An inclusive organization will work to find a meeting format that allows everyone to participate. (Stout 1996:135)

Organizations like TLC try to counter these problems through the use of formal meeting procedures, including intense facilitation and explicitly inclusive groundrules. Because TLC's members include both middle-class professional and low-income "grassroots" women, the organization's founders searched for a process that would insure that both groups of women could participate on an equal basis. They adapted their groundrules from the National Congress of Neighborhood Women's (NW) leadership support model. According to the NW handbook, while the use of formal groundrules may seem restrictive to a group's middle-class and professional members, low-income "grassroots" women find that it frees up their capacity to think and speak in a group setting and disrupts their patterns of being silent and withdrawn in a group of strangers. The groundrules are designed to even out disparities in members' levels of education, verbal fluency, and self-confidence.

TLC's groundrules are based on the following principles: (1) Speak from your own experience: all participants are considered experts—professional women may have specialized knowledge about housing development, but grassroots women have the expertise that comes from personal experience. (2) No putdowns, blaming, judgments, or unsolicited advice: this principle creates a safe environment in which participants of all backgrounds can share ideas without fear of ridicule or criticism. (3) Full participation: in discussions each participant is given an opportunity to speak. Even first-time participants are strongly encouraged to give their input. This principle guarantees that all participants, regardless of how articulate or aggressive they are, will have a chance to share their views. (4) Equal time for all: time-limits may be used during go-rounds, and interruptions, cross-talk, and speaking out of turn are not allowed. This principle helps keep the meeting moving forward and prevents a small minority from dominating the discussion.

In addition to regulating all discussions according to these groundrules, TLC's members use a step-by-step approach for decision-making that ensures each participant's views are included in the consensus process. This step-by-step approach is illustrated in the above vignette: an initial go-round allows each member to speak her mind without comment or interruption from the other participants. If a clear group consensus isn't apparent by the end of the first go-round, the go-rounds continue until consensus is reached. This process is based on the assumption that if participants listen with open minds to each other's views, they will eventually be able to reach a final decision that reflects the shared priorities of the whole group. One of TLC's founding members explained, "If you really take the time to do it, consensus emerges — it really emerges. I'm a very stubborn, self-directed woman, and I may go in thinking that I know how it's going to be. But in the process of going around and hearing these people I care about and who have ideas different than mine, I put mine out there and they put theirs out there and consensus emerges."

Inclusion and Equal Voice

As a result of its use of groundrules and go-rounds, TLC's meetings are very inclusive and participatory. In interviews, participants said that they had never had their opinions solicited and listened to in such a systematic way before. As one member put it,

> I think [TLC's] strength is using a model where when a woman comes into the process she really hears her own voice, and sometimes for the first time really feels heard. . . . Time after time, sitting in Templeton Leadership Circle meetings, I'll just remember women saying "I've been going to meetings for many years, all my life, and I've never been in a meeting where I felt so included." I think that was what was at the heart of the Templeton Leadership Circle in its early days, was people feeling very included and that they really mattered.

In contrast to the community-building approach to consensus-building, the women-centered method promotes genuine resident deliberation as part of the consensus process. The structured approach provides a safe and effective way for residents to voice their views, share their perspectives, and create a common vision through careful, empathetic listening. Each participant's opinions are incorporated into the group's decision, and no decision is finalized unless all the participants agree that they can live with it.

The women-centered approach is also far less vulnerable to manipulation by the organizer or facilitator than some of the other approaches to decision-making. The emphasis on "speaking from your own experience" and "equal time for all" helps to guarantee that the views of paid staff or core leaders will be given no more weight than any other member's views. And while some participants are likely to have more influence than others on the group's collective wisdom due to their moral authority, familiarity with the issues, or powers of persuasion, by the time the final go-round is complete, each member has at least had an opportunity to share her views and be heard. As one TLC member explained, this process ensures that every participant— regardless of whether they have formal expertise or previous experience with an issue—contributes to the development of the group's decision.

> I think that a lot of people, especially women, are hesitant to think that they have something to add, or that they have opinions that are worthy of saying, or that they have wisdom. And I think a lot of people have learned that they do have wisdom, and that people actually have made decisions based on their speaking from their experience. And that their lives, just their lives alone, is a lot of wisdom. And that just sharing day to day stories about their life actually helps guide policy.

This dynamic is particularly important in groups like TLC that have a diverse membership composition. Even though TLC's members include both low-income "grassroots" women and professional women, all the members' viewpoints are valued in the decision-making process.

The commitment to equal voice also fosters a strong sense of group ownership over the decisions. In interviews, several TLC board members admitted that they arrived at the Prospect Park meeting determined to reject the project. However, after listening to each member's views and getting a chance to express their concerns, these women became as enthusiastic about the project as everyone else. As one explained,

> The thing the process did was really build the commitment and the passion for it, and it also made the passion be really clear. It made it clear that, yes, everybody knew it was going to be hard, and everybody knew it was improbable, and everybody knew that it needed to be done, and they were going to make a commitment and do it. And, you know, a group that had . . . used a hierarchical process or Roberts Rules of Order process would have . . . probably very quickly made a decision, either

yes or no. And that wouldn't have built the kind of energy and the—really helping people understand what it meant to do it. . . . The process really allowed people to get that understanding. I was one of the ones, until the last meeting . . . saying "Don't do it. Don't do it." But in the end, it was the right decision, and I knew it. But it was only by going through that process that I got to that realization.

Thus, by making sure that each member's views are fully incorporated into the final product, the women-centered approach to decision-making builds group cohesion while creating decisions that are validated and endorsed by all the members.

Tensions Between Process and Product

Despite its clear benefits, unavoidable tensions exist between the women-centered model's highly inclusive process and the ability to be effective as an action-oriented organization. The insistence on including all voices and reaching full group consensus can make decision-making extremely time-consuming. Once TLC decided to take on the Prospect Park project, for example, the group spent meeting after meeting in intensive discussions and go-rounds on every aspect of the project, down to the most minute details. In addition to extensive board discussions about the financing details, the rehab plan, and the development of tenant management policies, smaller committees of volunteers met numerous times to develop consensus on the color schemes for the rehab, to plan parties for the tenants, and to decide on landscaping and design details.

As TLC grew and began taking on a greater number and variety of projects, this consensus-building process became unworkable. The everyday pace of decision-making intensified while the issues under discussion became increasingly technical and complex. For example, in contrast to the attention given to the minute details of the Prospect Park project, several years later the typical agenda for a single TLC board meeting included important decisions to be made on five to seven different issues or projects. With so many decisions to be made, TLC's detailed consensus-building process became increasingly unmanageable.

Faced with the challenges of trying to integrate its highly inclusive process with the fast-paced world of housing development, TLC gradually shifted toward an organizational structure more characteristic of a formal nonprofit organization than a community-organizing group. Now, several years later, TLC has become a mainstream community development corporation with only vestiges of its original consensus-building process still intact. Decision-making is primarily controlled by professional staff, and while many long-time members are proud of the organization's accomplishments in the community development field, they regret the change in the balance of power that accompanied the organization's growth:

> I think when it started out [the relationship between grassroots and professional women] was a good relationship, that each person had something to contribute. . . . When the complexity of running the organization instead of just creating it took place, the people who knew what it took to run it had much more information about what it took, and the people who were grassroots didn't have that information, didn't have those skills, and that gap began to widen. So then it was not as equal a relationship.

Difficulty Dealing with Conflict

Another difficulty with the women-centered approach to decision-making is that it doesn't deal effectively with the inevitable situations when consensus simply can't be reached. While power-based organizations take the presence of conflicting interests for granted, the women-centered organizations' consensus-building process is premised on the assumption that differences of opinion can be resolved through mutual sharing and respect: "Consensus norms reassuringly assume a harmony of interests. They imply a world where caring far outweighs aggression. . . . People imagine that difference, conflict, and aggression dissolve under consensus norms" (Baum 1997: 137–38).

While the emphasis on equal voice and careful listening does frequently enable participants to overcome differences of opinion and reach a compromise position, some differences simply cannot be reconciled. Without an effective mechanism for dealing with this reality, women-centered organizations risk being torn apart by such conflicts. For example, shortly after TLC completed the Prospect Park project, a routine board meeting discussion about whether to participate in the city's annual gay pride parade provoked a heated debate about TLC's relationship to the gay community. Several lesbian board members accused TLC's leadership of being homophobic, while other members argued that the group's public support of gay rights might alienate it from the city's African American community. The use of go-rounds and groundrules could not resolve the conflict, and a rift emerged within the membership that undermined the group's cohesion.

The challenges that these kinds of divisions posed to the group as a whole were exacerbated by the emotional intensity of the members' relationships to one another. One of the distinctive characteristics of the women-centered model is its emphasis on the interconnection between the personal and the public. Whereas most organizing models focus on people in their roles as public actors, participants in women-centered organizations are treated as whole people, with the joys, traumas, and dilemmas of their personal lives included as a part of each meeting. TLC used ongoing rituals such as the personal check-ins and appreciations to provide emotional support to every member, and members frequently shared intimate details from their private lives with one another. As one member explained, "we try to honor every woman. . . . If I'm going through a major crisis and I sacrifice to go to this [meeting], I want someone to at least acknowledge that. It's all holistic."

This holistic approach meant that when conflict did arise, it affected participants at a very personal level. TLC's conflict over the gay pride parade was thus intensely painful and emotionally draining. As one of TLC's staff put it, "the conflict ran deeply, because I think people took it really personally. . . . Templeton Leadership Circle, I think, was like a family to them. It was more than just an organization. It was their support group, their empowerment group." After operating as a harmonious family for so many years, the conflict was so emotionally intense that many members could no longer bear going to TLC's meetings. Several long-time friendships among TLC members were destroyed. And when no resolution could be reached, some of the group's founding members decided to drop out of the organization altogether.

Lewis Coser's study of conflict (1956) suggests that TLC's fate is common for groups that operate at such an intimate level. The emphasis on intensive participation and sharing gives members a personal and emotional tie to the group. As a result, when conflict occurs, the only way to resolve it is sometimes to break off the connections altogether: "In groups in which the total personalities of members are involved, internal conflict . . . would go so deep that it would touch directly on the consensual basis of group structure. No dissent can therefore be tolerated, and the dissenter must be forced to withdraw" (Coser 1956: 100). Without a built-in mechanism for dealing with irreconcilable conflict, internal discord can thus be extremely destabilizing for women-centered organizations.

In sum, the women-centered organizations utilize a highly participatory, formally structured approach to decision-making that gives all participants an equal voice and fosters genuine resident control over the process. The disciplined use of methods such as go-rounds and groundrules produces decisions with high levels of legitimacy and member buy-in. However, despite its clear benefits, this approach can be time-consuming and cumbersome, making it difficult for organizations to move efficiently from deliberation to action. In addition, the women-centered organizations' emphasis on interpersonal relationships, coupled with their lack of mechanisms for dealing with irreconcilable differences, make it difficult for them to deal effectively with internal conflicts.

THE TRANSFORMATIVE MODEL: UNITARY DEMOCRACY BASED ON SHARED OBJECTIVE INTERESTS

Like the women-centered model, transformative organizations emphasize the importance of intense individual participation in discussions and deliberations. But, whereas participation in an organization like TLC means sharing opinions based on one's own experiences, the transformative organizations encourage participation based on intellectual analysis and the application of abstract principles of social justice. In addition, whereas the women-centered organizations utilize a highly inclusive and structured meeting process in order to ensure that everyone is heard, the transformative organizations' meetings are characterized by a "personalized" politics (Lichterman 1995) in which participants are expected to jump in freely with their ideas without the guidance of formal structures or procedures.

JAG's small office was crammed full of people, and the energy level in the room was high. As I sat down I was handed a thick sheath of photocopied handouts to read. Books and papers filled every available space on the conference table, and the pile grew higher as more participants arrived at the meeting. After exchanging a few words of greeting with the other participants, I started to sift through the pile of papers, skimming through the text as I waited for the meeting to begin.

Two weeks earlier, at JAG's annual meeting, the organization's leaders had decided it would be useful to develop a comprehensive economic development platform for the neighborhood. This meeting was the first step toward that goal. JAG's leaders had invited any members who were interested in economic development to join the planning process and had asked them to bring ideas and suggestions to the meeting in order to get the discussion rolling. Three of the leaders had already researched and written draft proposals for the platform, while other members had gathered books and articles that they thought might be useful to the process.

Half an hour after the meeting was scheduled to start, Sandra, the facilitator for the evening, called everyone to order. She asked the group to do a quick round of introductions and then suggested reviewing the proposals and background materials that each member had brought. The three leaders who had written out their proposals each spent ten minutes summarizing their ideas and answering questions. Then the other members presented their contribu-

tions. One had brought a binder of materials from a series of workshops that JAG had sponsored three years earlier on the global economy. Another had brought several books published by an alternative press on sustainable economics, the environment, and urban planning. Others had brought informational materials produced by national progressive organizations whose work they admired. One graduate student announced that he had recently completed some research on the use of Tax Increment Financing10 around the region, and offered to share his findings. And several people had clipped newspaper articles from recent months that included data and statistics related to Chicago's economy.

Once all the members had shared their contributions, Sandra gave an update on the city's most recent Tax Increment Financing (TIF) proposal for the neighborhood. TIF districts had been springing up around the city over the past two years, provoking worried responses from community activists. The city's proposal for a new TIF in JAG's geographic area was the primary reason why JAG's members decided to create their own economic development platform for the neighborhood. Sandra had attended a recent informational meeting on the TIF held by the local alderman, and her description of the meeting provoked a lively discussion and debate. This segued into a lengthy discussion about other TIFs in the city and a heated debate about how JAG should respond to the TIF proposal.

After much discussion, but no resolution of the issue, Sandra suggested that they start working on developing JAG's principles for development. She directed the group's attention to a set of proposed principles that Danny, JAG's president, had drafted in preparation for the meeting and that Sandra had condensed into an easy-to-read chart. The group discussed each principle, analyzed it, and tried to come up with specific tools and techniques that could be used to measure whether each principle was being met. The conversation was lively as the members brainstormed ideas and suggested modifications or amendments to the proposed principles. Sandra did little as the facilitator. Instead, the conversation flowed easily as members energetically threw their ideas onto the table and debated relatively subtle policy distinctions. One debate revolved around the question of whether developers in a TIF should be required to contribute five percent of their profits to the community, or whether five percent of the TIF funds should go directly to the community, giving developers less money to invest in new projects. Another debate centered around how to define a socially responsible business—is an adult bookstore or a liquor store which pays its employees a living wage more or less socially responsible than a restaurant or hardware store which doesn't? At one point, one of the participants pulled out a book by a radical urban planner and suggested that

JAG's principles should be based directly on her writings, provoking lively arguments about whether her theories were even relevant to the discussion.

Two hours after the meeting began, no concrete decisions had been reached, but most of the participants didn't seem to care. Sandra suggested that they should wrap up the meeting. She proposed that they come up with some ideas for educational workshops or readings that might be useful in developing their principles. This provoked another lengthy discussion about the need to educate other residents in the community about these issues—a discussion that went on several unrelated tangents and extended the meeting for another half hour. Finally Sandra announced that she needed to leave. Still no decisions had been reached, but realizing how late it was, most participants started getting ready to go home.

Art, JAG's organizer, who had been relatively silent for much of the meeting, asked what the plan was for next steps. Given that no clear decisions had been reached, Sandra suggested that she and Danny work together over e-mail to develop a revised draft of principles to present at the next meeting. Everyone agreed. Then Art asked what position JAG should take on the TIF proposal, given that the hearings for the proposal would take place before the group would be finished with its platform. Despite the lengthy discussion earlier in the meeting on this topic, there was no clear consensus about what direction the group should take. A few people tossed out suggestions, without eliciting much response. Then Art casually laid out a proposal for action. His proposal incorporated some of the ideas that had circulated earlier in the evening, but was far more concrete and strategic than any of the earlier suggestions. A few participants raised some challenges to his proposed approach, but most were too tired by this point to engage in further debate. After a brief back and forth, Sandra asked if they were willing to go forward with Art's proposed plan. Most people nodded their heads, and those who didn't refrained from expressing any opposition. It was nearly ten p.m., and the participants were visibly relieved when Sandra finally declared the meeting adjourned.

Transformative organizations like JAG have a unitary conception of democracy based on the belief that low-income urban residents share the same basic interests. But whereas the other models of organizing base their decision-making processes on constituents' subjectively defined interests, transformative organizations make an implicit distinction between perceived and objective self-interests. Proponents of the transformative model believe that the political and economic structures that are at the root of urban problems produce a common set of objective interests among low-income and working-class residents. While these residents may not initially perceive their interests as being identical, this is because they interpret their experiences through the lens of dominant ideological frameworks that skew their perceptions of reality.[11]

Before community residents can make decisions about the neighborhood's priorities, transformative organizations believe that they must be introduced to alternative conceptual frameworks that will enable them to recognize their shared objective interests. Thus, in contrast to the community-building organizations—which believe that the neighborhood's stakeholders can build a common vision by consciously setting aside their differing interests and agreeing to disagree, and the women-centered organizations—which aim to build a collective consensus among participants through mutual listening, the transformative organizations believe that in order to reach a unified vision for the community, residents must understand the political and economic structures that underlie local neighborhood dynamics.

As discussed in chapter 3, organizations like JAG try to develop this understanding by engaging residents in popular education and critical reflection. JAG's meetings and discussions are an extension of this popular education process, providing participants with opportunities to hone their critical thinking skills through intense discussion and debate. The meetings also provide a framework within which more experienced members can critically analyze local issues in order to develop platforms and strategies to promote social justice at the local level. For this reason, the transformative organizations' meetings are intensely analytical, revolving around the application of abstract principles to local issues and involving extensive deliberation. Through these meetings, residents develop a common vision based on what they determine to be the community's objective interests.

Personalized Politics

If an organization's constituents all share the same objective interests, then it follows that they should be able to reach consensus through informal discussion and analysis, without the need for formal governance procedures. JAG's meetings tend to be loosely facilitated gatherings characterized by open-ended discussions and an expectation that people will insert themselves into the debate if they have something to say. Paul Lichterman (1995, 1996) refers to this style of democracy as "personalized politics," a culture of interaction rooted in a middle-class tradition of individualism that assumes a certain level of cultural capital. In order to participate effectively, participants must be able to keep up with the quick flow of discussion, articulate ideas clearly, and be comfortable engaging in abstract analysis and debate.

The lack of structure or real facilitation during JAG's discussions stimulates the free flow of ideas among participants, and generates a spirit of intellectual freedom and discovery. However, whereas JAG's core leadership—most of whom are middle-class activists and professionals—feel very comfortable in this kind of a setting, the lack of structure and the emphasis on abstract analysis tend to alienate and exclude JAG's less experienced and lower-income members.

The result is that JAG essentially operates as two separate organizations. The organization's middle-class, activist leaders focus their energy on conducting abstract policy analysis and developing organizational platforms and campaigns, while the group's low-income, less experienced participants tend to be involved in committees that focus primarily on solving very specific problems affecting their quality of life. While these meetings have some of the same flavor as the activists' meetings—the discussions are free flowing, animated, and highly participatory—the focus of the discussion is on the residents' own problems and experiences rather than theoretical policy analysis. For example, the discussions at JAG's Section 8 Committee meetings typically focused on participants' complaints about their landlords, the Section 8 program, and the conditions in their buildings.

As discussed in chapter 3, although members of both segments of JAG's membership lamented the lack of integration, they had little success in altering these divisions. Their difficulties in bridging the gap between the organization's two sides were exacerbated by the differences in the members' meeting styles. I observed several meetings in which JAG's leaders tried to bring together both types of members, but the efforts were rarely successful. For example, when Gladys, an elderly Section 8 recipient, came to a committee meeting composed entirely of experienced middle-class activists, she was heartily welcomed and encouraged to participate. However, her comments on the topic at hand focused on her personal experiences and observations rather than on the abstract policy-oriented analysis that was the focus of the group's discussion. While the committee listened respectfully and politely to her comments, they had difficulty integrating her personal observations into their political debate. As a result, ultimately most of her comments were ignored. Similarly, when several members of JAG's core activist leadership decided to lend their support to the Section 8 Committee by attending the committee's meetings, they sat silently, unable to find any meaningful way to participate. They were intent on listening to the participants talk about their experiences, but had nothing relevant to share from their own experiences.

The reliance on a meeting style that takes for granted a certain level of cultural capital can be especially problematic for organizations like JAG because it creates an imbalance of power along class and race lines within the organization. JAG's activist members tend to be middle-class whites, while the members of the Section 8 Committee tend to be low-income people of color. Because the activist leaders focus their energies on organizational policy questions and strategic planning, they end up having a disproportionate influence over the direction of the organization's work and its priorities.

Decision-making by Core Leaders

Another drawback of JAG's approach to democratic decision-making is that it rarely leads to genuine group consensus. In contrast to the women-centered organizations, which utilize a highly structured group process to create consensus, JAG's discussions were completely unstructured, with heavy emphasis on individual expression and abstract analysis and no agreed upon method for reaching decisions. JAG's meetings typically lasted three or four hours at a time, often ending without any clear decisions.

JAG's staff and core leaders frequently dealt with this dilemma by making the final decisions themselves. Faced with the need for some kind of decision about next steps, the members looked for guidance from these experienced activists. The staff and leaders were respected both for their intellectual and analytical skills, and for their knowledge about organizing and urban issues. In meetings of JAG's activist leaders, such as the one described in the above vignette, the members often delegated key policy decisions to one or two experienced leaders within the group and relied on JAG's organizer to guide their decisions about strategies. In meetings of JAG's less experienced participants—such as the Section 8 Committee—most of the strategic and analytical decisions were controlled by the organizer, with the implicit consent of the group.

For example, during most of the Section 8 Committee meetings that I observed, Art, JAG's organizer, let the group discussions proceed for more than an hour with little facilitation or direction. People felt very involved and included, but few decisions emerged from the process. Then, when the meeting was almost over and no decisions had yet been made, Art articulated his own detailed proposal for how the group should proceed. The participants typically accepted his proposal and endorsed it as their own. This strategy worked primarily because without a more carefully facilitated discussion, participants were unlikely to have clear thoughts or opinions about the final decision. In addition, many participants lacked confidence in their ability to analyze the underlying political and economic dynamics of their problems, making it difficult for them to develop clear proposals for action. As a result, when a well-thought-out proposal was presented to them, they were usually grateful and willing to support it.

Jane Mansbridge (1983) points out that this relegation of key decision-making to an "intellectual vanguard" is a common pattern within groups built around a shared ideology and a sense of common objective interests. If an organization's members have genuinely shared interests, trusting a small group of leaders to make decisions on behalf of the group as a whole is not undemocratic. Indeed, because JAG's leaders assume that the organization's constituents all share the same basic interests, they do not see the lack of genuine member participation in decisions as particularly problematic. Instead, they argue that this approach to decision-making is unavoidable. After all, despite JAG's emphasis on popular education and reflection, the reality is that at any given time a substantial portion of the participants will not have developed the critical thinking skills and knowledge necessary for effectively analyzing complex issues and generating appropriate platforms for social change. Pushing these members to make decisions would likely result in strategies that would be incompatible with JAG's overall ideological framework. Consequently, just as the power-based organizers resolve the tension between expertise and equal votes by using subtle manipulation, JAG resolves this dilemma by relegating much of the real decision-making authority to a small group of staff and leaders. JAG's president defended this practice, arguing that traditional conceptions of democracy are incompatible with an ideologically explicit organizing model:

> Participants [in JAG] don't have an equal voice. People in a leadership role have more voice. Formally there's always been a good-faith attempt to have some kind of ratification of decisions made by leaders, . . . [But] I think there's a lot of misguided utopian thinking among a lot of people interested in social change about democracy. I think democracy's a dialectical thing. . . . The role of leaders taking leadership is just as important as the role of mass participation.

Regardless of how necessary this method of decision-making might be as a way to preserve JAG's broader social justice framework, the lack of genuine member participation in much of the organization's actual decision-making remains problematic. JAG's staff and core leaders hold a disproportionate amount of power within the organization's policy-making and decision-making. And while many of the JAG members that I interviewed seemed resigned to this dynamic, they also expressed frustration over it. It was hard for participants to reconcile the highly participatory approach to discussion and debate with the far less inclusive process of decision-making. When there is such a clear disconnect between the group's discussion and its final decision, it is hard to feel invested in the process or the outcome. However, while this dynamic made many people uncomfortable, because of the tension between ideology and democracy, the dilemma was never satisfactorily resolved.

In sum, transformative organizations endorse a unitary approach to democracy based on the concept of shared objective interests. This approach promotes extensive deliberation and debate, giving community members an opportunity to analyze complex urban issues and critically assess different strategic options. However, this approach is rooted in a highly individualistic culture of interaction that requires participants to have significant levels of cultural capital if they are to participate effectively. In addition, because the model's explicitly ideological approach to urban change is incompatible with an open and inclusive approach to decision-making, the organizations often place actual decision-making authority in the hands of a small cadre of experienced activists.

CONCLUSION: BUILDING NEIGHBORHOOD-LEVEL DEMOCRACY

All of the organizations profiled in this chapter are committed to a democratic ideal, but they define this concept in widely varying ways. Each organization has a distinct conception of interest formation that shapes its approach to democratic decision-making, its methods of discussion and deliberation, how it identifies community priorities and how it develops strategies for action. While all the organizations approach neighborhood governance in a way that can be defined as "democratic," each approach entails different kinds of trade-offs among the four key democratic objectives introduced at the beginning of this chapter:

(a) promoting individual participation, inclusion, and equal voice;
(b) promoting genuine community deliberation over important issues;
(c) producing decisions efficiently; and
(d) creating decisions that further the organization's strategic objectives for the community in the wider public sphere.

Each organization excels in some of these areas and is less effective in others. And in the effort to resolve the tensions between these different objectives, many organizations rely on informal, behind-the-scenes decision-making strategies that can compromise the democratic nature of their governance structures.

Of all the organizations profiled in this chapter, the civic organizations are least effective at achieving the above objectives. Their free-for-all, open forum approach to democracy enables some community members to express their concerns, but does little to promote equal voice. And with no structure for discussions or for reaching decisions, the organizations frequently avoid deliberation and decision-making altogether.

The power-based organizations' adversary approach to democracy is very good at (c) producing decisions efficiently and (d) creating decisions that further the community's interests. The organizations also promote an ideal of participation and inclusion, but because there is often a tension between this objective and the other two, power-based organizations may resort to manipulation in order to ensure that the quality and efficiency of the decisions are maintained.

The community-building organizations' approach to neighborhood governance is most effective at achieving objectives (c) and (d). The organizations' rhetoric also focuses on the importance of individual involvement in decision-making, but in order to create effective comprehensive plans for the community they choose to rely on the decision-making authority of expert leaders. In addition, while the organizations emphasize the importance of building a shared vision of the common good through deliberation among multiple stakeholders, their approach does not allow much opportunity for real debate on important issues. Instead, their main technique for creating a common vision is by unifying the organization's members through rhetoric, symbolism, and charismatic leadership.

Of all the approaches to democracy, the women-centered approach is the most effective at promoting genuine inclusion and equal voice. In addition, the women-centered organizations excel at creating an atmosphere in which participants can engage in real deliberation and consensus-building. However, because of their emphasis on objectives (a) and (b), the women-centered organizations are not as good at achieving objectives (c) and (d). Decision-making in women-centered organizations is often extremely inefficient and time-consuming. In addition, because the organizations tend to define democracy more in terms of a process than a product, they don't place as much emphasis on the quality of the final decision as the other models do.

Finally, while the transformative organizations are also very good at (a) promoting high levels of individual participation and (b) fostering genuine deliberation, they may compromise the ideal of equal voice in favor of creating a free flowing atmosphere for intellectual exploration. In addition, while the organizations emphasize the importance of (d) producing effective strategies to further the community's objective interests, they experience a tension between this objective and the goal of democratic participation. In order to ensure that the decisions that are made are consistent with the ideological frameworks that drive the organizations' strategies, transformative groups may end up relegating decision-making to a small cadre of sophisticated leaders.

While this chapter focused on the *process* of democratic governance within community organizations, part III examines the *content* of these decision-making processes. Through an analysis of the case study organizations' issue priorities and action campaigns, the chapters in part III set out the tangible, on-the-ground consequences of the organizations' different approaches.

TABLE 5 Creating a Community Governance Structure

Model	Theory of democracy and conception of interests	Discussion and decision-making process	Implications for neighborhood governance
Power-based	Adversary democracy based on aggregation of individual members' potentially conflicting interests	Group discussion and identification of member self-interests followed by majority vote. Emphasis on formal protection of individual interests	Able to mediate among the interests of large numbers of people efficiently; produces decisions that are seen as fair and legitimate; tension between formal equality and effective decisions creates potential for manipulation and unequal influence
Civic	Unitary democracy based on the assumption that community members can develop decisions about neighborhood priorities without conflict or disagreement	Democracy as an open forum: no structure, facilitation, or decision-making rules	Lack of genuine deliberation; avoidance of controversy; avoidance of priority setting; lack of leadership accountability
Community-building	Unitary democracy based on a shared commitment to the common good despite potentially conflicting individual interests	Consensus guided by technically skilled leaders; communitarian approach with emphasis on group unity and speaking with one voice	Able to produce comprehensive community plans that are seen as legitimate and correct; enables diverse stakeholders to reach unity over a shared vision of the common good; lack of individual participation; potential for bias in definition of common good

TABLE 5 Creating a Community Governance Structure (*continued*)

Model	Theory of democracy and conception of interests	Discussion and decision-making process	Implications for neighborhood governance
Women-centered	Unitary democracy based on development of shared individual interests	Highly participatory, formally structured process of discussion; consensus based on interpersonal communication and mutual agreement	Respects the voice of each individual member; highly inclusive; produces decisions with high levels of buy-in and legitimacy; potentially very time-consuming and inefficient; difficulty dealing with internal conflict
Transformative	Unitary democracy based on shared objective interests	Emphasis on deliberation and debate as a vehicle for critical analysis and the development of an alternative vision for society. Consensus based on the leadership of experienced activists	Intellectually stimulating and analytically rigorous discussions; tension between democracy and ideology creates potential for decisions to be relegated to an "intellectual vanguard"

PART III

CREATING URBAN CHANGE

CHAPTER 6

DIAGNOSING AND FRAMING
THE COMMUNITY'S PROBLEMS

When Kyle Jenkins bought his first home, he was thrilled with the quiet, laid back atmosphere of his new neighborhood. So when a drug dealer moved in next door and began running a round-the-clock drug trafficking business out of his apartment, Kyle got angry:

"It was so blatant. There's a gate there and every time people go in and out the gate would slam and it would reverberate. It was twenty-four hours a day, and when I would walk my dog at 6:00, 6:30 in the morning, there would be a line of people waiting to get into his apartment to buy drugs. There was a line—every minute there would be somebody slamming the gate. . . . We couldn't take it anymore, because he was attracting every heroin addict and cocaine addict in the whole neighborhood, and it was starting to get scary. . . ."

Determined to put a stop to the problem, Kyle went to the local police station. After listening to his complaints, the officer on duty told Kyle he should get involved with his local CAPS organization. Kyle attended his first CAPS meeting the following week, where he had an opportunity to talk directly to the neighborhood's beat cops about the issue. Pointing out that they couldn't arrest and convict the drug dealers without ample evidence, the officers told him to keep detailed notes about everything he observed and to share the information with them on a regular basis. They also gave him tips for effectively navigating the police department's crime reporting system. Although Kyle was frustrated with the lack of an immediate solution, he felt empowered by his new role as the police's "eyes and ears" and was hopeful that once he was able to gather enough information, the police would be able to shut the drug house down.

Several miles away, new homeowner Peter Czerni was facing a similar problem. Shortly after moving into his new home, Peter learned from one of his neighbors that there was a drug operation down the street that residents had been trying to shut down for months. When a WON organizer knocked on his door several weeks later, Peter mentioned his concerns, and the organizer invited him to a meeting with his neighbors to discuss the problem. Thirty other residents showed up at the meeting, and WON's organizer worked with them *to develop a focused strategy for addressing the situation. "The funny thing about it," Peter recalls, "was that it was mostly a fight with the police. It was not really as much of a fight with the gangs. . . . The anger ended up getting directed towards the police." Deciding that the drug house was the result of police inaction and neglect, the group developed a step by step plan for pressuring the police commander to redirect his manpower and resources to target the situation. As taxpayers, they believed the police commander had a responsibility to comply with their demands, and if he refused, they were prepared take their demands over his head. "We had to adopt a very aggressive, confrontational sort of strategy and map that out and be prepared for anything. . . . We had to understand who the police commander reports to, and who he reports to—ultimately the mayor." After a series of protests and several negotiating meetings, the police finally responded to the residents' demands. They barraged the drug house with intensive surveillance, made numerous arrests, and eventually shut the drug operation down.*

The chapters in part II examined the impact of different models of community organizing on the development of urban residents' capacity to engage in collective action. Part III will explore how the case study organizations translate this capacity into concrete action to change the material conditions and quality of life within neighborhoods. People often assume that once the residents of a given community have the capacity to work together, the solutions to the neighborhood's problems will be obvious.[1] In reality, even though residents may share a common sense of dissatisfaction with their conditions, the nature and source of this dissatisfaction can usually be interpreted in a number of different ways. By providing a structure and framework for decision-making about local issues, community organizing groups shape the way residents interpret and diagnose their experiences. Consequently, the approach that residents take to address the neighborhood's problems will vary depending on the organizations they're involved with.

Kyle Jenkins and Peter Czerni both had the same problem—a drug house nearby. But because the organizations they got involved with had very different theories of change, the men ended up framing and interpreting their problems in very different ways. CAPS, a civic organization, defined Kyle's situation as a technical problem stemming from the police's lack of sufficient information. In contrast, WON, a power-based organization, framed Peter's situation as an issue of police accountability. "[Our approach] is different from a civic model in that . . . our underlying philosophy is that if you don't have power you can not create change," WON's organizer explained. "The system is predicated on power. . . . When we're going over things, it really is about power, and we discuss these concepts explicitly." These distinctions in the organizations' interpretations of the men's experiences resulted in different strategies for solving the problems and, ultimately, very different outcomes.

This chapter examines the ways that community organizations translate residents' concerns into clearly defined problems. This process of social construction is an integral feature of all community organizing. As Alinsky put it, "In any community, regardless of how poor, people may have serious problems—but they do not have issues, they have a bad scene. . . . What the organizer does is convert the plight into a problem" (1971: 119).

Sociologists refer to this process as the development of a "collective action frame"—" 'schemata of interpretation' that enable individuals 'to locate, perceive, identify, and label' occurrences within their life space and the world at large" (Snow et al. 1986: 235). By defining individual experiences as part of a broader set of problems or issues, collective action frames help residents to see the value of working together to create change. Furthermore, by offering causal explanations for residents' experiences, collective action frames shape residents' conceptions of the urban change process and their perceived solutions to the neighborhood's problems (Snow and Benford 1992).

Each model of community organizing has its own collective action frame, shaped by a distinctive theory of change. I begin my analysis of each model by examining these theories of change. Then I explore how these conceptual frameworks impact the way that community organizing groups diagnose the neighborhood's problems, identify the solutions to these problems, and implement these solutions through specific strategies and tactics.

Throughout the chapter, I will illustrate my analysis by describing how the case study organizations approached the issue of urban crime. As the stories of Kyle Jenkins and Peter Czerni demonstrate, the visible presence of drug dealing and gang activity in many urban neighborhoods has made public safety an issue of concern for many low- and moderate- income urban residents. Because of the issue's salience, even though the case study organizations all worked on a wide range of different issues, public safety was the one issue that appeared on all of their agendas.

The purpose of this chapter is primarily descriptive rather than evaluative. My aim is to articulate and explain the case study organizations' distinctive conceptions of urban problems and their approaches to change. The differences between these approaches clearly have important implications for the organizations' effectiveness in achieving urban change. Chapter 7 will take up this issue through a detailed and critical evaluation of the organizations' campaigns.

THE CIVIC MODEL: RESTORING SOCIAL CONTROL

The civic model defines urban problems with a collective action frame that focuses on the breakdown of the neighborhood's social order. The model's proponents argue that in stable communities, strong social bonds and well-functioning social control mechanisms ensure conformity to shared rules and norms. In contrast, they believe that the anonymity and disorganization that characterize today's inner-city neighborhoods provide fertile ground for a wide range of problems to emerge (Hunter 1995; Sampson 1995; Wilson and Kelling 1989).

Based on this diagnosis, the model's proponents advocate solutions to urban problems that focus on strengthening the mechanisms of formal and informal social control at the community level. Mechanisms of *informal* social control include peer pressure and social networks that ensure conformity to shared norms and standards of behavior. *Formal* social control mechanisms, on the other hand, utilize the authority of the state—as represented by the police and city services system—to impose sanctions on deviant behavior and enforce order. Civic organizations work to restore both formal and informal social control by building social ties among neighbors, establishing community-wide norms, and mobilizing the city services system to respond to local problems.

CAPS and CAN: Translating Residents' Concerns Into Social Control Problems

Like most community organizing groups, CAN and CAPS begin the process of defining the neighborhood's problems by asking residents to identify their most pressing concerns. In contrast to the other organizations in this study, however, CAN and CAPS don't have any systematic procedures for accomplishing this task. Instead, the organizations simply give residents an opportunity to voice their concerns during the informal free-for-all at their monthly meetings. Whatever problems are identified through this process are then dealt with in an ad hoc manner on a case by case basis.

In many cases (as described in chapter 5), the problems that participants raise are never addressed at all by the organization. When they *are* addressed, it is through an approach that implicitly defines all the neighborhood's problems as issues of social control. CAN and CAPS' participants tend to assume that whenever a problem emerges in the neighborhood, it must be the result of a failure in the neighborhood's social control apparatus.

For example, every time residents complained at CAN meetings about potholes, CAN's leaders attributed the problem to a breakdown in the Department of Streets and Sanitation's maintenance protocol. Viewing the city services system as a straightforward, complaint-driven, administrative apparatus, they assumed that once information goes into the system, it is processed, and the situation is dealt with according to formal rules and procedures. When problems like potholes weren't addressed in a timely manner, participants assumed that either the city department responsible for dealing with that particular issue hadn't been given the necessary information, or the information hadn't been prioritized correctly.

Any evidence of a breakdown in the city's formal social control apparatus worried CAN and CAPS participants because they feared that if signs of disorder weren't addressed quickly, the neighborhood would deteriorate even further. Arguing that a neighborhood that looks uncared for will attract further incivility—an assumption commonly referred to as the "broken windows theory" (Wilson and Kelling 1989)—participants insisted that small problems left unattended would enable bigger problems to emerge. "[A] lot of times basic city services is at the heart of why a crime has sprung up," one CAPS member explained. "My favorite example is a street light is out. All of a sudden people are hit with purse snatching. It's never really happened there before. Why? Well, you've got two street lights out."

While such breakdowns in the city's formal social control mechanisms were cited as the most immediate cause of the neighborhood's problems, participants also blamed the neighborhood's lack of shared norms and standards of behavior for creating an environment in which such problems could emerge. "[The] primary problems are probably lack of communication amongst us, and [lack of] expectations of that old non-defined word, standards," one participant explained. "I think our expectations are different not only along cultural lines but are also different along economic lines. And there is not a clear, if you will, acceptable level of behavior."

For example, when residents came to CAN meetings to complain about problems like drug dealing, loitering, and graffiti, CAN's members attributed the problems to the neighborhood's lack of acceptable behavioral norms. As one local landlord and CAN member put it, "We cannot let lawless people and people who have no clue as to what it means to be socialized to cause the kinds of problems they're causing and to destroy things."

CAN and CAPS members believed that it was up to the neighborhood's property owners to serve as gatekeepers for the community by enforcing basic social and behavioral norms and keeping undesirable elements out of the community. By not exercising proper control over their buildings, they argued, irresponsible landlords contributed to the physical deterioration of the neighborhood and enabled criminals to take over the streets. As one participant explained, "We have a tremendous amount of absentee landlords, which has led to a lot of the problems. They're not here to oversee. . . . Unless they're being held liable for some of the things that are going on, they don't really want to do anything about it. The drugs and the gangs, a lot of that wouldn't exist in the neighborhood if you didn't have landlords who let it exist."

CAPS and CAN: Solutions and Strategies

In their effort to strengthen the neighborhood's social order, CAN and CAPS' first priority was to bring local problems to the attention of the appropriate department within the city services system. "A lot of what we do," explained one CAN leader, "is remind government organizations that they need to be doing things that they should have been doing anyway. Like fixing street signs or repairing sidewalks or recapping all the fire hydrants."

Viewing city government as a bureaucratic system that operates according to formal rules, the organizations' participants assumed that in order to get the city to respond to neighborhood problems, they simply needed to follow the correct procedures. Thus, each time a problem was raised at the organizations' meetings, CAN and CAPS participants worked to identify the city department that could most effectively address the problem, the appropriate liaisons within that department, and the necessary procedures for accessing the services. They expected that once they submitted their complaints through the city's established channels for citizen input, the city services system would kick into gear to address their concerns.

In addition to trying to mobilize the city services system to eradicate existing problems, CAN and CAPS members tried to preserve the neighborhood's stability by wiping out small signs of disorder as soon as they occurred. Participants engaged in neighborhood clean-ups and beautification projects both on their own and as a group. One CAPS member explained the theory behind this approach: "The viaduct at the end of our block, it's all white. Occasionally it's got graffiti on it. We take it out immediately. Just paint over it. They find it really discouraging because it's not worth them taking the risk of getting arrested putting it on there if within less than twenty-four hours it's gone." Similarly, participants served as the city's "eyes and ears," monitoring the neighborhood's public areas on an ongoing basis to keep the city informed about problems as they arose. "If I see a hazardous situation, I'll report it," one member explained. "If I see a light out I'll call. If I see an abandoned car, I'll keep my eye on it for a few days and then I'll call. That's the day to day kind of stuff, and a lot of people do that."

In an effort to strengthen the informal mechanisms of social control in the community, CAN and CAPS also worked to build social connections among the neighborhood's "responsible" residents. "What I envision is that

EXAMPLE: CAN'S APPROACH TO CRIME AND SAFETY

When CAN's members got together to talk about the neighborhood's problems, the issue of crime was a frequent topic of discussion. CAN's approach to crime focused primarily on the issue of "problem buildings." Participants complained that the preponderance of crime-ridden apartment buildings in the area was ruining the neighborhood's reputation and undermining their property values. After a particularly bad spate of muggings and purse snatchings, one local property owner decided to take matters into her own hands. Tapping into her personal and professional networks, she contacted twenty of the neighborhood's most "responsible" landlords and invited them to a meeting. Declaring that it was time to let the "riff raff" and "low-lives" know that "it's our turf, not theirs," the group hammered out a coordinated strategy for re-establishing order and stability in the neighborhood.

In their brainstorming sessions, the group's members all agreed that the primary blame for the neighborhood's crime problems rested on the poor management practices of the problem buildings' owners. As one put it, "[If drug dealers are] allowed to sell their drugs or hang out in someone's building or establishment, then that [building] owner and that business owner becomes the problem. There could be drug dealers that dealt for twenty years, but if they come on this stoop in front of my building and I let them sit there, I'm the problem."

The group decided to use peer pressure to force the neighborhood's landlords to abide by a set of common standards for tenant screening and property management. "We're talking about [creating] standards and forcing people to live up to them. . . . It's social pressure to conform to social norms," one participant explained. The group developed a "Landlord Manifesto" outlining standards of behavior and codes of conduct for managing apartment buildings, and then tried to get all of the neighborhood's landlords to sign it.

In addition, the group tried to use the threat of formal sanctions to force the worst landlords to clean up their acts. They reported several landlords to the city for code violations in the hope that the steep fines would convince the owners to give up their buildings. They also worked closely with the police, regularly documenting their observations and reporting their findings. Many offered their own buildings to the police for surveillance purposes. And when the problems at two property owners' buildings got particularly bad, participants asked the alderman's office to set up private meetings with the landlord, the alderman, CAN's leaders, and the police to rake the landlords over the coals.

you can walk down the street and greet a neighbor and know they live in that building or that building. And your neighbor will greet you as a neighbor, as opposed to hi from a passing stranger," one participant explained. Another participant added, "It's trying to establish a super-family, if you would. Not necessarily as close as a family, but at least second cousins—so you're not afraid to talk to people on the street because you already know them. And strangers get noticed that way."

To facilitate the development of shared norms and rules of behavior among the area's residents, the civic organizations also tried to increase the percentage of responsible homeowners and middle-class residents in their neighborhoods. Arguing that such residents would have a greater sense of investment in the community and a lower tolerance for disorder, many participants believed this shift in the area's demographic composition was essential for creating a more stable neighborhood. In the words of one CAPS member, "I think all of us want to see a more middle-class community. . . . Middle-class families don't want gangs of thugs roaming around and causing social chaos and robbing and stealing and mugging people. That's not safe for their children. They don't want to see kids running on the streets throwing bottles and breaking bottles and throwing up gang signs." To achieve this goal, the organizations' members frequently lent their support to private development initiatives designed to replace low-income renters with homeowners.

THE POWER-BASED MODEL: BUILDING THE COMMUNITY'S CLOUT

Whereas the civic model frames the neighborhood's problems in terms of social control, the power-based model frames neighborhood problems as a function of the struggle for influence within the public sphere. Proponents of the power-based model view almost everything that happens in urban neighborhoods as the result of decision-making by economic and political powerholders. Espousing a pluralist conception of the polity (Dahl 1961), the model depicts the public sphere as an open arena in which competing interest groups battle it out. Steven Lukes (1974) refers to this as a "one-dimensional" conception of power because it implicitly defines power as a zero-sum game in which winning is premised simply on whichever group has enough raw clout to get its way.

The power-based model's proponents believe that this interest group system essentially works, but only if all interest groups are included at the bargaining table. Since urban residents are usually not so well organized as other traditional interest groups, the model's proponents argue, they don't have enough clout to participate effectively in the public sphere. As a result, their interests and needs are typically overlooked when decisions are made about urban issues. As one power-based organizer put it, "The problem in the neighborhood is that the neighborhood is not as organized as it should or could be, and that neighborhood people are not going to have the amount of power that they need to really have. All the institutions in the neighborhood and politicians—all these people who traditionally have positions of power and make decisions about how the neighborhood is going to be—the problem is that residents don't have that same kind of power."

The solution to this problem is to build residents' power to fight for their interests within the public decision-making process. Because low-income and working-class residents typically don't have access to traditional sources of power—such as money—their most important resource is their numbers. Thus the most effective way to address the community's problems is by bringing together large numbers of residents to pressure economic and political powerholders to concede to their demands.

WON and UNITE: Translating Residents' Concerns Into Issues of Power

In order to identify and diagnose the neighborhood's problems, WON and UNITE use a step-by-step approach that is a standard feature of power-based organizing. As the first step in this process, the organizers talk one-on-one with the neighborhood's residents, through both doorknocking and housemeetings, to identify their most pressing problems and concerns. Next, the organizers work to translate the general "problems" identified by residents into specific "issues" with clear demands. When residents are asked about their concerns, they usually state their grievances in fairly vague terms—gangs, crime, bad public services. In order to make the power relations at the root of these problems as transparent as possible, the power-based organizations hone in on specific manifestations of the broader grievance. So, for example, WON translated residents' concerns about poorly maintained streets into a list of specific streets and alleys that needed to be repaved.

Once the issue has been defined, the organizers work with residents to identify *the* political official or economic powerholder who has the authority to resolve the situation. This individual—usually referred to as the "target" or the "enemy"—then becomes the focus of the organization's campaign. By placing responsibility for the issue on a public actor, the power-based organizations locate the problem within the wider public sphere. And by focusing their blame on a *specific* public actor, the power dynamics underlying the problem become clear: what may have initially seemed simply like a frustrating situation is now directly attributed to the actions (or inaction) of a person with power. As one organizer put it, "Issues are not caused by systems. Issues are caused by people in the system who are not doing their job" (Trapp 1986: 5). This personalization of the issue makes it easy for politically inexperienced residents to perceive their grievances as the direct result of a lack of responsiveness to residents' interests within the public sphere.

Finally, the power-based organizers highlight the fundamental imbalance of power at the root of the problem by using familiar metaphors that draw from residents' everyday experiences with power. For example, WON's organizers frequently describe the abstract concept of public accountability by referencing the relationship between an employer and an employee. As one member put it, "As far as local government and government agencies, it's always been our policy they work for us. We're their bosses and they should come and do as we ask them." Thus, through a carefully orchestrated process of issue framing, the power-based organizations define residents' problems as a function of unequal power relations within the public arena.

WON and UNITE: Solutions and Strategies

This framing of the issues shapes the strategies that WON and UNITE use to solve neighborhood problems. Generally speaking, every power-based campaign revolves around one central goal—to force the target to concede to residents' demands. To achieve this goal, the organizations must first build enough clout to convince power-holders to take them seriously. This requires numbers. Through doorknocking and house meetings, power-based organizers and leaders try to "agitate" the neighborhood's residents to get involved in the campaign by appealing to their basic self-interests.

Once they have recruited a large enough group of supporters, power-based organizations engage in public action to demonstrate their power. Lacking the stable, reputational clout that comes from having money or corporate power, the organizations typically rely on public confrontations with their targets in order to demonstrate their numbers and gain influence within the political decision-making process. As power-based organizer Shel Trapp explains, "Through the use of confrontation, the community can get to the bargaining table, not because they are liked, not because they have good ideas, not because they want to save their community, but because they are respected and in some cases feared" (Trapp 1976a: 19).

A typical WON campaign begins with a public meeting where the target is forced to respond to the organization's demands in front of hundreds of angry residents and the media. In addition to presenting the target with a clear demonstration of WON's power-in-numbers, the organization also uses a variety of tactics to polarize and intensify the conflict. Such tactics include forcing the target to respond to each demand with a simple "yes" or "no" response (making it impossible for the target to avoid a direct answer); using well-coordinated audience cheers and chants to intimidate the target; and using seating arrangements designed to make the target feel trapped.

If a target refuses to cooperate with residents' demands, power-based organizations intensify the conflict. Asserting that the ends justify the means, power-based organizations are infamous for their willingness to do whatever it takes to achieve their goals. As one organizer put it, "It's a war. It's two forces clashing. You can't avoid getting your hands dirty. The way to get change is power. With power it doesn't matter what tactics you use. There are no rules. . . . We're talking about a war, and a war always has casualties." WON's signature tactic is to load residents into school buses and pay surprise visits—better known as "hits"—on the homes or offices of a campaign's targets. Typically striking at night or on weekends, the goal is to embarrass the target in front of his neighbors, and make it clear that his reputation won't be safe anywhere unless he concedes to the group's demands.[2]

Using these and other tactics, power-based organizations escalate the confrontation until the target agrees to negotiate. Once they gain a seat at the bargaining table, the organizations typically reframe their confrontational stance into a more professional and collegial approach. As WON's director explained, "We fight in order to get to the table. Once we're at the table, if we don't have to fight with someone again, we don't." However, to avoid the risk of cooptation, the organizations insist that their relationships with targets remain impersonal and business-like. WON's organizers referred to this approach as "the iron fist and velvet glove"—you can negotiate with powerholders, but it must be based on an understanding of the power you could leverage if you needed to.

Once they have reached an agreement with the target over their demands, WON's members continue to monitor the situation to make sure the target follows through. And they remain prepared to apply additional pressure if necessary to force compliance. Finally, when the demands have been met, the group celebrates its victory and begins the process of identifying the next campaign.

EXAMPLE: WON'S APPROACH TO CRIME AND SAFETY

At the start of every new WON campaign, the group's organizers spend several weeks knocking on doors in the neighborhood to find out about the issues of greatest concern to local residents. During these doorknocking sessions, complaints about crime come up more often than any other single concern. The organizers respond to these complaints by using a systematic, step-by-step approach which is illustrated by the following example.

After talking one-on-one to several dozen residents about their concerns with prostitution, drug houses, vandalism, robberies, and abandoned houses, John, WON's organizer, invited them to come to a meeting to develop a coordinated strategy for addressing crime in the neighborhood. He began the meeting by asking each participant to name the crime situation that was of greatest personal concern. This exercise resulted in a list of several dozen "hotspots" from around the neighborhood. The creation of the list transformed the participants from a collection of individuals into a united group with a specific set of issues and demands.

John pointed out that if the police were more responsive to residents' concerns, the hotspots wouldn't exist. He proposed inviting the police commander to a public meeting where residents could demand that he respond to their concerns. At the meeting, the residents confronted the commander with their list of hotspots and demanded that he commit additional manpower and resources to address the problem locations. Faced with hundreds of angry residents and a bevy of news cameras and reporters, the commander agreed.

Several weeks later, residents gathered to evaluate the effectiveness of the police's response at each of the hotspots. Although the police had taken action on almost every single item on the list, many had not been resolved. The residents concluded that they needed to do more to increase police responsiveness in their neighborhood. Along with residents from other neighborhoods in WON's organizing area, they decided to launch a campaign to demand that the city assign twenty-five additional police officers to their police district.

After several unsuccessful attempts to get the city's highest police official—the Superintendent—to attend a public meeting to discuss these demands, WON staged a well orchestrated "hit" on the city's central police headquarters. Waving placards, chanting, and singing songs, dozens of WON participants protested at the headquarters in front of rush hour traffic, TV cameras, and numerous passersby. In response, the Superintendent's next-in-command agreed to meet with the group, launching a series of intensive negotiations.

THE COMMUNITY-BUILDING MODEL: STRENGTHENING THE
COMMUNITY'S SOCIAL AND ECONOMIC FABRIC

Whereas the power-based model's collective action frame focuses on the community's lack of clout within the public sphere, the community-building model focuses on the health and vitality of the neighborhood itself. Viewing the neighborhood as a holistic organism, the model's proponents believe that the deterioration of the community's internal fabric is at the root of most urban problems. They argue that without a strong social and economic infrastructure, urban neighborhoods cannot effectively respond to their residents' needs.

Given this diagnosis, proponents of the community-building model stress that in order to solve urban problems, communities must redevelop themselves from within. "Even the poorest neighborhood is a place where individuals and organizations represent resources upon which to rebuild. The key to neighborhood regeneration, then, is to locate all of the available local assets, to begin connecting them with one another in ways that multiply their power and effectiveness, and to begin harnessing those local institutions that are not yet available for local development purposes" (Kretzmann and McKnight 1993: 5–6). To accomplish this goal, community-building organizations work to build partnerships among local stakeholder institutions, government agencies, and the private sector in order to strengthen the neighborhood's social support systems and economic base.

PACT and CO-OP: Translating the Neighborhood's Problems Into a Comprehensive Understanding of the Community's Internal Fabric

Like the power-based organizations, PACT and CO-OP begin their analysis of the neighborhood's problems by trying to systematically identify local residents' most pressing concerns. But whereas the power-based groups work to translate residents' concerns into one specific, clearly defined issue, PACT and CO-OP take a much more comprehensive approach. Viewing the neighborhood as an organic, interdependent whole, community-building organizations believe that all of the neighborhood's problems can be traced to a common set of underlying community dynamics. In order to understand this broader picture, PACT and CO-OP use research, expert analysis, discussions with local stakeholders, surveys of residents, and public forums to assess the entire array of problems in the community. Then, by focusing on the interconnections between the various problems, they develop a comprehensive assessment of the neighborhood's needs.

For example, when PACT was first formed, its founders spent months studying and analyzing the history and dynamics of the neighborhood's current problems. Through this process, they determined that virtually all of the problems were connected to a common thread—the deterioration of the neighborhood's social and economic fabric. According to PACT's leaders, the neighborhood's high rates of unemployment and poverty, its problems with gangs and youth violence, and the impending threat of gentrification and displacement could all be traced to the community's historic lack of economic self-sufficiency. As PACT's chair put it, because of the community's lack of control over its own development, "[the government has been] able to dump all the scattered site housing in one spot and . . . developers were able to buy up all this land and put their type of development on there, take our industrial sites, take our factories and build quarter of a million dollar lofts."

Drawing on the results of their comprehensive community analysis, PACT's leaders concluded that this economic decline was also linked to an erosion of the neighborhood's social fabric. They argued that the lack of social connections among residents and a pervasive culture of negativity had weakened the neighborhood's internal spirit of resilience. As one explained, "There are people who have given up hope. . . . [T]here was a time in Port Angeles when you just thought nobody cared. You know, it was no man's land. We didn't know what was going to happen. And so, you know, here you have a neighborhood there was a perception it was one of the worst neighborhoods in the city. And people felt hopeless." Furthermore, PACT's leaders argued that the historic lack of cooperation among the neighborhood's institutions had eroded the community's ability to address its own needs: "There was some silo thinking," one institutional leader explained, "where each one of us is a silo doing our own thing and not looking at what's going on around us, and in many cases competing unnecessarily among each other when the community as a whole is being disregarded."

PACT and CO-OP: Solutions and Strategies

In order to address these problems, PACT and CO-OP developed comprehensive neighborhood plans designed to rebuild the community's economic and social infrastructure in a holistic way. As the introduction to PACT's comprehensive plan explained, "The future of the Greater Port Angeles community rests on our ability to enhance economic opportunities for our residents. . . . We want to offer our community all the resources to develop in a healthy, sustainable way." In an effort to achieve this goal, PACT worked to attract employers to the neighborhood, promote local entrepreneurship, and revitalize the neighborhood's commercial areas. "[We] want to protect the jobs that are there and also to attract and create new businesses and to develop the workforce for the jobs that are available. And [we] want commercial development—[we] want to develop the commercial corridors. And the industrial corridors," one member explained. In addition, PACT's leaders worked to build partnerships with outside corporations and businesses in order to attract private investment to the neighborhood. By rooting these partnerships within a comprehensive vision for the neighborhood's future, they hoped to attract needed resources while enabling the community to retain control over its own development.

Along with promoting economic development, PACT and CO-OP's comprehensive plans sought to strengthen the community's social fabric. As described in previous chapters, PACT and CO-OP built relationships and a shared vision among a wide array of different stakeholder groups and engaged them in collaborative projects to address the neighborhood's needs. In contrast to traditional social services, which try to solve problems through the intervention of outside experts, these programs focused on addressing residents' needs by building the community's own capacity to help its members. "[We] give people credit for who they are," one CO-OP member explained, "[we] see people from a much more positive point of view, and . . . just because someone is unemployed or has a health or behavioral health problem, it doesn't mean that they don't also have a lot of strengths." Many of the organizations' programs focused on building mutually supportive relationships among residents. For example, CO-OP developed a peer-to-peer counseling program in which former welfare recipients were matched up with current recipients to help ease the transition to self-sufficiency. Similarly, CO-OP addressed the lack of preventive health care services in the neighborhood by training local residents to provide health information and referral services to their neighbors and friends.

In order to leverage the necessary funding and support to make these programs a reality, PACT and CO-OP worked to build strong partnerships between the community and local government entities. The organizations' leaders emphasized that without government support, implementation of their comprehensive community plans would be impossible. "There's no way we could have an organization that's not linked to the government in the sense of having that open communication with them, inviting them to our table to sit down with us so we can hopefully get laws and policies passed that will help the people from the community get the empowerment that they need," one PACT leader explained.

In an effort to secure this support, PACT and CO-OP sought to build collegial, consensus-based partnerships with local officials and policy-makers—partnerships that were rooted in the organizations' claims to legitimacy as

EXAMPLE: PACT'S APPROACH TO CRIME AND SAFETY

A few years after PACT was first formed, several of the neighborhood's churches decided to join the organization in an effort to respond to their congregation members' rising concerns about crime. Most of the congregation members viewed the crime problem as a law enforcement issue and wanted PACT to do something about it. However, in the process of developing a comprehensive plan for the neighborhood, PACT's members began to see crime as just one piece of the community's overall social and economic decline. They concluded that the neighborhood's gang problem was directly connected to the neighborhood's lack of economic opportunities and support networks for youth. Consequently, rather than viewing the gang members as criminals, PACT embraced them as members of the community who, like all Port Angeles' residents, were suffering the impacts of the neighborhood's complex social problems. As PACT's organizer put it, "You might say there's no way to solve gangs, just lock them up. But we look at our family and friends and we know people on the streets, and we don't want them in prison. I know—my cousin's out there. It will take us all working together to solve the problems."

By leveraging the community's existing assets in new ways, PACT's members developed an integrated web of services and programs for at-risk youth. The centerpiece of PACT's strategy was to bring together local churches to provide recreational opportunities for youth as well as support and counseling to gang members. This strategy was modeled on the nationally acclaimed work of Eugene Rivers in Boston (Crowe 1999). Rivers coordinated a network of pastors that offered counseling and mentoring to gang affected youth, successfully defusing much of the gang-related violence in Boston. Building on Rivers' model, PACT worked with local pastors to create "sanctuary zones" in and around the churches to provide safe spaces for local youth to engage in sports and recreation. In addition, some of the pastors began ministering to local gang members and providing them with advice and support. And the churches worked with the police to develop a system for reducing the violence associated with gang warfare.

PACT also brought together the area's youth agencies and job training organizations to develop a set of streamlined mentoring and employment programs for youth. As one of PACT's organizer's observed, "Some of the [organizations], where they thought the issue of public safety was an issue that was never going to be won, are now starting to see maybe something can be done, and maybe something more than locking kids up can be done. There is hope for rehabilitating our young people in our community rather than just putting them away somewhere." The organizations worked together to sponsor job fairs and job preparation workshops to connect local residents to jobs. And they leveraged government funding to create a peer-mentoring program to connect at-risk youth with successful young adults who were trained to assist the youth in accessing job training and employment opportunities.

the voice of the community. PACT and CO-OP used the breadth and diversity of their memberships to convince government leaders that they could effectively represent the interests of the entire neighborhood. For example, in an effort to strengthen its legitimacy in the eyes of local government, CO-OP merged with another preexisting collaborative in the same neighborhood. Government officials applauded the merger because it created one unified "voice" for the neighborhood, providing an easy vehicle for government agencies to partner with the community.

In addition to emphasizing their ability to represent the entire community's interests, PACT and CO-OP tried to gain acceptance as the official policy-setting and planning bodies for their neighborhoods. By emphasizing the technical and professional merits of their comprehensive neighborhood plans and the skills and capacities of their member institutions, the organizations hoped to convince local government to adopt their plans as blueprints for local development and policy-setting.

THE WOMEN-CENTERED MODEL: BUILDING FAMILY-FRIENDLY COMMUNITIES

The women-centered model traces the problems facing low-income women and their families to their historic exclusion from mainstream community decision-making structures. Because the issues affecting families are typically defined as domestic problems to be addressed in the private sphere, the model's proponents argue, low-income women and their children are left to deal with their problems in isolation, without external support or public solutions. Similarly, even though women have historically played a central role in building communities, they have largely been excluded from formal leadership roles. As a result, the public and private institutions that serve families' needs—social services, schools, housing—frequently fail to take into account the unique interests and conditions of the families themselves when they design their services.

Proponents of the women-centered model argue that in order to make communities work for women and families, issues that are commonly relegated to the private, domestic sphere must be translated into community issues with public solutions. In order to do this, women must be given the opportunity to develop a vision for themselves, their families, and the community as a whole. This vision can then become the basis for the creation of new programs and services to meet families' needs. In order to implement these strategies, the model emphasizes the importance of building face-to-face interpersonal relationships and hands-on partnerships between neighborhood women and local public and private institutions.

PILOT and TLC: Translating Private Problems Into Public Issues

Emphasizing the connection between the private and public spheres, women-centered organizations work to identify the community's problems by focusing first and foremost on participants' personal lives. The organizations create safe, nurturing environments in which members can talk about their personal and family problems and provide support to one another around these issues. As one PILOT organizer explained, "In the typical community organization, there's a dividing line between the public and the private, and you don't talk about the personal stuff within the organization. . . . [But] a lot of the issues that families are wrestling with are issues that cross those borders—childcare, whether a mother can get out to a GED or ESL class."

Once participants have begun to tackle these problems on a personal level, PILOT works with them to explore the linkages between these seemingly private concerns and broader community issues. Through the sharing that happens in the support group setting, common problems surface: "What generally happens is the parents in the room are all wrestling with the same issues. . . . If one of them can't learn English because the classes are at nighttime and her husband won't let her go to them, or if one of them can't get adequate daycare or is mad about something at the school—her kid isn't learning to read or whatever—usually, it's a pretty general problem. So it's the same kind of stuff."

As the women realize that what they had viewed as private troubles are actually common problems shared by the group, the public dimensions of the problems become clear. Situations that participants may have once assumed were the result of their own personal failings are re-framed as community problems. "The personal issues that everyone's feeling bad about and guilty and why am I a failure, turn out to be issues of, well English classes are at the wrong time and at the wrong location, [and] no, people should not have to all hire reading tutors for their kids to learn how to read in the third grade, you know."

PILOT's organizers attribute these problems to the fact that low-income urban neighborhoods are not "family friendly." Women and families' voices aren't included in the development of the neighborhood's institutions. And most of the services that low-income families rely on don't take into account their unique circumstances and needs. As one PILOT organizer put it,

A community should be a good place to bring kids up. You should be able to get the resources and support you need in that community. And our analysis of the problem, and why communities aren't like that has to do with the fact that families are rarely the ones that set the agenda in the community. . . . It's set by outside interests, developers, business people who don't necessarily live in that community. It's set by professionals who come in from the outside, bureaucrats at the board of education, social service bureaucrats, government bureaucrats. . . . And what we think is that parents are the people who know best what it would take to make the community family friendly.

PILOT and TLC: Solutions and Strategies

In an effort to build more family friendly neighborhoods, PILOT and TLC work to make local institutions and services more responsive to the needs of low-income families. PILOT fosters the development of face-to-face relationships between parents and the administrators of local institutions in an effort to build greater empathy for families within those institutions. Just as interpersonal sharing enables PILOT's participants to discover the public side of their private problems, PILOT's leaders hope it will enable these administrators to learn about parents' vision and needs. As one of PILOT's founders explained, public administrators are often "visibly moved with the parents' stories of the complexity of their lives and with their energy to help improve their communities and their children's schools." The hope is that this increased empathy will translate into programs that better meet families' needs.

In addition, women-centered organizations work to create new programs and services to address issues related to women's domestic responsibilities and family concerns, such as child care, education, schools, housing, and safety. For example, TLC's members rehabilitated low-cost apartment buildings to make them better suited to meet the needs of single mothers and their children. And in an effort to address the lack of educational and recreational resources for the neighborhood's children, TLC's members developed an after-school tutoring and summer reading program.

Unlike traditional social services, these programs are designed and run by the parents themselves. Even though in most cases the participants have no previous experience with program development or service provision, by working together they gain the skills necessary for making the programs a success. As a result, women-centered organizations' projects tend to be very hands-on and community-based.

In addition to addressing families' needs, these projects frequently result in the creation of safe, nurturing spaces in the community where women can gather and support one another—"spaces that are the moral equivalent of an inclusive, egalitarian, nurturing family" (Belenky, Bond, and Wein-

EXAMPLE: PILOT'S APPROACH TO CRIME AND SAFETY

When the mothers in PILOT's parent teams talked about their visions and goals for their families, many shared a concern for their children's safety. In particular, the mothers worried about their inability to keep their children safe in neighborhoods where violence, gang warfare, and drive-by shootings were a daily fact of life. The walk to and from school each day was particularly troublesome for some parents. As one mother explained, "Walking down the street with my kids, it was dangerous for all of us. . . . We had heavy gang stuff going on in our area."

In one PILOT parent team, once the mothers discovered that other parents shared their concerns, they realized that this was not a problem they needed to tackle in isolation. They decided to form their own "parent patrol" to monitor the streets and provide the children with oversight and protection during their daily trek to and from school. "[It's] very important that someone be out when the kids are coming to school and going from school," one mother explained. "I believe it will lower the crime rate of children being victims. . . . If they see someone standing out there, an adult, no stranger's going to come up and do something to a child. It will also lower the rate of children getting hit by cars."

With the support and enthusiasm of so many mothers, the parents were confident that they would have little difficulty recruiting volunteers for the patrol. However, they knew that in order to make their vision a reality, they would need to reach out and build partnerships with a variety of local institutions and organizations. Toward this end, the mothers met with representatives from the local police department. They discussed their idea and built an ongoing partnership in which the police provided them with arm-bands, training, and a commitment to bring instant back-up support whenever it was needed. Similarly, the local school provided the parent team with access to a desk and a phone for emergency calls. And the team developed a partnership with a cell phone company that provided them with walkie talkies so that they could communicate with one another during the patrol. Finally, local stores worked with the parents to provide an organized network of "safe havens" for the neighborhood's children.

Thanks to a team of committed parent volunteers and a strong web of support, the women created an ongoing patrol that operates five days a week at the beginning and end of the school day. Teams of five to ten parents fan out into the streets surrounding the school to keep an eye on the children as they walk. With their access to walkie talkies and police back-up, the parents are confident they will be able to deter potential criminal activity. "It builds sort of a safety net for the students," one parent volunteer explained. "With the gangs or prostitutes, seeing the presence of an authoritative figure . . . is a deterrent for setting up shop there. . . . It makes a huge difference."

stock 1997: 265). For example, PILOT's parent teams developed parent rooms in their children's schools where parents could gather for socializing, problem-solving, and mutual support. "Their vision is to reconnect people," one PILOT organizer explained. "Creating the school as a gathering place where community gets built, and not just a 9 to 2:30 building for young children to get academic education, but a recreational center and a cultural center."

In order to secure the necessary resources and technical support for these hands-on projects, women-centered organizations work to build what PILOT refers to as a "web of support"—reaching out to local businesses, organizations, institutions, and government to identify potential partners. As PILOT's organizer explained, "We like to see partnerships develop, so for example, the parents who can't take the English classes because they're at nighttime and across gang lines, ask the social service agencies to run the classes during the daytime while the kids are in school, at the local school, with childcare. And that makes a family-friendly English class." The result is collaborative projects where community residents are the ones calling the shots, and local partners provide essential funding, in-kind services, and support.

THE TRANSFORMATIVE MODEL: CHALLENGING UNJUST SOCIAL STRUCTURES

The transformative model frames the problems facing urban neighborhoods as localized symptoms of broader systemic injustices. Like the power-based model, the transformative model's theory of change emphasizes urban residents' lack of power within the public decision-making process. However, whereas power-based organizers believe that the "system" basically works as long as residents are sufficiently organized to participate in it, the transformative model's proponents believe the system itself is at the core of the problem.

In contrast to the power-based model's pluralist conception of the public sphere as an arena in which residents can battle it out with other interest groups for a piece of the pie, proponents of the transformative model believe that the very structure of the public sphere makes it impossible for disempowered communities to achieve their goals. The model's proponents argue that unequal power relations permeate all aspects of society—our culture, our educational system, the media, our political system—creating a self-reinforcing web of inequality. Even the interest group process itself is shaped, both directly and indirectly, by these underlying power relations. As a result, they argue, the structure and agenda of the public decision-making process serve to protect and reinforce the interests of society's most privileged elites. Steven Lukes (1974) refers to this dynamic as the second face of power.

Furthermore, the model's proponents argue, because the dominant conceptual frameworks of mainstream society are the product of these broader power relations, the very way that we perceive and understand the world is skewed to protect existing power imbalances. When urban residents identify their problems and concerns, their perceptions are shaped by the interests of those in power. Thus, residents tend to accept dominant political and economic arrangements as natural and inevitable, even though these arrangements may not serve residents' needs. Lukes refers to this ideological and cultural power as the third face of power.

On the basis of this theoretical framework, proponents of the transformative model believe that urban problems can only be solved through a radical restructuring of the dominant political, social, and economic institutions. They argue that in order to create meaningful change, we must introduce new conceptual frameworks into the public arena and challenge the terms of the public debate. And they suggest we must make community organizing part of a long-term process of social movement building to transform society's institutional arrangements.

JAG: Translating Residents' Problems Into Broad Social Structural Injustices

JAG's leadership believed that most of the neighborhood's problems were the result of deep-seated structural inequalities that systematically empower one group at the expense of another. Like the other organizations in my study, JAG began its assessment of the neighborhood's problems by talking to residents one-on-one about their concerns. Then it used a step-by-step process to translate these concerns into an analysis of society's underlying social, economic, and political dynamics. "JAG's leadership has made a conscious decision to be more—I don't know if ideological is the word or not, but certainly more conscious about the attitude that we're bringing into the kinds of issues, and looking at broader political, social, and economic forces," JAG's director explained. "We're looking at problems being an outgrowth of an unjust economic structure, and a power structure that does not respond to the needs of those people. Fairly simplistically, that's what the problems are." In particular, JAG attributed most of the neighborhood's problems to the failures of the capitalist system and to America's unjust class structure. (Other transformative organizations, such as those associated with the Center for Third World Organizing, place primary emphasis on other structural dynamics, such as racism.)

In order to facilitate this framing process, JAG used popular education to help its constituents understand the connections between their daily struggles and broader social justice issues. JAG sponsored community workshops examining the connection between local problems and global economic and political dynamics. For example, in response to residents' concerns about the impending gentrification of the neighborhood, JAG organized a series of educational workshops on globalization, neoliberalism (i.e. free market economics), and the connection between global economic trends and urban development. The organization also engaged its participants in guided reflection and analysis about local issues.

Through this process, JAG encouraged its participants to view the neighborhood's problems within the context of broader structural trends. For example, JAG interpreted tenants' concerns about losing their affordable housing and local merchants' concerns about being displaced by national chain stores as the symptoms of a global economic shift that had transformed the patterns of urban development in Chicago.

JAG: Solutions and Strategies

Because of the complexity of the transformative organizations' analytical framework, their strategies for addressing the neighborhood's problems tend to be multidimensional. JAG worked on several fronts simultaneously, trying to address residents' immediate needs—such as tenants' impending loss of their housing—while at the same time trying to contribute to longer term structural change. As JAG's director explained,

> Overthrowing the entire system as a result of some community organizing campaigns? That's foolish. On the other hand, if we're not conscious of what's happening on this larger scale while we're doing some of the more immediate things and try to make those connections, then we're equally foolish. . . . I've said many times, community organizing adds up to far less than the sum of its parts. And I don't know why that is, but it's absolutely true. And those of us who don't recognize that are going to keep doing a lot of work around small things that don't change much.

Because of this dual focus, JAG's strategies included both short-term fights in response to specific instances of injustice in the neighborhood as well as long-term efforts to challenge the terms of the local debate about economic, political, and social issues and to introduce an alternative vision for society.

The tactics that JAG used to achieve these goals reflect the transformative model's multifaceted conception of power. In order to fight specific neighborhood problems in the short term, JAG relied on strategies similar to those used by power-based groups. For example, JAG was involved in numerous small-scale campaigns to get local landlords to provide better services to their tenants. Because these campaigns revolved around a straightforward power relationship between the tenants and their landlord—i.e. "one-dimensional" power—JAG focused on organizing the tenants into large tenant councils in order to increase their power vis-à-vis the landlords. The tenants confronted the landlords as a unified bloc, and when the landlords didn't accede to their demands, JAG intensified the pressure by organizing public protests, media campaigns, and hits on the landlords

While these direct confrontations between tenants and their landlords primarily involved one-dimensional power, JAG was also engaged in longer term strategies to address the second and third dimensions of power. These strategies revolved around popular education and symbolic action as well as direct confrontation. JAG tried to alter the nature of the public debate about neighborhood issues by challenging the range of choices offered to residents through the mainstream political process. As part of this effort, JAG's members met with local politicians and leaders to try to educate them about the limitations of existing paradigms and to introduce them to JAG's alternative vision. And the organization's leaders worked to get articles and letters to the editor in the local papers to publicize their framing of the issues. JAG also used protests and actions to insert JAG's perspective into the political debate. But in contrast to power-based organizations, which use protests to display their clout and thus will not stage a protest unless they can mobilize enough people to make an impressive showing, JAG's protests served more of an educational and symbolic role and thus tended to be relatively small.

JAG not only tried to change the terms of the public debate, it also worked to create alternatives to mainstream forums for public decision-making. Arguing that the existing structures for public input—such as government-sponsored public hearings on neighborhood issues—were inherently biased, JAG's leaders refused to participate in these forums, even as protestors. Instead, the organization tried to provide opportunities for residents to engage in a more open and egalitarian decision-making process about local issues. For example, when the local alderman organized a series of community planning meetings, JAG argued that the process was premised on a preexisting set of assumptions about what good development is and that the framework was too narrowly defined to provide residents with an opportunity for genuine deliberation and decision-making. JAG invited residents to an alternative planning meeting where participants worked with architects and planners to create their own development plans for the community, complete with maps and drawings.

EXAMPLE: JAG'S APPROACH TO CRIME AND SAFETY

Like residents in most urban neighborhoods, many of JAG's constituents were concerned about the neighborhood's gang activity, violence, and highly visible drug trafficking. Many of these residents assumed that the problems could best be solved through increased police presence and more aggressive law enforcement efforts in the area. But JAG's staff and core leaders viewed the neighborhood's crime problems as symptoms of broader structural injustices, not simply a lack of sufficient law enforcement. They resisted residents' efforts to form an anti-crime committee within the organization, trying instead to use education to move residents toward a more nuanced understanding of the issues. As one member put it, "Nobody wants to be shot at. You want to feel like your kid can go outside. . . . It's very complicated and in some ways you can't blame people [for being concerned about their immediate safety], but in other ways you want them to look at the broader picture and why these problems are here and try and do something about that as well as deal with the immediate problem. And that gets back to education."

Most of JAG's leaders believed that existing law enforcement practices not only couldn't solve the neighborhood's crime problems but were actually harmful to the community. They perceived mainstream policing strategies as draconian and repressive and were critical of residents who participated in the CAPS program and tried to push for greater police activity in the area. As one JAG member explained, "CAPS has real problems in that it's mostly the white, long-term landowners who participate in the meetings and tend to identify those African American youths who stand on the corner, since they're African American and young then they must be gang members. Then, . . . since they're identified as potential gang members, they can be abused more by the police and they can be criminalized by the police. And then they're locked away in that enormous complex of [prison] facilities we have."

According to many of JAG's leaders, current law enforcement practices would need to be radically restructured before they could offer a viable means for maintaining the community's safety. As one put it, "You're going to have to take apart the whole city police department to fix it."

Instead of trying to drive out the area's criminals through increased law enforcement, JAG focused on trying to change the terms of the local debate about crime and safety issues. JAG's leaders viewed the neighborhood's problems with gangs and drugs as the inevitable products of an economic system that doesn't provide viable employment opportunities for low-income communities of color and a legal system that criminalizes the poor.

In one-on-one discussions with residents and through community meetings and forums, JAG's leaders tried to challenge the dominant assumption that the best way to improve a neighborhood is to drive out those who engage in criminal activity. Instead, JAG's leaders tried to educate residents about alternative economic strategies that would better serve low-income residents' needs and turn them away from crime. In addition, JAG's members worked to educate residents about their rights vis-à-vis the police and to provide them with tools for handling potential police harassment and abuse.

CONCLUSION: APPROACHES TO URBAN CHANGE

The variations in community organizations' collective action frames can have a dramatic impact on residents' perceptions of a neighborhood's problems and the strategies they use to address these problems. As summarized in table 6, each community organizing model entails a distinct approach to urban change. Because of these differences, even though urban residents may share similar experiences and concerns, their responses to these experiences can vary considerably.

The differences between these approaches have important implications for the nature of the case study organizations' on-the-ground work. The next chapter will examine this work in more detail in an effort to evaluate the impact and effectiveness of these different approaches.

TABLE 6 Diagnosing and Framing the Community's Problems

Model	Diagnosis of the problem	Prescribed solutions	Strategies and tactics
Civic	Neighborhood's problems are the result of social disorder stemming from a lack of shared norms and standards of behavior and ineffective mechanisms of formal social control	Solution is to activate formal mechanisms of social control through the city services system to tackle existing problems and to rebuild informal social order to prevent further problems	Submit complaints through city's bureaucratic system; enforce shared norms and standards; fix "broken windows"; build ties among neighbors
Power-based	Neighborhood's problems are due to residents' lack of clout within the public sphere and the pluralist interest group process	Solution is to organize residents into large, coordinated blocs to pressure powerholders to give in to their demands	Build the organization, confront powerholders through public meetings; create pressure through actions and protests; negotiate; monitor
Community-building	Neighborhood's problems stem from a weakening of the community's internal social and economic infrastructure	Solution is to rebuild the community through comprehensive neighborhood-based programs, services, and economic development strategies	Develop comprehensive plan; build partnerships with government and businesses based on legitimacy and professionalism; leverage the resources and support to implement the plan
Women-centered	Neighborhood's problems result from the fact that the institutions at the core of community life aren't responsive to the vision and needs of women and families	Solution is to create resident-run programs and services that address families' needs while at the same time making local institutions more family friendly	Build interpersonal relationships with government and institutions to make them more responsive to families; create working partnerships with local organizations and institutions to implement resident-run projects
Transformative	Neighborhood's problems are the symptoms of systemic social, economic, and political injustices	Solution is to address immediate problems while connecting local issues to broader political and economic structures	Use popular education, protest, and symbolic action to fight unjust situations and to alter the terms of the public debate

CHAPTER 7

TAKING ACTION: STRATEGIES AND OUTCOMES

CHAPTER 6 described the different explanatory frameworks used by each model to interpret the community's problems. This chapter analyzes the implications of these different "theories of change" for the effectiveness of the case study organizations' on-the-ground work. Through a detailed examination of a typical campaign for each model, I explore the impact of different community organizing strategies on the everyday lives of urban residents and the broader public sphere.[1]

I begin my analysis by evaluating how each model's organizing strategies affect the public decision-making process. Genuine popular participation in the public sphere is not only a necessary prerequisite for a truly democratic society, it is also essential to the process of urban change. Thus, I evaluate the extent to which the organizations' campaigns connect residents to public decision-makers, shape the allocation of public resources, and influence the broader public policy agenda.

The second part of my analysis focuses on the campaigns' impact on local residents' material conditions and quality of life. Do the campaigns effectively solve the specific problems they were designed to address? Do they lead to actual improvements in the lives of ordinary residents? And finally, what kinds of visible changes do they create in the neighborhood and the community?

THE CIVIC MODEL: CAPS' SANDWICH WORKS CAMPAIGN

When residents of the Cranston neighborhood gathered to discuss local crime and safety issues at the area's monthly CAPS meetings, a frequent target of their complaints was a small restaurant located on one of the neighborhood's busiest commercial strips. Arguing that the restaurant was unclean, in disrepair, and a hub for local drug dealing and gang activity, residents were outraged that it was allowed to remain in business. "They're open all hours of the night," longtime CAPS member Dwight Burge explained. "We've never heard of a submarine shop staying open until 4, 4:30 in the morning, and all kind of little kids and bums and gang bangers and thugs hanging out there all hours of the day. It's unheard of."

Even though the booths were broken and rusted and most of the tables were missing, the Sandwich Works attracted large numbers of youth—allegedly gang members—who menaced passersby and made the area unsafe for law-abiding residents. "It was a nice set up when they opened," Dwight continued. "[But then] they ripped the tables out. [The owner] did the worst thing he could do which is put telephones inside the store, which needless to say that's not used for emergency calls, that's used for drug activity." In addition to the apparent gang activity, the excessive litter and debris on the sidewalk surrounding the premises upset residents who lived nearby or had to pass the restaurant on their way to the train.

Month after month, CAPS participants begged the police to do something about the problem. The police agreed to do what they could, but they also pointed out that increased enforcement really wasn't the answer. With the recent repeal of Chicago's anti-loitering law, the police could not arrest youth for loitering on street corners unless they were actually engaged in criminal activity. And the police insisted that despite their best efforts, they hadn't been able to catch the youth in the process of committing any crimes.

After months of listening to the police give this argument in response to residents' complaints, several longtime members decided it was time to consider other approaches. However, changing the direction of the conversation proved difficult. New participants kept showing up at the CAPS meetings to ask the police to do something about the Sandwich Works problem, and they weren't usually very sympathetic to the claim that there was nothing the police could do. In response, longtime members and the police ended up spending much of their time explaining why, after months of trying to deal with the situation, it still wasn't resolved.

To show their support for the police, several longtime members eventually decided it was time to step to the plate. At the suggestion of the police sergeant and the CAPS facilitator, they agreed to organize some "positive loitering" sessions in and around the restaurant. They reasoned that if the police couldn't do anything to stop gang members from loitering, then it was up to them as residents to reclaim the space. The idea was discussed with some enthusiasm for several meetings, and eventually participants set a date and got organized. When the day came, ten CAPS participants met at the Sandwich Works and spent an hour "loitering" both inside and outside the restaurant. While they were there, most of the youth dispersed, but within minutes of their departure, the corner's usual occupants returned.

Frustrated with their failed efforts to drive away the gang members, the participants gradually shifted their focus from the youth to the restaurant's owners. As Dwight explained, "They're well aware of what's going on. They hide behind the bullet proof glass [in front of the counter]. When it gets a certain time, they hide behind that and then whatever goes on out there goes on out there and nothing else is said about it. . . . If you own a business and [troublemakers] are standing out there, tell them to get away from the business or call the police. And if you're not doing either—if you're just a window peeker and close your shades, you're the problem."

In an effort to shut down the business or, at the very least, force the owners to address the situation, CAPS participants started working with the police and liaisons from various city departments to identify city ordinances that they could use to target the sandwich shop. Through an ad-hoc process over the course of several months, they came up with several potentially promising tactics. These ideas were typically suggested by the city services staffers who attended the CAPS meetings on a sporadic basis, but because no one was officially responsible for following up on these suggestions, many of the ideas were never put into motion. In a few cases the CAPS facilitator, the police, or the city staffers themselves took the initiative to contact the appropriate agencies and submit a formal complaint. This was usually followed by weeks of waiting, brief updates on the situation at the monthly CAPS meeting, and, ultimately, disappointment.

For example, when police told residents about a new enforcement program the city was using to shut down businesses that had been cited for multiple code violations and illegal activity, the residents decided the Sandwich Works would be a perfect candidate for the program. When the CAPS facilitator announced at the following meeting that he had contacted the city department in charge of the new program and provided them with the necessary information, many participants felt sure that this strategy would get rid of the restaurant once and for all. When nothing happened for several months, they began complaining that the city must not be doing its job. Eventually one of the city's lawyers informed them that the Sandwich Works wasn't eligible for the program because there was no record of illegal activity or arrests on the premises.

Hearing residents' frustrations, a staff member from the local alderman's office who occasionally attended the CAPS meetings suggested they contact the health department. Residents embraced the idea, joking that the restaurant must be in violation of every health code in the books. The alderman's staff person offered to make the necessary phone calls, and the following month reported to an elated audience that Sandwich Works had failed the health de-

partment's first inspection. Ultimately, however, this strategy also ended in disappointment when the restaurant resolved the code violations in time for the follow-up inspection several weeks later and was allowed to remain in operation.

Of the various strategies that participants tried, they achieved perhaps their greatest success by working with the city's License Commission. The idea for this strategy came from a police sergeant assigned to a different beat who sat in on one of the group's monthly meetings. The CAPS facilitator followed up on the suggestion by issuing a formal complaint about the Sandwich Works with the city's license commissioner. The complaint resulted in a hearing at the bureau's offices with the commissioner, the restaurant's owners, representatives from the police department and alderman's office, and several CAPS participants. At the hearing, the residents joined with the police and the alderman in castigating the restaurant's owners for causing the neighborhood so many problems. Then the license commissioner threatened to revoke the Sandwich Works' business license unless the owners agreed to clean up their act. He insisted that they call the police at the sign of any problem and that they maintain a regular schedule of cleaning around the premises. And he encouraged them to work with the neighborhood's law-abiding residents to maintain order in the area.

Within several weeks of the hearing, the owners ripped out all the tables and booths from the restaurant, converting it into a carry-out deli. The overall cleanliness of the building improved, and the number of youth hanging out inside the premises declined significantly. However, while residents were pleased to see some positive change in the situation, the problems with loitering and gang activity in the area continued. After some initial optimism, complaints about the sandwich shop once again became a regular feature of the CAPS monthly meetings.

Civic organizations define urban problems as the product of a breakdown in social order. Consequently, their organizing strategies focus on mobilizing the community's formal and informal mechanisms of social control. The Sandwich Works story illustrates the potential limitations of this approach. By providing residents with a direct connection to the city services bureaucracy, CAPS was able to influence the provision of basic city services in the neighborhood. But relying on the city services system to solve neighborhood problems is an extremely limited, and ultimately not very effective, problem-solving approach. Furthermore, while giving residents the opportunity to interact with city workers can help residents to access information about how city government works, it doesn't actually engage residents in the public sphere or make local government more accountable to the community.

Positive Impacts of CAPS' Approach

Civic organizations like CAPS serve a useful role in urban neighborhoods by helping to connect residents to the city's established mechanisms for solving local problems. The CAPS meetings provide residents with information about how the city services and policing systems work while giving them an opportunity to communicate directly with the city services employees responsible for addressing problems in their neighborhood. Such a forum is essential for building a well-functioning city services infrastructure. By giving residents clear information about city laws and ordinances and direct access to the various city departments, organizations like CAPS help to democratize the provision of city services.

Opening up the communication between residents and city workers is especially important in cities like Chicago where city government tends to be disconnected from residents and civic life. Described by one observer as a "machine politics of secrecy," Chicago's government has traditionally been very hard for citizens to access (Kretzmann quoted in Ferman 1996: 118). Information about government is usually closely guarded, and residents are often denied even the most rudimentary information about public services: "Basic information needed to understand how the City works, to assess how well services are provided and to determine who is responsible for various city programs is incredibly difficult to obtain. Simple questions like what an agency actually does, the total amount of money an agency spends, and the names of people who run the agency are difficult to answer" (former Chicago alderman Dick Simpson, quoted in Ferman 1996: 118).

Organizations like CAPS not only enable residents to acquire this information, but also help them to navigate the city's complex bureaucratic systems. In the process, the organizations undercut the city's informal, behind-the-scenes processes for resource allocation and decision-making. Chicago's city services system has historically been controlled by the political machine— a system of political quid pro quo in which local aldermen provide services in exchange for electoral support. The civic organizations allow residents to bypass this system by working through official bureaucratic channels to get things done. As a police commander involved with the CAPS program put it, "I'm a lifelong Chicagoan, and as you may know, in the past, the only way to get anything done was to go through the alderman, and then you owed the alderman. But the way this is set up, it really levels the playing ground for everyone. Everyone is entitled to—and gets—a good level of city services" (Chicago Policing Evaluation Consortium 1999: 73).

Through this process, organizations like CAPS enable residents to solve certain specific neighborhood problems affecting their quality of life. By linking residents to the city's Health Department, for example, CAPS enabled them to force the Sandwich Works' owners to improve the restaurant's sanitary conditions. Similarly, through their connection to the License Commission, CAPS participants were able to address some of the restaurant's exterior maintenance problems. Through these small but tangible improvements, CAPS made a positive contribution to the neighborhood's physical environment.

Limitations of CAPS' Approach

Despite these contributions, the civic organizations' approach to urban change also has significant drawbacks. First, while CAN and CAPS enabled residents to take advantage of existing avenues for accessing city government, they did little to actually encourage resident participation in the public sphere. Through CAPS and CAN, residents were able to access information about city policies, but they did not gain any influence over the formation or implementation of these policies. Instead, the organizations provided a forum for individual residents to solve their problems by bringing them to the attention of city bureaucrats. Residents essentially remained passive consumers of government services rather than active citizens engaged in decisions over resource allocation and public priority setting.

This problem was exacerbated by the civic organizations' lack of effective follow-through. Providing residents with information about how to access the city services system is only useful if residents actually do something with that information. But because CAN and CAPS operated as unstructured forums with no staff or formally designated leaders, it was up to the individual discretion of each participant to take action on the ideas presented at the meetings. As CAN's president explained,

> I think sometimes people come to our meetings and, maybe this is a good thing because maybe they perceive us as being more organized and powerful than we really are. But the thought is, okay I'm going to register a complaint with CAN. And then CAN will take care of it. We're sort of like the complaint bureau. Or I'm going to call CAN's attention to a particular issue, and then it will be like our massive bureaucracy will swing into action in dealing with it [laughs]. . . . The work that needs to be done on those issues, because there is no staff, because it is such a lean organization and it is really grassroots, . . . the work has to be done by that person. . . . And more often than not, people aren't interested in doing that.

With no process for turning residents' concerns into an organized campaign, and no mechanisms for insuring adequate follow-through by participants themselves, much of the information that was exchanged at CAN and CAPS' meetings never resulted in further action. With the Sandwich Works campaign, the only ideas that generated any action were those that either the citizen facilitator or specific city service workers took the initiative to act upon.

Even when participants did follow through in contacting the appropriate city departments, they weren't able to hold the city accountable for responding to their requests. CAN and CAPS' meetings were designed to provide a forum for individual residents to engage in direct interactions with the police and other city service workers (see chapter 5). When these workers didn't effectively respond to residents' requests, the residents complained amongst themselves, but they rarely did anything to hold the police accountable. Because they were acting as individuals rather than as a unified group, they were afraid that if they tried to push their demands, they would be singled out as troublemakers. As one participant explained,

> [The police] don't quite often do what they say they're going to do. There's some problems with the CAPS program, and that's the main problem, in a nutshell—no response. And you can talk about some serious issues and they just don't do anything about it. . . . And then citizens don't follow through and they don't say 'Hey, I complained about this. What was done? I want to see a follow-up.' And nobody does that, because you don't want to alienate them. You don't want to be considered a troublemaker. So it's a weird situation the citizen is in, you know.

If the CAPS meetings had enabled residents to approach the police as a unified group rather than as supplicating individuals, the residents likely would have been able to pressure the police to fulfill their promises. Instead, by defining residents as passive consumers of city services, the CAPS approach made each resident dependent on the police's good will in order to get problems solved.

Many CAPS participants dealt with this dynamic by trying to ingratiate themselves with the neighborhood's police officers, apparently believing that this was the most realistic strategy for ensuring an adequate response to their problems. As described in the Sandwich Works story, when newcomers accused the police of not doing their job, long-time participants frequently tried to shield the police from these criticisms, pointing out that they had been working on the issue for months. Some members took their support for the police one step further, using scanners to keep track of police activity, roaming the streets to help the police look for suspects, and encouraging the police to provide them with information about ongoing investigations so they could help track down the perpetrators. In this respect, instead of providing an opportunity for residents to shape government priorities and actions, CAPS turned residents into the police's allies and informants. Rather than trying to change the way the police did business, residents focused on becoming accepted as police insiders.

In addition to their limited ability to hold government accountable, the civic organizations were not very successful, even under the best of circumstances, at actually solving the neighborhood's problems. Because civic organizations view local government as a technical and administrative apparatus that operates according to formal rules, the organizations rely entirely on the city's official bureaucratic procedures to get things done. Almost all of CAN and CAPS' interactions with local government were with low-level city workers who had no discretion to solve problems outside of the officially sanctioned procedures set up by the city services bureaucracy. For example, despite residents' constant insistence that the police drive the "gangbangers" away from the Sandwich Works corner, with no law enabling the police to arrest loiterers, there was little that the individual beat officers who attended the CAPS meetings could do. Similarly, although residents were convinced that the restaurant's pay phones were one of the main factors attracting the drug dealers to the premises, the police insisted their hands were tied. Even though the city had an agreement with Chicago's primary phone service provider that enabled the police to remove pay phones for safety reasons, because the Sandwich Works phones were owned by an independent provider, the police had no legal authority to remove them.

CAPS' participants seemed to accept such limitations as a given. If there weren't specific ordinances or procedures already in place for solving a particular problem, the participants typically concluded that they had no other recourse for addressing the situation. Thus, instead of working to identify other strategies outside of the formal confines of the city services system, CAPS participants defined their strategic options entirely in terms of the available legal and bureaucratic tools.

This approach can be quite limiting since the city's available tools tend to all be of one kind. The city services system is the social control arm of local government, designed to respond to problems by establishing order through the imposition of formal sanctions. For example, the police's problem-solving framework is oriented around arresting people, threatening them with arrest, or punishing them in other ways in order to establish control. This framework rules out a wide range of other possible solutions. As one CAPS participant explained,

There is a contingent [within the organization] that thinks we really need more job training and counseling and things so that people won't need to be in gangs because they can do something else for a living. . . . [But,] I think when it comes down to it, there are only a certain number of specific things that we can do. As much as some people would like to have more job training or whatever, it doesn't matter. If there's fifteen guys who don't live there sitting on the steps of your building and they don't leave when you ask them to, then the police have to come and make them leave. Ideally take them away, but who knows. So there's like kind of a theoretical level where people are like "if they really wanted to solve the problems, we'd have to debate these issues and do these things which are much larger social and legal issues." And then the consensus at the meeting says these are way beyond the scope of anything we can do in CAPS at the beat level. At the beat level there are certain things we can do, and if all we're doing is pushing these people into [a neighboring suburb], in a certain very selfish level we don't care because then they're not here. . . . There's no point in our talking about [larger policy issues] at the beat meeting because it's not what a beat meeting does.

The civic organizations' tendency to define all the neighborhood's problems within a social control framework not only limits the range of available strategies, it also enables the organizations to ignore the interests and perspectives of other social groups within the community. In defining the Sandwich Works problem, CAPS participants focused exclusively on their own perspectives as neighbors and passersby who were uncomfortable with the loitering at the restaurant.[2] From the perspective of the neighborhood's low-income residents, however, the Sandwich Works problem was less a problem of social control than a reflection of the community's lack of resources. During CAPS participants' positive loitering episode, they watched a small group of middle-aged women who were clustered around the restaurant's phones take turns making calls. Clutching utility bills and other paperwork, the women were clearly using the phones for essential household business. When the women overheard the CAPS participants complaining about the phones, they explained that many of the area's low-income residents were dependent on the Sandwich Works phones for emergencies and other necessary calls. The CAPS participants dismissed their pleas, explaining to them in patronizing tones that their campaign to shut down the phones was for the good of the entire community.

This disregard for the perspectives and experiences of other social groups can fuel a tendency toward draconian and oppressive strategies. Determined to restore the neighborhood's stability, CAPS participants frequently asked the police to do whatever was necessary to drive the disorderly elements out of the community—even if that meant violating some residents' civil rights. In a typical comment, one participant explained, "Years ago if someone was disturbing the peace it was a clear-cut issue. It was like get your rear-end off the street or go to jail. And nowadays it's all this personal freedom and legal rights. And I kind of feel in a way that the pendulum has swung too far." Participants frequently asked the police to harass local youth, even if they couldn't arrest them, and requests to "beat up the bad guys" were not uncommon. Many participants blamed the American Civil Liberties Union for the neighborhood's problems, arguing that contemporary civil liberties laws make it impossible for the police to maintain control.

In sum, civic organizations can help to democratize the provision of city services by connecting residents directly with the city service system, but their approach to organizing provides residents with a very limited set of tools for actually solving the neighborhood's problems. Because the organizations connect residents to local government through individual-level interactions with low-level bureaucrats, residents have little ability to actually affect public decision-making or hold the city accountable. Similarly, while the organizations can create small, tangible improvements in the neighborhood's physical environment, the civic model's social control framework can result in strategies that are divisive, narrow in scope, and limited in their effectiveness.

POWER-BASED MODEL: WON'S CAPITAL IMPROVEMENT CAMPAIGN

When Matt Galloway was hired by the Westridge Organization of Neighbors (WON) to organize residents in the Dunkirk neighborhood, he began by knocking on hundreds of doors throughout the area. "It's the most basic tool we use to find issues and discover what they are," he explained. "That's what every organizer who works here does. It's the first thing they do when they start here, is they knock on, . . . four hundred or five hundred doors."

After several weeks of talking to residents about their problems, Matt concluded that the issue of greatest concern to the majority of Dunkirk's residents was the deplorable state of some of the neighborhood's streets and alleys. Although residents had cited a variety of different problems in the community – school overcrowding, racial tensions, gang violence—the pothole issue was the one problem that infuriated almost every resident he talked to. Many complained of frequent flat tires or damage to their cars while others said they

feared for their children's safety on the dilapidated streets. As one resident ex-
plained, "It was horrible. My husband in two months had five flat tires. So [of
course] I was upset."

Residents' anger was exacerbated by the fact that some of the neighbor-
hood's blocks seemed to be in pristine condition while theirs were in a state of
decay. Some claimed that the alderman's supporters got their streets and alleys
repaired and paved regularly while the rest of the neighborhood was ignored.
To Matt, who was looking for an issue that would galvanize the area's resi-
dents into action, this seemed the ideal starting point for a new campaign.

Matt organized a meeting for area residents to discuss the problem and de-
velop an action plan. After several minutes of discussion, he asked partici-
pants to each name the street or alley that had caused their household the
greatest aggravation. As residents named the specific locations of the prob-
lems, Matt compiled the trouble spots into a list. Through this process, he
translated the general "problem" of poorly maintained streets into a very spe-
cific "issue" with a clear set of demands which became the focal point of the
group's campaign.

Next Matt asked participants what they thought the group should do to
solve the problem. Some suggested writing letters to the city. Others joked
they'd be better off paving the roads themselves because the city certainly wasn't
going to listen to them. After several minutes, Matt posed some questions to
the group: "Who's in charge of making decisions about which streets get
paved?" Several people replied, "Alderman Otten." "And who pays the alder-
man's salary?" People looked around at each other as a few tentatively an-
swered, "us?" Matt nodded. "Everyone here pays taxes, and you have no input
into where your taxes are being spent. One person is making those decisions."
A few residents argued that the alderman didn't care what they wanted be-
cause they weren't citizens and thus couldn't vote. But one resident who had
already been involved with several WON campaigns said emphatically, "It
doesn't matter. We're neighborhood residents and taxpayers and he should be
accountable to us."

By the end of the meeting, the residents had agreed that if they wanted their
streets and alleys paved, they needed to hold Alderman Otten accountable.
Matt suggested that the best way to do this was to set up a meeting where the
alderman would be forced to respond to the community's demands. He pro-
posed inviting the alderman to a large public meeting where they could pre-
sent him with their list of streets and alleys. The participants agreed, and a
date was set.

To prepare for the meeting, Matt trained the residents in basic door-
knocking techniques, and they used these techniques to talk to hundreds of
their neighbors. The issue resonated with many of the area's residents, and al-

most three hundred people showed up for the meeting. At the meeting, several leaders testified about the problems they had experienced as a result of the neighborhood's poorly paved streets, and then they presented the alderman with their list of demands: seven streets and twenty-five alleys to be paved within the following year. Arguing that "it's our tax money, and we deserve to see how it's being spent," they also demanded that he provide them with a detailed account of how he planned to spend his $1 million capital improvement budget in the upcoming fiscal year. The leaders were aggressive and direct, and their speeches were punctuated by loud shouts and chants from the large audience. Caving into the public pressure, the alderman agreed to meet with the group to engage in more detailed negotiations.

At the negotiating meeting, a small group of resident leaders tried to get a firm commitment from the alderman on a timeline for fixing the streets and alleys on their list. Once out of the public spotlight, however, Alderman Otten refused to give in to their demands. He told them that their aggressive behavior was inappropriate and that they should be ashamed of themselves. And he argued that he couldn't negotiate with them because all the decisions about capital improvements in the ward were made by his "committee." When pressed to explain who this committee was, he called in a small contingent of surly looking men who sat silently through the rest of the meeting. Several of WON's leaders confronted the men in the hallway after the meeting, and it soon became apparent that they were political lackeys who had been called in to intimidate the residents during the negotiations.

Frustrated and angry, the leaders left. The following week, they convened a meeting to decide what to do. After updating other residents on the alderman's actions, several leaders proposed that it was time to intensify the pressure. They announced that a school bus was waiting outside to take them to the alderman's house, and quickly asked for a group vote on the idea. When it was clear that the proposal had almost unanimous support, Matt sent a large poster-sized letter around the room for all the residents to sign. It read as follows:

"As residents of this ward and as city taxpayers we deserve real input into how capital improvement dollars are spent and what happens with other aspects of our neighborhood. We simply want a voice in the decisions that affect the quality of life for our families. It is not unreasonable to ask your office to make commitments to the community. . . . We have been willing to meet with you in good faith and have been willing to compromise. We look forward to the day that your office might be willing to do the same."

Within minutes, the letter was signed and the residents had boarded the bus, chanting and singing as they drove the short distance to the alderman's house.

The bus pulled up at a large brick house, and the residents began streaming out, chanting, waving placards, and shouting for the alderman. Inside the house a hand pulled back the curtain to peek outside, but nobody came to the door. Members of the group ran to neighboring houses to leave flyers explaining the reason for their "visit" while others continued to call for the alderman. After fifteen minutes had passed, it was clear the alderman was not going to come out. The chanting reached a frenzied pitch as several of the group's leaders solemnly pasted the poster-size letter from the community to the alderman's door. The group filed back onto the bus, chanting and singing, and loudly warning the alderman that they would be back.

At the residents' next meeting, they decided to pay an unannounced visit to the alderman during his regularly scheduled neighborhood office hours the following week. Their goal was to catch him off guard in a situation where he would be forced to meet with them. Otten, however, had sent one of his supporters to spy on the planning meeting, and thus received ample warning of the planned visit. Not sure what acts of aggression this group might be capable of, he called the police department and asked for their protection. At the last minute, he also faxed his capital improvement spending plan for the upcoming fiscal year to WON's office. WON's staff were pleased to discover that the plan included two-thirds of the streets and alleys from their list.

When the time for his office hours arrived, the alderman seemed both surprised and wary when an orderly and respectful group of fifteen residents arrived to thank him for working with them. He refused to acknowledge that their pressure tactics had had any influence on his capital improvement plan. WON's members were nonetheless convinced that their aggressive organizing was the sole reason for the favorable new budget. Viewing this outcome as an effective resolution to their campaign, the group declared victory and went out to celebrate their success.

Framing urban residents' problems as a function of the struggle for influence within the public sphere, power-based organizations like WON work to build residents' power to fight for concessions at the political bargaining table. The implications of this approach are well illustrated by WON's Capital Improvement Campaign. Through the campaign, WON successfully engaged hundreds of residents in the public decision-making process. By altering the balance of power within the neighborhood, WON was able to influence the allocation of public resources in the community, creating concrete improvements in residents' daily lives. Unfortunately, however, the very techniques that enabled WON to be so successful also made nuanced deliberations over public policies and priorities difficult. And while WON effectively fought for concessions from within the political system, its efforts had little impact on the larger structure and framework of the political decision-making process itself.

Positive Impacts of WON's Approach

The power-based groups' organizing techniques enable them to effectively mobilize large numbers of residents into unified, well-coordinated blocs. By doing one-on-one recruitment and focusing their organizing around the issues of greatest concern to the neighborhood's residents, WON and UNITE were able to consistently turn out hundreds of residents for each of their campaigns. In addition, by building the list of demands for new campaigns around individual participants' specific grievances—such as the list of streets and alleys in the Capital Improvement campaign—WON gave residents a strong motivation to become personally and actively involved in all stages of the campaign.

Once residents were involved, the power-based organizations' methods of cutting and framing the issues enabled inexperienced participants to understand the basic concepts of pluralist power and the interest group process. By focusing on clearly defined, winnable issues and a specific target, the organizations successfully convinced participants of the importance of building clout and engaging in public confrontation in order to achieve their goals. The aggressive tactics that emerged from this process, along with the organizations' substantial displays of people power, altered the targets' calculations of their own self-interests. As one WON leader put it,

> An alderman basically can't turn his back on WON, because the alderman's got to realize that WON has got a lot of power, and it could make or break an alderman, to a certain extent. And the same way with the police department. WON probably could make enough stink, you know, through confrontation with the police department where, you know, a commander could be transferred out. . . . They might not like us all the time, but they still respect us and they'll deal with us.

WON and UNITE thus succeeded in gaining influence over the decisions of key power brokers and political leaders.

Through this process, the power-based organizations also created alternative mechanisms for governance and resource distribution at the local level. In a direct challenge to traditional city services bureaucracies, which promote individual-level relationships between residents and government, WON and UNITE mobilized their members to interact with government as a powerful group rather than as passive service recipients. Moreover, whereas the city services system reacts to problems on an ad hoc, piecemeal basis, the power-based organizations created mechanisms for systematically identifying the interests of the community's residents and translating these interests into political victories.

In the Capital Improvement Campaign, this alternative governance process enabled WON to undermine the alderman's efforts to use his control over public resources for traditional patronage purposes. According to Alderman Otten's critics, he routinely used public resources to reward his supporters and punish his enemies. Residents claimed that he conducted door to door "surveys" and voter polls prior to elections in order to identify his political opponents and then routinely ignored their requests for city services. Thus, while he paved his own street and those of his political supporters every year, he left the rest of the streets to crumble and decay.

The informal allocation of city services based on a system of quid pro quo and political favors is a common feature in many large US cities. By organizing residents to confront Otten, WON created a far more equitable framework for neighborhood governance. They forced him to develop his budget priorities based on the interests of a critical mass of the neighborhood's residents rather than political favors, and by making him publicize the budget in advance, they constrained his ability to use his access to city services to reward residents for voting for him. Thus, WON's campaign helped to democratize the allocation of public resources in the community.

By strengthening residents' influence within the public sphere, WON and UNITE secured numerous concessions from local powerholders in the form of improved public services and resources for their neighborhoods. These victories created visible improvements in the material conditions and quality of life for local residents. In addition to gaining freshly paved streets and alleys, WON's participants used similar campaigns to ensure that several of the neighborhood's schools received capital improvements, thousands of residents with flooded basements received a new sewer system, several local landlords evicted their drug dealing tenants, the local library received new computers, and several local parks got new recreational programs and facilities.

Limitations of WON's Approach

WON and UNITE's approach made them among the most effective organizations in my study. However, the very techniques that enabled them to be so successful at mobilizing large numbers of residents and winning concrete victories also had significant trade-offs. First, in order to implement these techniques, organizations must be able to commit substantial staff time and organizational resources. The power-based approach to change requires the mobilization of hundreds of residents for each campaign. Recruiting, organizing, and training these residents is an incredibly staff-intensive process. Just doing one-on-one interviews with hundreds of residents at the start of every campaign, let alone all the work that must come after this stage, takes hundreds of hours of staff time. Without adequate staff support, this approach is thus unlikely to succeed. As Matt put it,

> If I'm not there and [the other organizers are] not there in the neighborhood and we're not pulling all the things together and we're not spending the time doing one on one conversations and organizing everyone to doorknock on their block or in the neighborhood, it would never happen. And when we're gone, it's not just going to continue on. I think it's ridiculous to think just because these people are really good leaders that they're going to necessarily be able to maintain this. Because [the other organizers] and I work sixty hours a week to maintain it. And even then, if we aren't working really hard, it starts to fall apart. But at the same time, you look at the President of the United States and he has how many staff? The guy's got like four hundred staff or something ridiculous. And this neighborhood has six staff. So I don't know how much of a weakness that is as much as it's a reality.

The model's staff-intensive approach was not a problem for WON and UNITE, both of which were able to leverage enough funding to maintain fairly large staffs. But for organizations unable to raise the necessary funds, this issue can pose a significant obstacle.

In addition to requiring significant staff time, the specific techniques that power-based organizations use to convince residents to get involved can impose limitations on the scope of the organizations' work. While building campaigns around the "gut-level" grievances of the majority of the neighborhood's residents is what enabled WON to mobilize so many people, this technique restricted the organization's campaigns to a narrow range of least-common-denominator issues. Even though the residents in WON's neighborhood faced numerous issues of greater weight and importance than the potholes in their alleyways, WON focused its campaign around this relatively mundane problem because it was the one thing that most residents mentioned during Matt's doorknocking. Although Matt acknowledged that there were more significant issues affecting residents' quality of life, he insisted that in order to build the neighborhood's power, it was necessary to focus on whatever issues were most likely to get residents involved with the organization.[3]

WON's avoidance of more complex and pressing issues limited the scope of its impact on residents' quality of life. Even more worrisome, by appealing to residents' most basic frustrations and concerns, WON occasionally produced campaigns that discriminated against certain members of the community. For example, in the 1980s, when the threat of "racial change" made the area's majority white ethnic residents fear for their safety and property values, WON's work took on a racist, exclusionary cast. The centerpiece of these efforts was a campaign to create a legal mechanism that would enable white residents to recoup the equity in their homes if the arrival of African American and Latino residents in the neighborhood hurt their property values. The campaign fostered divisions among old and new residents and heightened the neighborhood's reputation as a white racist enclave.

Similarly, the power-based organizations' techniques for translating residents' problems into issues of power ultimately limited the scope of their influence within the public sphere. Converting complex problems into winnable issues with a clearly defined "target" makes it easier for inexperienced residents to understand the power dynamics underlying these problems. And by demonizing the targets, power-based organizers are able to galvanize residents into taking an active role in the organization's direct action campaigns. However, simplifying the issues in this way can make it difficult for residents to engage in more nuanced deliberations about public priorities.

For example, at the annual gathering of National People's Action, WON's national network, the convention's lead organizer declared, "We come to Washington to show people how to do their business because nobody here knows how to do any business but lining their pockets. We're here to unline their pockets and take it back to our community." While this depiction of government officials makes it easy for residents to get fired up about confronting them, it ignores the complexities of the political process. To the extent that political officials aren't responsive to local residents' concerns, it is usually not a simple consequence of overt greed or corruption but rather because the political decision-making process involves inevitable trade-offs among different priorities and interest groups.

This tendency to ignore the complexities of the political decision-making process is exacerbated by the power-based organizations' emphasis on using a yes/no framework to present the community's demands. While framing the demands this way effectively wrests control over public negotiations away

from the powerholders, most policy issues cannot necessarily be dichoto-
mized into a yes or no answer. By forcing officials to interact with the residents on these terms, power-based organizations can create impossible situations for political leaders faced with competing interest groups or demands.

For example, in their campaign to get a new library for the neighborhood, WON's leaders demanded that the "targets" commit to funding the library within the next year and insisted on a simple "yes" or "no" answer. It
quickly became apparent that the demands being issued did not make sense
given the complexities of the policy decisions involved. But instead of allow-
ing the targets to discuss the issues in detail in order to generate a more constructive dialogue, WON's leaders kept demanding that the officials simply
answer the questions as posed, grabbing the microphones away from them
and shouting them down when they tried to explain the competing interests
at stake, and leading the audience in raucous chants in an effort to get the
officials to concede. The officials tried to explain that the planning and bud-
geting process for new libraries takes at least five years and that over a dozen
equally needy neighborhoods—many of which had made their requests
years earlier—were already on a waiting list to receive new libraries.

After the meeting, residents attributed the officials' lack of cooperation to
greed and corruption—as if they were benefiting personally from not spending their budget on the community.[4] In reality, the officials were grappling
with the reality of having far too few resources to respond to a long list of legitimate community needs. As one official explained in a follow-up letter,
"My response [to your demands] will be the same . . . as it is for all organizations and neighborhoods now seeking consideration for a new library after
2001. As you can appreciate, we must treat all requests equitably through our
public hearing process and not in a piecemeal fashion." By simplifying the
public decision-making process into a battle with evil powerholders, WON
ignored the complex public policy questions at the heart of the situation,
making effective negotiations with these powerholders difficult.

This dynamic is linked to another potential drawback of the power-based
approach. While fighting for specific concessions within the political arena
may enable organizations like WON to change the way public resources are
distributed, it doesn't change the overall structure of local government or
the nature of political decision-making. In other words, while power-based
organizations may be very effective at winning a bigger piece of the pie for
their communities, they have little impact on the nature of the pie itself. In
fact, by working to get political officials to incorporate the community's interests into the political decision-making system, power-based groups may
inadvertently lend legitimacy to that system (Boggs 1986).

This critique can be better understood if we think about the power-based organizations as players within a political game. The power-based model represents an extremely effective set of game-playing strategies that fit well within the structure and informal "rules" of a pluralist political system. These strategies enable power-based organizations to win important concessions from other players. But as Michael Burawoy (1979) points out in his analysis of social relations on the shop floor, playing a game generates consent with respect to the rules of that game. Construing the political sphere as a game obscures the social relations and structural inequalities that underlie the political arena. Rather than focusing on transcendent needs or a broad social vision, the power-based organizations focus on playing the game well. Ultimately, playing the game becomes an end in itself, and the organizations come to view any choices outside of those conferred by the game as utopian.

This dynamic is illustrated by WON's interactions with Alderman Otten. In order to win concrete concessions for the neighborhood, WON's leaders couldn't afford to challenge Otten's overall legitimacy as the neighborhood's political leader. Although WON's leaders privately criticized him for being corrupt and unethical, they never questioned the system that had granted him his power or the basic foundations of his political leadership. Instead they focused on finding the most effective ways to alter his calculations of his own self-interests so that he would give in to their demands. Even though their interactions with him were confrontational, their participation in this political game legitimated his role. WON's members accepted the terms and conditions governing the game being played, and while this made it possible for WON to win an important victory, it constrained the organization's ability to challenge the larger institutional structure of the political system itself.

In sum the power-based organizations in my study were able to achieve significant improvements in the material conditions and quality of life of local residents. By effectively organizing large numbers of residents to fight for specific concessions, WON and UNITE altered the balance of power within the public sphere, leading to important changes in the distribution of public resources and government services. However, the techniques at the heart of this success entailed some potentially significant trade-offs. In particular, in the effort to engage inexperienced residents in the public sphere, WON simplified complex political issues, precluding more nuanced deliberations over public priorities. In addition, the emphasis on being effective players within the larger political game prevented the power-based organizations from challenging the larger structure and framework of that game.

THE COMMUNITY-BUILDING MODEL:
PACT'S REDEVELOPMENT CAMPAIGN

When the founding members of Port Angeles Collaborating Together (PACT) first started working together, they agreed that their number one priority must be to halt the process of gentrification that was threatening to destroy their community. The neighborhood, which had been the center of Chicago's Puerto Rican community for several decades, was starting to feel the effects of rising property values and rapid redevelopment. PACT's leaders wanted to make sure that their community didn't become Chicago's next yuppie enclave, a shift they feared would displace most of the existing residents and destroy the neighborhood's cultural roots. As one member put it, "One of the biggest challenges we face is how do we address this development that's taking place in the community. How do we make sure that the people who are here stay here. . . . Because these developers have the big bucks to come in and develop blocks at one time, now [the existing residents] are being kicked out, without [the residents] having anything to say about it."

PACT's leaders believed that if they were going to prevent the wholesale displacement of the Puerto Rican community, they would need to become active participants in the urban development process. "Gentrification has happened [in the past] because it's an open process, but we haven't understood it and we haven't been there to voice against it," explained PACT's director. "[We] want to make sure the community controls what happens. We need full control of what takes place in our community." With the community in control of the development process, PACT's leaders argued, the neighborhood could be revitalized for the benefit of existing residents rather than outside speculators or realtors. "I would like to see the picture of this community, the structure, the way it's put together, look like a Hancock Park [an upscale Chicago neighborhood[5]], but with the current people that are here now," PACT's chair explained. "[A] lot of new businesses in the area, a lot of new homeowners. . . . But that change is going to happen for the good of the people who are here and by the people who are here."

In order to achieve this goal, PACT worked to develop a comprehensive plan for community-controlled redevelopment in the neighborhood. The planning process began with extensive research and analysis to identify the neighborhood's assets and needs and to assess the feasibility of various development options. PACT hired a professional consulting firm to conduct a land-use study of the neighborhood, enlisted researchers at a local university to develop an analysis of the neighborhood's economy, conducted surveys of local residents, held focus groups at several local schools, and held several community planning meetings.

Based on this research, PACT's director and staff worked with the professional staff of its member institutions—including the directors of several community development organizations, business associations, and housing organizations—to craft a detailed redevelopment plan for the neighborhood. The plan included proposals for affordable home ownership, economic development, commercial development, and job creation as well as a vast array of complementary social services—child care, health care, youth programs, job training, and cultural programs.

PACT's leaders knew that they would need significant government support and private investment if they were going to get their ambitious programs off the ground. In an effort to secure the necessary funding, they submitted an application to have Port Angeles designated as a federal Empowerment Zone[6]—a designation that would have provided more than $10 million in public subsidies and private investment over a ten-year period.

Several months later, when their Empowerment Zone application was rejected, PACT's leaders turned to their local alderman for advice. He suggested they apply to the City's Department of Planning and Development to have Port Angeles selected as a Redevelopment Area. He explained that Redevelopment Area status would enable the city to acquire and consolidate property in the neighborhood through the use of eminent domain. By working in partnership with the city, PACT could use this tool to gain control over the neighborhood's land, an important step in enabling the organization's members to implement their redevelopment plan.

Seizing upon the alderman's proposal, PACT's leaders set to work, fine-tuning their plan to fit with the city's Redevelopment Area guidelines. They held additional planning meetings and worked with staff from the city's Department of Planning and Development to craft their application for Redevelopment Area designation. The plan included a detailed acquisition list of vacant lots and abandoned buildings in the neighborhood as well as proposals for converting these properties into affordable housing, green spaces, and commercial enterprises.

Once the plan was complete, PACT's leaders prepared to present it to the city's Community Development Commission, an appointed body that acts as official gatekeeper for redevelopment proposals in the city. After working so closely with the alderman and other city policy-makers to develop the plan, PACT's leaders felt assured that their proposal would be approved. With the organization's broad membership base and home-grown professional expertise, the city could hardly deny its legitimacy as the appropriate policy-setting body for the Port Angeles community.

Several days prior to the hearing, however, PACT's members discovered *that a group of Port Angeles property owners—primarily white newcomers to the area—were organizing in opposition to the plan. Worried that their status as the community's official voice would be put in question, PACT's members mobilized several dozen people to attend the hearing. In addition to using their numbers to demonstrate the community's support for their plan, PACT's leaders used a sophisticated computerized presentation to emphasize the plan's technical merits and its compatibility with the city's official development priorities. PACT's testimony successfully quelled the opposition, and, with the Community Development Commission's blessing, Port Angeles was designated as a Redevelopment Area. Several weeks later the city offered PACT $2 million in grants and loans to kick-start the redevelopment process.*

In order to oversee the plan's implementation, PACT's director appointed a steering committee of PACT members, made up of representatives from the neighborhood's community development organizations, banks, business associations, churches, and several block clubs. In addition, representatives from the mayor's office, the Federal Department of Housing and Urban Development, the city's Department of Planning and Development, the alderman's office, and other local elected officials were invited to participate in the steering committee in an advisory capacity. As PACT's staff explained in a letter to the organization's members, "Every effort has been made so that all sectors affected and all decision-makers are at the same table."

As the implementation process began to move forward, PACT's director and staff met with Chicago's mayor and other top officials to solicit the city's support for specific components of the plan. Assuring them that the city was in full support of PACT's proposal, the mayor assigned his housing and development staff to work with PACT on the implementation process. PACT worked with the city's Department of Planning and Development to acquire vacant land and abandoned properties in the community and secured a commitment from the city's Department of Housing to help the group construct new single-family homes on several of these lots through the city's affordable homeownership program. The Chicago office of the Federal Department of Housing and Urban Development assigned two professional consultants to help PACT secure additional public and private funding sources for their plan.

Once these public sector partnerships had been established, PACT's director began meeting with corporations and small businesses to draw private investment to the community. In an effort to attract a full-scale grocery store to the neighborhood, he contacted representatives from several national grocery chains to invite them to open stores in Port Angeles. When these efforts were unsuccessful, he traveled to Puerto Rico and convinced a Puerto Rican grocery chain to use Port Angeles as a base for expanding its operations throughout the Midwest. Similarly, PACT's staff worked with the neighborhood's business association to develop plans for a Puerto Rican restaurant district that would attract customers from all over the city to spend their money in the community.

As the development process moved forward, many of PACT's member institutions worked to reorient their own organizational agendas to fit with the broader Redevelopment Area plan. Using the city's $2 million as a revolving loan fund, the neighborhood's community development corporations began planning affordable housing and commercial development projects for the lots and vacant buildings identified on PACT's acquisition map. Because no single agency had the capacity to implement some of the more ambitious proposals, they formed joint ventures for collaborating on several initiatives.

PACT's members knew the redevelopment process would not be a short-term undertaking and that stemming the tide of gentrification altogether might be impossible, but they felt confident that because of their work, the area's existing residents would be the ones to benefit. As Julio, PACT's director, put it, "If we allow private developers to develop, prices will go skyrocketing, like in Burville [a nearby gentrified neighborhood]. But in Burville there wasn't a community initiative like this. We as a community have been empowered to control this."

Through the development of homeownership opportunities for existing residents, PACT's members believed they could create a permanent foothold for the Puerto Rican community in the neighborhood: "In Burville we didn't have control because we didn't own anything, we rented. I'm not moving and I'm encouraging everyone to buy and stay here," Julio declared. In addition, members were confident that by creating economic opportunities for the area's residents and revitalizing the neighborhood's commercial districts, they could enhance the entire community's quality of life. Julio explained, "We all believe in a healthy community. We all have a right to make our future one that will benefit us. . . . We want to make sure those areas that are dilapidated and not serving this community any purpose start doing so. We're here to successfully put forward a project that will benefit all of us."

Community-building organizations work to address urban problems by redeveloping the community's internal social and economic infrastructure. PACT's Redevelopment Area campaign provides a rich example of the strengths and limitations of this distinctive approach. By providing a vehicle for comprehensive planning and policy development at the neighborhood level, PACT enabled the community to influence the public decision-making process. And by building partnerships among diverse institutions and organizations, PACT strengthened the neighborhood's internal capacity to create programs and services to meet its needs. However, in order to implement these programs, PACT became dependent on the good will and financial support of its local government partners. This enabled local government to shape the direction of PACT's campaigns and ultimately limited the scope of PACT's influence over the broader public policy process.

Positive Impacts of PACT's Approach

Whereas power-based organizations provide a mechanism for bringing residents' specific interests into the public decision-making process, community-building organizations like PACT provide a mechanism for comprehensive policy development at the neighborhood level. The emphasis on comprehensive planning enabled PACT to take into account complex trade-offs among different groups' interests in a way that the civic and power-based organizations could not. Approaching the neighborhood's problems holistically, PACT tried to reconcile the interests of different stakeholder groups within the neighborhood to create a vision for the community as a whole. By working to negotiate among competing interests in an equitable manner, PACT gained legitimacy within much of the community and the wider public sphere as the official voice for the neighborhood.

PACT's comprehensive plan provided a template for program development, resource allocation, and priority setting within the neighborhood. The plan enabled the community to maximize its internal resources and to exert a certain amount of control over public and private interventions in the neighborhood. In cities like Chicago where neighborhood "planning" tends to be rooted in politics rather than principled policy-making, this kind of comprehensive planning can produce guidelines for rational, community-controlled development. As a result of PACT's efforts, the development of vacant land and abandoned buildings in Port Angeles could be shaped by a cohesive vision rather than the uncoordinated actions of profit-seeking speculators or ad-hoc government interventions.

In cities like Portland where local government is already committed to extensive planning and community involvement in policy setting at the neighborhood level, having a single unified voice that represents the interests of the community as a whole helps to facilitate this partnership building process. CO-OP provided a vehicle for Portland's city and county governments to dialogue with the community about its priorities, develop shared agreements, and create a comprehensive vision to guide public and private investment in the neighborhood.

PACT and CO-OP's emphasis on comprehensive planning not only enabled the organizations to gain legitimacy in the eyes of local government, it also resulted in sophisticated strategies that took into account the complexities of the neighborhood's problems. PACT's Redevelopment Area plan addressed multiple issues simultaneously and sought to create synergistic interactions among each individual strategy. By using eminent domain to seize abandoned buildings and vacant lots owned by speculators, PACT hoped to prevent the rapid escalation of local property values while turning land that would have eventually become expensive condo developments into affordable homes. In addition, by putting the lots into productive use, PACT helped to rid the neighborhood of long-time eyesores, in the process boosting residents' sense of optimism and pride in their neighborhood. Furthermore, by creating locally based commercial development opportunities, PACT aimed to expand the amount of wealth in the community, thereby giving more residents the capacity to become successful homeowners. Through these and other similarly complex strategies, PACT and CO-OP addressed the immediate symptoms of the neighborhood's problems while at the same time contributing to longer term solutions.

By developing collaborative partnerships among a wide range of stakeholders from both inside and outside the neighborhood, PACT built the community's internal capacity to implement these complex strategies. In other words, whereas the power-based approach enables residents to win improved government services or to secure the passage of government policies favorable to their interests, the community-building approach expands the community's ability to create programs and services to address its own needs. This is especially important for addressing issues that can not be resolved effectively through government intervention. For example, WON might use its power to win public funds for a community center or for affordable housing, but without organizations in the neighborhood with the capacity to implement these programs, this would be a hollow victory. Similarly, the designation of Port Angeles as a Redevelopment Area would have done little to further PACT's vision without the existence of community development corporations, social service agencies, and business incubators willing to collaborate to realize this vision.

Through this combination of comprehensive planning and collaborative partnerships, the community-building organizations had a significant impact on the material conditions and quality of life in their neighborhoods. While PACT and CO-OP's comprehensive plans will take years to implement, the organizations have already created visible changes in the daily lives of many neighborhood residents. In its first year of implementation, PACT's Redevelopment Area project created new homeownership opportunities for dozens of moderate-income community residents, brought a much-needed full-service grocery store to the neighborhood, took key tracts of land out of the control of real estate speculators, and increased the stock of affordable housing in the area.

Limitations of PACT's Approach

PACT's achievements were unfortunately counterbalanced by some significant trade-offs. First, while PACT's emphasis on developing a common vision among all the neighborhood's stakeholders enabled it to strengthen the community's internal capacity, the effort to build consensus among such a diversity of groups limited the scope of PACT's work. In order to get multiple stakeholders to agree on a single vision, that vision must be rooted in conceptual categories that all the stakeholders can accept and understand. PACT's plan for preventing the displacement of the Latino community thus had to be rooted in a set of principles that the neighborhood's banks, hospitals, nonprofits, businesses, and residents could all agree on. In the urban development arena, the only framework that is widely accepted and understood is that of the free market. Consequently, when PACT's members created a shared vision for gaining community control over the neighborhood's development, it is not surprising that this vision focused on the ideals of economic growth, capital investment, and business development.

While this framing enabled the neighborhood's diverse array of stakeholders to work together, it did not necessarily represent the most appropriate strategy for achieving PACT's overall goals. The free market operates according to its own logic and on its own terms. It may be possible to redirect the market to achieve certain community objectives, but ultimately, once market forces are unleashed, the resulting development is just as likely to displace residents as it is to benefit them. For example, by promoting economic development and physical revitalization along Port Angeles' main commercial strip, PACT helped to meet residents' needs for goods and services, but in the process it also made the neighborhood more attractive to outside investors and upper-income residents. Without mechanisms to protect the community from the pressures of market forces—such as by taking housing out of the market altogether—PACT's approach was as likely to catalyze the gentrification process as it was to halt it. By framing its strategies within the dominant market framework, PACT thus limited its ability to achieve the goal of maintaining Port Angeles for existing residents.[7]

Another drawback of the community-building approach is that in order to implement a comprehensive community plan, the organization must be able to secure substantial support from established government institutions and political powerholders. The need for significant ongoing government funding and assistance is one of the primary reasons why organizations like PACT and CO-OP choose to engage in collaborative rather than confrontational relationships with local officials. As one PACT leader explained, "It's very much necessary. We're talking about a housing development in a certain area where the alderman controls the zoning, a lot of things, controls the land, controls the realtors. There's a lot of things that the alderman controls. Being opposed to him head to head will not get anywhere, unless you want to do some political organizing to politically oust him and by the time that is said and done, four or five years go by."

While PACT and CO-OP's friendly relationships with government enabled them to secure important resources for implementing their comprehensive plans, their dependence on government support meant that the organizations' agendas were often shaped by government priorities. For example, when PACT first developed its comprehensive plan, its intention was to apply for Empowerment Zone (EZ) designation. As a result, the plan emphasized economic development, job creation, job training, and private investment, all of which were central requirements of the federal government's EZ application process. When PACT's application was unsuccessful, the organization reframed its goals to focus almost exclusively on the physical development of the neighborhood in an effort to fit within the priorities of the city's Redevelopment Area program.

In some cases, PACT and CO-OP's dependence on public sector support not only shaped the direction of their work, but actually enabled local government officials to exert direct control over the organizations' agendas. For example, CO-OP's government partners sat in on all of the organization's meetings, and while they had no voting power, they nonetheless had a significant impact on the group's decisions: "Even if you don't vote, if you tell people 'if you don't do it this way you won't get the money,' you've influenced how the vote gets out," one member explained. "It's hard for [the member agencies] to be really objective when comments are made by the county or the city because they'd risk cutting their own throats by challenging the views of their funders." After CO-OP's members spent several months discussing their vision for a particular project, a representative from the mayor's office who attended one of their meetings warned, "The city's going to say we have lots of initiatives and lots of dollars [invested] in this area. If what you're looking for is for more dollars from the city for what you're coming up with, the city is going to say you need to get involved in what is already funded." Given this input, the group abandoned its initial idea, concluding that without funding there was no point in moving forward with additional planning.

Whereas power-based organizations use public pressure to alter government programs and priorities, PACT and CO-OP's reliance on government support meant they had to accept the government's existing agenda and try to work within it. In situations where the government's priorities weren't in line with the community's goals, this constrained PACT and CO-OP's ability to achieve their objectives. For example, both PACT and UNITE were interested in creating a coordinated job placement center for their communities. Using a typical power-based approach, UNITE organized hundreds of people to stage a protest at the state capitol to demand funding for the center. In response to this public pressure, after a series of negotiating meetings, the official in charge of administering public aid programs statewide gave UNITE a $100,000 grant, unconnected to any of the state's existing funding streams or the government's programmatic priorities. In contrast, PACT's leaders pursued their goal by arranging a meeting with the Director of the Mayor's Office of Workforce Development to see whether their center would fit within the city's existing strategies for job placement. When they were told that it would not, they were disappointed, but rather than trying to change the city's priorities, they asked the Director to suggest ways they could fit their work into the city's existing programs. One year later, UNITE's center was up and running. Meanwhile, PACT's leaders were still trying to figure out how they could fit their plan into the available funding streams.

PACT and CO-OP not only had little influence over government priority-setting, they also had difficulty holding their government partners accountable even when their goals fit well with existing government programs. Community-building organizations work to build partnerships with government on the basis of their legitimacy as the unified voice of the community as a whole and their technical expertise as planners and community developers. Consequently, PACT's interactions with public officials usually took place in small closed-door meetings where PACT's professional staff, representing the collective vision of the entire membership, tried to convince the officials of the technical merits of their plan. In other words, whereas WON's interactions with the alderman all involved large numbers of residents, few of PACT's members (let alone the neighborhood's average residents) were invited to participate in the organization's meetings with the mayor and other city officials. On the one hand, this dynamic enabled PACT to enter into technically complex, sophisticated deliberations with its government partners. On the other hand, it made it very difficult for PACT's members to hold these government partners accountable to the community.

For example, after meeting with the mayor in an effort to secure city support for PACT's comprehensive plan, Julio announced that the mayor had been so impressed with PACT's work that he had said "yes to everything." Julio was so pleased to have PACT's work validated by Chicago's power elite that he was willing to take the mayor's verbal promises of support at face value. Expressing skepticism, one member later said, "I really do hope I'm wrong, but it seems to me that the mayor and city are slick enough to use that very sense of strength and this false confidence and contentment. [Julio] said 'we went into the mayor and he said yes to everything.' Yes to what? Yes to what? I didn't see anything specific on the table that he committed to. . . ." When several members suggested that PACT's leaders create a written agreement with the city to clarify and formalize their obligations, Julio scoffed at the idea, insisting that such skepticism was misplaced. "I can put it on paper," he replied, "but I'll tell you this group has the support of every single elected official in the area." Because most of PACT's partnerships with government were mediated by Julio and the other lead staff, the organization was forced to rely on the mayor's verbal commitment, with little capacity to hold him accountable to his agreement. In contrast, if the mayor's commitment had been made in front of a hundred community members, even if it were just a verbal agreement, he would have had much greater difficulty reneging on his promise.

This dynamic can be particularly problematic when the government's vision for the neighborhood isn't in line with the community's. Although PACT's primary goal was to prevent the gentrification of the Port Angeles neighborhood, many of the organization's government partners were known throughout the city as promoters and facilitators of the gentrification process. Chicago's mayor had long been criticized by advocates for affordable housing for his support of upscale development throughout the city, and even Port Angeles' alderman—one of PACT's closest supporters—had been accused by residents in other parts of his ward of fostering gentrification. Thus, while PACT's partnerships with government officials may have been a strategic necessity, these relationships made the organization vulnerable to cooptation and manipulation. Expressing a fear voiced in private by a number of PACT's members, one member said, "I'm afraid that PACT may be being used by the city and local politicians, even without their own consciousness, to gentrify Port Angeles. I'm becoming more and more convinced that that's the subtext of the meeting with the mayor and all of this interest [by the city in forming a partnership]. . . . I hate to say this because I feel like a fool, but it's using PACT to allow the city to come in and start planning the gentrification process." PACT's dependence on government support, its lack of influence over broader public policy debates, and its inability to hold its government partners accountable made this risk of cooptation especially worrisome.

In sum, the community-building organizations provide an important vehicle for comprehensive planning and policy development at the neighborhood level. Through partnerships among diverse stakeholder groups and government policy-makers, the organizations enable the community to identify a synergistic combination of programs and services to address the neighborhood's complex needs. However, the effort to build a common vision among all the neighborhood's stakeholders can constrain the scope of the community-building organizations' work. Furthermore, in order to implement these complex strategies, the organizations typically require significant government funding and support. At best, this means the organizations must frame their work to fit within existing government priorities. At worst, it can make them vulnerable to manipulation and cooptation at the hands of local political leaders.

THE WOMEN-CENTERED MODEL: PILOT'S COMMUNITY CENTER CAMPAIGN

When a group of twenty parents at Paxton School completed PILOT's ten-week leadership development and team-building training, they were excited to be able to start making a difference in their community. Over the weeks, they had developed the skills and self-confidence they needed to make changes in their own lives and the lives of the people around them. They had learned how to create step-by-step action plans for achieving their goals. And they had discovered the value of building a web of support to help them attain these goals.

During the final weeks of the training, the team had also worked together successfully to implement a group project. In an effort to strengthen communication between parents and teachers, they had organized a well-attended parent-teacher potluck. The success of this small project left the parents feeling energized and excited. They knew that if they set their minds to it they could create even greater changes in their school and their community.

In the process of discussing their personal goals, the parents had discovered that they shared many of the same basic desires: several wanted to learn English, several more wanted to earn their GED (high school equivalency diploma), and almost all the parents wanted to be able to get better jobs. As one parent explained, "You know how things are today, if you don't have a GED or a high school diploma you can't get a job. And I say it from personal experience."

While many of the parents had tried to take advantage of adult education classes offered in other parts of the city, their limited incomes, heavy domestic responsibilities, and lack of childcare made it extremely difficult for them to access these resources. Most of the classes were far away, at inconvenient times, and didn't provide adequate accommodations for children. Given these conditions, the parents decided that what their community needed more than anything else was a center for adult education that was designed to meet the specific needs of families with young children. Paxton's principal suggested that the parents organize their own center within the school, and offered them full *use of the building's facilities if they could find the programs and resources to make their vision a reality.*

Realizing that they couldn't accomplish this goal on their own, the parents decided to reach out to the community for help. "We needed to know what else was out there in our community, what other families wanted and needed, and who else could help," one parent explained.[8] The parents developed a detailed survey questionnaire, and after receiving training in doorknocking and one-on-one outreach, they hit the streets. Over the next two months, as they talked to more than 700 residents about their problems, their assets, and their dreams, the parents were surprised to discover how warmly they were received. "We went door to door and asked our community what they wanted, what was important to them. That was a horrifying experience too, because I know I [never] open my door for anyone," parent Angela Turner recalled. "But people were very willing to share, very anxious to share, and I was very surprised."

Through the outreach process, the parents discovered that many residents shared their desire for adult education. In fact, there was overwhelming support for their proposal to create a community center in the school. The parent team organized a community meeting to present the results of their research and to launch an action-planning process for the project. Almost fifty people from the school, the community, and local agencies attended the meeting. After summarizing the outreach process, the parents announced the five program areas that had been identified as priorities during their research: (1) adult education and job training; (2) programs for children; (3) child care; (4) family support activities; and (5) prevention programs for parents and teens.

The parents invited community members to work with them to design programs to address each of these priorities. The challenge of creating these programs from scratch seemed overwhelming, but with PILOT's help, the parents began to build the partnerships they needed to make the programs a reality. Angela Turner explained, "We were afraid, we had never done anything like that before. We didn't have any so-called special skills that we thought we needed to have to do this type of thing. We got a lot of encouragement from PILOT and others to, you know, yes you can do it, you can do anything. And we felt that way. We were afraid, but we did feel that way. And then we looked up and we were meeting with directors and deans and principals and aldermen and people I know I never would have talked to in my life, would have been horrified to."

In an effort to secure the necessary resources and support to implement their programs, the parents met with representatives from a wide range of public institutions, private agencies, and nonprofit organizations serving children and families in the community. They met with the Dean of Chicago's City Colleges system to explore the possibility of creating a satellite campus for

GED and ESL classes at their center. The Dean offered to provide the instructors and materials for the classes on the condition that a minimum of a
hundred participants would commit to enroll. Although it took several weeks
of additional outreach and recruitment, as well as some additional pressure on
the City Colleges, the parent team eventually had enough students enrolled,
and the City Colleges signed on to the project.

The parents also developed relationships with the administrator of a local
social work agency who eventually offered to create a family support program
at the center, and the head of a local youth services agency who offered to provide security at the school. And through the support of dozens of community
volunteers, they organized free child-care as well as tutoring, sports, and recreation programs.

Several months later, the parent team celebrated the Paxton Community
Center's grand opening with a ribbon cutting ceremony and family activity
night. Joining the parents in their celebration were dozens of community residents and their children, key community leaders, representatives from the various partner organizations, and several state and local elected officials. Within
weeks, several adult education classes were up and running with full enroll-
ment and an enthusiastic group of students. And while parents studied, their
children participated in free childcare and youth activities. Over time, the program grew to include a number of additional programs such as citizenship
classes and Boy Scouts. The parents elected a community-based advisory
board to guide the center's work. And, with the help of their partner organizations, they leveraged the funds to hire two part-time parent coordinators to
oversee the center's programs and activities.

Since its founding, the center's adult education classes have become among
the most popular and successful GED and ESL classes in the city, with some
of the highest rates of completion in the entire City Colleges system. And over
time, as new PILOT parent teams have emerged in schools throughout the
city, many have been inspired by Paxton's success to create their own school-
based community centers, with programs and offerings tailored to meet their
community's needs.

Women-centered organizations attribute many of the problems in urban
neighborhoods to the historic lack of input or control by low-income families over the programs and institutions that shape their lives. To address this
situation, organizations like PILOT and TLC work to provide the neighborhood's families with an opportunity to develop a vision for their community
and to build the partnerships necessary to make this vision a reality. PILOT's
Community Center campaign provides a good illustration of this approach.
Through the campaign, PILOT connected residents to local public and private institutions, ultimately making these institutions more responsive to

families' interests. And PILOT enabled its participants to develop concrete programs and services to directly address their needs. However, because of PILOT's commitment to creating resident-run, all-volunteer programs, the overall impact of these programs was limited in scope. And while the parents' face-to-face relationships with public institutions may have changed the perspectives of individual staff within those institutions, they had little impact on the broader public decision-making process.

Positive Impacts of PILOT's Approach

Women-centered organizations provide women and families with an important mechanism for influencing public decision-making in their neighborhoods. By giving women who have been alienated from public life the opportunity and the skills to build a collective vision for their community, organizations like PILOT challenge the traditional institutional arrangements in low-income urban neighborhoods. Public institutions designed to serve families' needs—such as schools, community colleges, and social service programs—typically treat women and families as passive clients and consumers. Organizations like PILOT turn this traditional relationship on its head, redefining the women as experts who know best how to address their families' needs.

By building face-to-face relationships between parents and the staff and administrators of these local public institutions, organizations like PILOT help to make the institutions more open and responsive to neighborhood families. For example, when Paxton's parent team first met with the lead social worker at a local agency to share their idea for a community center, the social worker immediately started trying to tell them what to do. She was enthusiastic about the team's vision, but skeptical that a group of untrained and inexperienced parents could develop their own community center. In response, the parent team members asserted their leadership, emphasizing that they wanted to partner with the agency to provide some specific programs, but that the families of the community would be the ones driving the project. Over time, as she started to form relationships with the parents, the social worker developed a new understanding and respect for their leadership. She began advocating for the parent team's program within her agency, and eventually was able to offer the team a substantial commitment of support in the form of staff time, funding, and programs. As a recent evaluation of women-centered organizing projects around the country concludes, "Strengthening the community's public and nonprofit institutional response to families . . . break[s] down the 'us/them' sense between institutions and those they serve, and . . . mak[es] these institutions more welcoming of, accessible to, and used by the community" (O'Donnell and Scheie 1999: 20).

In the long run, such relationships have the potential to transform the culture within these institutions. For example, one of the teachers at Paxton School, writing in PILOT's newsletter, asserted that because of the relationships that were formed through the community center project, "Today at Paxton there is a new attitude towards parents, a new culture of cooperation, communication and pride. . . . This project brought about a huge transformation, building new, constructive relationships among teachers, parents, and kids. . . . Both parents and teachers say the program helped them understand and appreciate each other better." These changes have altered the way the school operates, creating a more open, family-friendly educational environment rooted in ongoing partnerships between parents and staff.

Through this process, women-centered organizations are able to create important changes in the material conditions and quality of life of local residents. As a result of PILOT's Community Center campaign, hundreds of neighborhood residents were able to benefit from Paxton's classes and recreational programs. That same year, members of Paxton's parent team used similar techniques to create a parent patrol, to develop a parent room in the school, and to get involved as volunteers in their children's classrooms.

The hands-on nature of these programs and services makes them especially rewarding for the organizations' members. In contrast to the community-building organizations' comprehensive, professionally designed programs, women-centered organizations' projects are developed and controlled by small teams of inexperienced women. This hands-on involvement gives the participants a sense of direct ownership over the projects and a strong feeling of personal accomplishment. For example, one TLC member compared the group's first project to the experience of giving birth: "That was so neat. That stands out. That was really something. It was just like being in childbirth. You have birthed a child, and then you've got the child on their feet and off and running." Similarly, PILOT's Angela Turner said her involvement with the Paxton community center gave her a lasting sense of personal accomplishment: "What I like best is knowing that what I have done has permanently changed the school and the community. I like thinking that when my kids have moved on, the center will still be here—it will outlast me."[9] This deep, personal sense of accomplishment provides an important level of material benefit that is impossible to achieve through government-run services or professionally administered programs.

Limitations of PILOT's Approach

Despite the benefits of this approach, framing complex urban problems as something that a small team of women can address through volunteer-led programs and services has some inevitable drawbacks. Like most urban problems, the issues that PILOT and TLC's members tried to address were complex and multifaceted. But when the members developed hands-on strategies for solving these problems, they ended up focusing only on the problems' most immediate and visible manifestations. This dynamic is certainly understandable, but it inevitably limits the scope of the organizations' work. For example, the establishment of the Paxton community center effectively responded to residents' immediate needs for remedial education, providing a valuable service in a neighborhood where a substantial proportion of the adult population doesn't have a high school diploma. But while this is an important step in helping local residents to find employment, it does nothing to address the other, more complex dimensions of the problem, such as the reasons why so many of the area's residents have never received a high school diploma in the first place.

Although PILOT and TLC's participants were often aware of the limited reach of their small-scale projects, they had difficulty expanding the scope of their work. As discussed in previous chapters, TLC's efforts to increase the scale of its work undermined the integrity of its original leadership team to such an extent that the organization eventually ceased to be identifiable as a women-centered community organizing group. TLC began as a group of women who wanted to address the lack of affordable housing for families. During the first year of the organization's existence, its members focused on a volunteer-intensive project to renovate a small, four-unit apartment building to create family-friendly housing. The success of this project inspired the group to begin pursuing larger, more ambitious rehab efforts. But the demands of these more complex projects forced the original group of volunteers to become dependent on a growing contingent of professional staff and consultants. And while the women in TLC's leadership team continued to provide these professionals with guidance and oversight, eventually the complexity of the group's projects made it impossible for them to offer meaningful advice or direction. As a result, TLC eventually became a staff-controlled, bureaucratically run community development corporation. TLC's experience suggests that if women-centered organizations are to retain the benefits of a team-centered, highly participatory approach, their strategies must remain fairly small in scale.

The impact of the women-centered organizations' strategies is further limited by the methods they use to influence government and the public sphere. Women-centered organizations try to alter the internal culture of public institutions by building face-to-face relationships between residents and the staff and administrators of those institutions. By sharing their personal stories and collective vision in small, friendly meetings, the Paxton parent team altered the perspectives of individual administrators within the public schools, the City Colleges, and local social service agencies. But while these relationships enabled the parents to shape the way these individual agencies served families in the community, they did not have a significant impact on the broader public decision-making process. Changing the views of individual institutional administrators one person at a time does not necessarily produce broader system-wide change within the institutions as a whole. Thus, while PILOT and TLC's efforts led to concrete changes in the way specific departments and staff members within these institutions conducted their business, these relationships rarely had any meaningful impact on the institutions' overall policies and priorities.

For example, PILOT's parent leaders built a strong one-on-one relationship with a key member of the Chicago School Board in an effort to secure a public commitment to creating funding for parent designed and controlled community centers in all of Chicago's schools. After meeting with a small group of parents and being touched by their stories of personal transformation, the School Board member pledged his support for their project. This support eventually led to an offer by the School Board to fund community centers in four of the schools in which PILOT parent teams were active. This offer of funding was a welcome boost to those schools' efforts, but it was a far cry from the broader policy changes the parents were hoping for. It didn't increase the overall voice of parents in the Chicago Public Schools' agenda-setting process, nor did it reflect a systemic shift in the School Board's policy priorities. Furthermore, because the funding wasn't part of a broader expansion of the public resources "pie," it most likely resulted in a shift in resources away from other equally deserving priorities.

Several of TLC's founding members cited this dynamic as one of the ongoing dilemmas of their approach. Because of TLC's friendly, nonthreatening relationships with local government administrators and the relatively small scale of their projects and demands, the organization became an easy and cheap way for government agencies to fulfill their obligations to the low-income community without having to change their broader policies and priorities. As one longtime TLC member put it:

> I think we came along just when they needed to look like they were being fair, giving everyone opportunities. And we fell into their lap, and we were easy to manage and everybody looked good, and we gave them lots

of [public relations] points, and cost them nothing. . . . I think that we represent this token kind of female, lots of cultural diversity, kind of thing. And so it serves them and it costs them very little money to pay tribute to those principles. So if you look at the amount of money . . . we're scraps that they can toss off the table and it makes them look really good. We're kind of the golden child that serves their needs.

Thus while the interpersonal relationships that PILOT and TLC developed with the staff of local public institutions enabled them to secure resources and support for their projects, the relationships did not necessarily enable the residents to impact the wider decision-making process about public policies and priorities.

In sum, women-centered organizations help to improve the material conditions and quality of life in urban neighborhoods by creating volunteer-run programs and services to meet residents' basic needs. In addition, by building partnerships among local institutions and small teams of grassroots women, the organizations make these institutions more responsive to the voice and leadership of the neighborhood's families. However, although the hands-on nature of the organizations' projects makes them particularly rewarding for the participants, it tends to limit the scope and the scale of their impact. And while the organizations often develop supportive relationships with local government agencies, these relationships do not necessarily translate into broader changes in the public agenda.

THE TRANSFORMATIVE MODEL: JAG'S HIGH ROAD DEVELOPMENT CAMPAIGN

For more than twenty years, the Justice Action Group (JAG) has organized residents of Chicago's Dalton neighborhood around housing issues. Over much of that time, the central focus of JAG's work has been the fight for tenants' rights vis-à-vis their landlords. But in the mid-1990s, JAG's leaders began to see a dramatic change taking place in the landscape of affordable housing issues in their neighborhood. As the pressures of gentrification started to impact the local property market, the very existence of affordable rental housing in the neighborhood came under threat. Rents were rising and many rental units were being torn down to make way for upscale condominiums.

Faced with this new reality, JAG's leaders struggled to develop a new direction for their work. The neighborhood's problems seemed to be a direct result of broader market dynamics. Realizing that there was little they could do to alter the market itself, JAG's leaders concluded their best hope for saving affordable housing was to introduce an alternative framework for development in the *neighborhood. As JAG's president explained, "Our vision is that, no, gentrifi-cation is not inevitable. None of these changes are inevitable. . . . Resources [could] be developed in ways that are more equitable. . . . There's a lot of or-ganizations that avoid that whole question and they're just trying to get a few more crumbs, get a few more units of affordable housing. . . . [But] there is the potential to have a whole different approach to development."*

In an effort to create a more equitable and sustainable economic frame-work, JAG's leaders decided to create a set of guidelines that they could use to critique and reshape the local development process. After researching and ana-lyzing the dynamics of economic development in Chicago and elsewhere, they concluded that the neighborhood's patterns of gentrification were part of a larger shift toward neoliberal economic policies world-wide that inherently benefited large-scale developers and financiers at the expense of local popula-tions, particularly the poor. Denouncing this dominant approach to develop-ment as "Low-Road" development, they worked to develop a framework for de-velopment that would prioritize the needs and interests of the community's resi-dents, particularly its low-income residents, over those of outside investors and businessmen—an approach they termed "High Road"[10] development.

In the process of creating this High Road vision, one of JAG's core members visited the Mondragon Cooperative in Spain—a well-known worker owned and controlled cooperative—and others attended an annual gathering of or-ganizations around the U.S. committed to "sustainable development." The graduate students in the group examined the academic literature on urban de-velopment. And, the organization's core members shared articles, books, and ideas that they had gathered from their other activist affiliations. Over a pe-riod of several months they discussed, debated, drafted ideas, exchanged feed-back and revisions over e-mail, and debated some more.

The resulting platform challenged the underlying premises of "value-free" growth and market-oriented development as well as the dominant political frameworks for decision-making about neighborhood development. The plat-form's introduction framed the development issues in the neighborhood within the larger, global economic climate: "Sometimes it appears that there is no al-ternative to the Low Road; some say that in today's world the community can not afford to be selective and should take whatever jobs and investment it can get. JAG rejects this way of thinking, and draws on the experience of High Road development in other communities."

JAG's proposals for "High Road" development included a requirement that all commercial and industrial businesses recruited to the neighborhood pro-vide living wage, high-quality jobs targeted for local residents; that all devel-opers receiving public subsidies and government resources be required to con-tribute to the advancement and well being of local residents through job train-

ing, child care, community centers, and youth programs; and that new industries recruited to the neighborhood have a demonstrated record of responsible environmental practices including minimizing reliance on extractive nonrenewable materials and a commitment to pollution prevention and waste minimization. The platform also called for the creation of legal mechanisms to regulate housing prices, such as a fair rent commission and rent control, as well as across-the-board restrictions on market rate development, such as required set-asides of affordable housing on all new developments. Finally, the platform emphasized the importance of developing long-term economic arrangements at the neighborhood level—such as cooperative housing and worker-owned co-ops—that would effectively insulate rental housing, jobs, and basic goods from the private market.

Once the platform was complete, JAG used it to frame its organizing efforts in the neighborhood. When the local alderman announced that he was planning to designate one of the neighborhood's commercial streets a Tax Increment Financing (TIF) District, a popular development tool that JAG's members viewed as one of the most potent symbols of Low Road development, JAG's members worried that the designation would lead to the loss of additional affordable units in the neighborhood. Although the city had scheduled a public hearing about the matter, JAG's members decided that trying to oppose the TIF through the public hearing process would be a waste of time. With the public hearing's agenda and decision-making framework defined and controlled by the city's power holders, JAG concluded it would be impossible for the community to gain any real voice in the process. Instead, JAG's members decided to use popular education to generate opposition to the TIF and to alter the terms of the debate about urban development within the neighborhood.

Over a period of several weeks, JAG's members met privately with the alderman and other key neighborhood leaders to share their concerns about using TIF as a development tool and to explain the "High Road" alternatives. They also organized several meetings and workshops to introduce their framework to area residents. And several members wrote letters to the editor of the local newspaper to publicize their views. The TIF proposal passed, but JAG's members remained committed to the long-term process of challenging the dominant assumptions about development in the neighborhood.

Several months later, JAG's leaders discovered that the alderman was secretly engaged in a planning process for yet another TIF in the neighborhood. This time they seized the opportunity to shape the terms of the local debate about the issue before it could be defined by the official public hearing process. JAG organized a large community forum to educate residents about TIF and to promote a public discussion about how development should hap-

pen in the neighborhood. The forum attracted more than 150 people and provoked lively debate. While JAG invited one local pro-TIF activist to speak, the
bulk of the speakers focused on the devastating effects that TIFs had had on
other neighborhoods. By the end of the meeting, an issue that had previously
provoked little public interest in the neighborhood had become the subject of
heated public contestation.

With the issue now on the table, the alderman and his supporters felt compelled to hold their own forum to respond to the concerns JAG had raised. In
an effort to regain control over how the issue was framed, they invited developers from other neighborhoods to discuss the benefits of TIF and to emphasize
the "win-win" nature of this development tool. While the forum was clearly designed to build support for the TIF, it helped to stoke the growing public debate over the issue.

In the months that followed, JAG continued to talk to residents about the
dangers of TIF and the principles of high-road development through several
small community meetings and numerous one-on-one discussions on the
street. In addition, the organization joined with several nonprofit organizations, churches, and tenants' groups to organize a march for diversity and affordability, with opposition to the TIF as one of its central platforms.

Shortly after the march, when a reporter asked the alderman about the
progress on the TIF, the alderman denied that he had ever had any plans for a
TIF. Even though he had already apparently earmarked city funds for a TIF
feasibility study, he claimed that the TIF was simply a figment of JAG's collective imagination. JAG's members concluded that their opposition had convinced the alderman to back away from his plan, and they declared victory.
While they knew this was only a small step in their larger struggle to stop gentrification, they saw it as an important sign that they had started to have an
impact on the broader debate about development in the neighborhood.

Transformative organizations view the problems facing urban neighborhoods as localized symptoms of broader systemic injustices. Consequently,
the organizations aim to address these problems by challenging society's
dominant institutional arrangements. JAG's High Road Development
campaign provides a good illustration of both the benefits and the limitations of this approach. By challenging the prevailing framework for urban
development, JAG successfully altered the terms of the local debate about
housing and economic growth in the neighborhood. However, JAG's lack
of internal capacity and organizational clout as well as the ambitious nature of its agenda constrained its ability to win concrete concessions from
local powerholders and decision-makers. As a result, the organization had
only a limited impact on the material conditions and quality of life in the
neighborhood.

Positive Impacts of JAG's Approach

Unlike most of the other organizations in this study, transformative organizations have the potential to alter the structure of public decision-making about urban issues over the long-term. As the above story illustrates, while JAG's organizing strategies did not necessarily stop the process of gentrification, they did begin to create a shift in the framework of local debates about neighborhood development. As Art explained, "I think we've been successful in putting things on the agenda. Politicians and developers and even the community council [a homeowners' group] are talking about things they never would have two years ago. And at least, whether they mean it or not, I don't know, but at least they're claiming to be addressing the concerns of JAG."

Through its educational forums, media campaigns, and protests, JAG challenged the dominant assumption that growth and private development are necessarily beneficial and desirable. Prior to JAG's involvement, condo conversions, new commercial developments, and Tax Increment Financing projects were presented by the alderman, developers, and other neighborhood organizations as "win-win" initiatives that would benefit the entire community. And for the most part, the broader community accepted this framing. Through JAG's organizing efforts, urban development was gradually redefined as a contested issue that was directly related to larger struggles over class, race, and community control. JAG's popular education work forced the local alderman and other community leaders to acknowledge the organization's concerns when making decisions about neighborhood priorities. As a result, even though these powerholders didn't ultimately accept or necessarily abide by JAG's principles, these principles became incorporated into the public debate about local development.

JAG's approach also expanded residents' perspective beyond their immediate neighborhood to engage them in public deliberations about the city's overarching policies and priorities for development as a whole. Whereas most of the other organizations in this study focused on securing concrete concessions for their neighborhoods, JAG's platform was designed to alter the urban development paradigm for the entire city. In other words, instead of simply trying to win a bigger piece of the pie—an approach that typically means fighting with other communities for resources—JAG tried to alter the overall nature and configuration of the pie itself.

Limitations of JAG's Approach

While JAG was thus successful at shifting the framework of political debate in the neighborhood, it was less successful at creating concrete changes in the community's material conditions or quality of life. As JAG's president explained, "The reality's been that we've tried to raise a few voices opposing the establishment's agenda, [but] have done very little to be advancing [any] kind of alternative." The primary obstacle to JAG's success was the complex and challenging nature of its goals. JAG's principles of High Road development were fundamentally at odds with the organizing principles of the urban "growth machine"—the powerful coalition of politicians, developers, realtors, corporations, and large institutions that controls the urban development process in most U.S. cities (Ferman 1996; Logan and Molotch 1987). Challenging the power of this coalition as well as the validity of the growth agenda upon which its power is based is a Herculean task. As JAG member Lucy Crain explained, "I don't think JAG has been completely successful in achieving its goals. And I think the biggest reason is that there's just too many forces allied against it. . . . I feel like the forces of politics and money that are lined up against JAG are just enormous, and it feels like a David against a Goliath."

By taking a radical stance against the dominant approach to growth and development in the city, JAG marginalized itself politically, making it difficult for the organization to achieve any short-term victories. As Lucy pointed out, given the local alderman's control over neighborhood development, getting him to buy into JAG's agenda would have been a big step forward. But because of the power of the pro-development forces within urban politics, such support would have been tantamount to political suicide for the alderman: "The alderman is in a very tough spot. He's not going to be able to get anything done unless he can hobnob with the mayor, unless he's a friend with the mayor. And I don't think he can be a friend with the mayor and really try to prevent gentrification in the neighborhood. And so he's in this really tough spot. And he's either going to do what the mayor wants him to do, or he's going to lose his job, because they'll nominate someone else and get him out of here unless he does what they want him to do."

JAG might have had more success in implementing at least some elements of its agenda if it had had enough clout to apply political pressure on the alderman and other power brokers. To build this kind of clout, however, JAG would have had to convince a critical mass of residents to buy into its agenda—a task that would have required a significant amount of in-depth popular education work. In addition, to get these residents actively involved in the organization's campaigns, JAG would have had to do the kind of intensive recruitment and leadership development work that made the power-based groups' organization-building activities so successful. But in contrast to WON and UNITE, which each had at least four full-time organizers at any given time, JAG struggled to raise enough money to support even one full-time organizer.

While it is impossible to know for sure all the reasons for JAG's lack of popularity with funders, the explicitly ideological nature of its agenda was at least part of the problem. Even the most liberal mainstream funders seemed to be uncomfortable with JAG's overt criticism of many of the basic tenets of the United States' economic and political systems and its emphasis on long-term social structural change. As one JAG member speculated,

> I know other community based organizations that seem to be well funded. There might be a particular thing about JAG. [JAG] might be just one level of challenge to the status quo, so that for the foundation to commit puts them on another side of an issue — not quite so community service, not so much a white endorsement of social concern, but somebody who is working in there to challenge the order of things. And that might be a little bit too vocal, too clear, for the power structure, including the donors, the foundations, to commit to that . . . [or] to be comfortable with them.

Regardless of whether the funders actually disagreed with JAG's goals, in reality most foundations are unwilling to invest in initiatives that do not lead to tangible short-term outcomes and measurable improvements in residents' quality of life. As Art explained, JAG was unwilling to make the trade-offs that an emphasis on short-term outcomes might entail: "I think [JAG's] main strength is . . . the possibility for really creating change that may in fact be long term and sustainable. I think a lot of local organizing based on fairly immediate, small-scale victories tends to, even though it may be the intention of groups to do more, it ends up being pretty immediate stuff. I think if you really do want something changed, that we need to be thinking beyond that." Whatever its merits, JAG's emphasis on long-term change rather than visible short-term outcomes impeded its ability to raise enough money to do the kind of base-building and leadership development work that made the power-based organizations so successful.

This lack of capacity, combined with the ambitious nature of JAG's proactive agenda, severely constrained the organization's ability to alter the material conditions in the neighborhood. Even though JAG was able to shift the *terms* of the public debate, its efforts ultimately had little concrete impact on the neighborhood's quality of life. The only tangible effects that JAG had on the neighborhood resulted from its efforts to stall new development projects that were likely to harm the area's low-income residents. As one member explained, "I think we're pretty good at putting out fires. . . . I think where there have been some real threats in our neighborhood, I think [our] attention has been drawn there and that's where [much of our] work is done." For example, JAG's core members joined forces with the tenants of several subsidized apartment buildings to fight local landlords' efforts to turn the buildings into market rate condominiums. Through such efforts, JAG was able to stop several Low Road development projects from moving forward. While this did not result in any lasting change in the developers' priorities, it did help to slow the gentrification of the neighborhood. As one member put it, "I've begun to realize what would happen if there weren't people like us who are confronting the powers that be—how much swifter things would move against us and the poor if there wasn't somebody out there going to the mayor's office and saying this is not right and trying to attract attention. It doesn't really work [to prevent gentrification], but it slows things down."

JAG succeeded in building enough clout to veto specific development proposals by mobilizing diverse groups of residents around their shared opposition to these projects. However, whenever JAG tried to move from simply opposing a project to actually pursuing an alternative proposal, it soon became clear that few of its allies or coalition partners were willing to support its broader agenda. For instance, after JAG successfully worked with a group of tenants to save their building from being razed, the group met to strategize about the building's future. JAG's leaders saw this as an opportunity to push for the creation of a tenant-run cooperative. They proposed finding a nonprofit to buy the building and then giving control over management to the tenants themselves. Most of the tenants, however, insisted that all they cared about was getting decent maintenance, and that they didn't want control of their building. As one tenant put it during a strategy session, "We're not asking for the tenants to be in charge, we just want a cleaning service and management that works."

Without broad-based support for its alternative vision, JAG was unable to win concessions to its High Road agenda within the public sphere. By successfully vetoing several proposed Low Road developments, JAG helped to keep gentrification at bay, thus preventing residents' material conditions from getting worse. But without the capacity to achieve its broader proactive vision for the neighborhood, the organization was unable to *improve* residents' overall quality of life in any lasting or meaningful way.

In sum, by challenging the dominant frameworks for urban economic development, JAG altered the terms of the public debate about the neighborhood's future. In doing so, the organization helped to lay the foundation for potential long-term changes in the public decision-making process. However, because JAG was not able to build enough internal capacity or clout to implement its proactive agenda, its immediate impact on local residents' quality of life was fairly limited.

CONCLUSION: STRATEGIES OF URBAN CHANGE

Each model of community organizing embodies a distinct set of strategies for solving neighborhood problems and addressing residents' needs. The comparison of the case study organizations' campaigns in this chapter demonstrates the unique contributions as well as potential drawbacks of each of these approaches, as summarized in table 7.

Clearly, some strategies of urban change are more successful than others. However, no single approach can effectively address all the problems affecting urban neighborhoods. By examining the case study organizations' experiences, we can begin to assess which kinds of strategies are most likely to succeed in a given context and situation. Just as importantly, we can also anticipate the distinct trade-offs of even the most successful strategies.

This chapter focused on community organizing's direct impact on urban residents' quality of life and the local public sphere. In doing so, it left several key questions unanswered: What effect do the kinds of campaigns profiled in this chapter have on residents' material conditions and the nature of the public sphere over the long haul? Is community organizing capable of generating long-term changes in the overall structure and framework of urban politics and society? These questions will be explored further in the next chapter.

TABLE 7 Strategies and Outcomes

Model	Public sphere: Positive impact	Public sphere: Limitations	Material conditions: Positive impact	Material conditions: Limitations
Civic	Connect residents directly with city government. Undermine patronage system	No impact on public decision-making—just connect people to existing system. No ability to hold government accountable	Some limited ability to solve certain small-scale problems by imposing social control	Reliance on city service system's existing tools to solve problems. Solutions tend to be narrow in scope and potentially divisive
Power-based	Alter balance of power. Create alternative form of governance	May preclude nuanced deliberations over public priorities. No impact on the structure of the public sphere itself	Achieve concrete changes in the distribution of public resources and government services	Limited ability to change things that government can't solve through public services or programs
Community-building	Provide a vehicle for comprehensive planning. Impact the way government implements its priorities in the community	Dependence on government limits impact on broader public priority setting. Potential for cooptation	Enable community to implement holistic programs to address neighborhood's complex needs	The need to build a common vision among multiple stakeholders can limit the scope and effectiveness of the strategies
Women-centered	Make public institutions more responsive to the voice and leadership of women and families	Building one-on-one relationships with public administrators has little impact on the broader public priority setting process	Create community-based programs and services to directly meet residents' needs	Projects tend to be small in scale and limited in scope
Transformative	Shift the terms of the public debate—alter the framework of the public sphere	Not enough clout or influence to gain significant changes in public priorities	Able to sometimes stop externally driven policies and projects that would harm the community	Limited ability to implement a proactive agenda

CHAPTER 8

WIDENING THE SCOPE: ORGANIZING FOR BROADER SOCIAL CHANGE

If community organizing is to live, it must change. . . . I don't mean to suggest that traditional community organizations have not made some significant strides. Our process of finding and developing grassroots leaders is an important contrast to the notion that the only people that can solve problems are anointed experts. We have helped people understand that their opinions count, that there is power in numbers, and that, even though there may be conflict within an organization, democratic decisions are possible. We also have contested for and won power. . . . However, if we have any hope of affecting larger societal issues and continuing to be relevant to our own constituents, we have to create space for discussing and developing a collective vision.
—Gary Delgado (1998: 18–20)

What will it take for community practice to live up to its goals of effecting social and economic justice in the 21st century? . . . [U]nless organizing can both build on and surpass a local focus, the goal of a democratic society will fail. We will end up with internally directed local democracy and corporate control of everything else. . . . Clearly the opposition has to be constructed from the ground up, but it must also connect to global concerns and developments. Nothing short of large international alliances can stop the corporate march to the 'end of history' (Brecher and Costello, 1994).
—Robert Fisher and Eric Shragge (2000: 13–14)

THE ANALYSIS in chapter seven demonstrates the powerful impact that effective community-based organizing can have on urban residents' quality of life. Depending on the specific model an organization chooses, grassroots community-based organizing can be a valuable tool for addressing some of today's most pressing urban problems.

In an increasingly globalized world, however, not all problems can be addressed at the community level. The problems experienced by urban residents are typically rooted in political and economic structures that are anything but local in their origins (Brecher, Costello and Smith 2000; Castells

1983; Fisher 1994; Gould, Schnaiberg, and Weinberg 1996; Halpern 1995; Logan and Molotch 1987). To what extent can community organizing move beyond the local neighborhood to address these broader institutional arrangements?

This chapter explores the potential for grassroots, community-based organizing to contribute to broader social structural change. Because this examination involves a widening of the scope of my analysis beyond the local dynamics of individual community organizations, my methodology in this chapter differs somewhat from that used in previous chapters. While my analysis draws on the experiences of the case-study organizations, it also relies heavily on existing sociological research on the social movements of the past. Building on the insights offered by this literature, I analyze the potential connection between community-based organizing and the formation of broader movements for social change. I then assess the potential for different models of organizing to contribute to the process of movement building.

In exploring community-based organizing's broader potential, I do not intend to minimize the importance of its many contributions to the quality of life in urban neighborhoods. My aim throughout this book has been to demonstrate the powerful role of community organizing in strengthening democracy, building community capacity, and solving urban problems. Regardless of whether or not community organizing can ultimately transform the broader institutional arrangements that shape urban neighborhoods' underlying conditions, its contributions at the local level are nonetheless essential.

WHAT IS THE CONNECTION BETWEEN COMMUNITY ORGANIZING AND SOCIAL STRUCTURAL CHANGE?

An examination of the ongoing legacy of community organizing in America's cities inevitably leads to the question of whether grassroots, locally based initiatives can affect the structural roots of urban problems (Fisher 1994; Halpern 1995). Despite numerous community organizing "victories" over the past few decades, the conditions for low-income and working-class urban residents are, to a great extent, worse now than ever before. While effective community organizing has no doubt improved the quality of life for many urban residents, few locally based organizing initiatives have been able to permanently alter the root causes of urban problems. As *The Nation's* JoAnn Wypijewski puts it,

A neighborhood organization can build fifty or even 500 homes, and for those fifty or 500 families that's a very good thing. It may retrain 500 workers, and again for those 500 the experience might be transformative. In an era when government has shunned its responsibilities, these actions to fill the breach are noble, possibly even "empowering," but . . . even if replicated 500 times they would not begin to attack the core problems of homelessness or joblessness or insecurity or the vast disparity between wealth and poverty. (Wypijewski 1997: 18)

While locally based strategies are essential for combating the symptoms of urban problems, the problems themselves can not be resolved at a local level. As Robert Halpern concludes in his analysis of neighborhood-based strategies to address poverty, "The historic experience with neighborhood initiative suggests that it is at best an ameliorative, not a transforming, problem-solving strategy" (Halpern 1995: 221).

Social scientific research on urban problems helps to explain why locally based organizing is so limited in its long-term impact. To illustrate, let's take a closer look at the approaches to crime overviewed in chapter 6, focusing on the two campaigns with the greatest impact on residents' quality of life—WON's police accountability campaign and PACT's crime prevention strategies.

The violence and instability associated with gang warfare and drug trafficking significantly undermine urban residents' quality of life, making the resolution of these problems a priority for many community-based organizations. WON addressed the issue of urban crime by organizing residents to pressure the city's law enforcement agencies to be more responsive to the community's concerns. Through protests, public confrontations, and negotiations, the organization won a commitment from the police to target manpower and resources toward key neighborhood hotspots. These victories improved residents' sense of safety and well-being by increasing their confidence in the police. Over time, the increased law enforcement activity also helped to shut down several drug operations and remove several known criminals from the neighborhood.

But social science research on urban crime suggests that WON's approach is unlikely to solve the neighborhood's safety problems in the long run. Despite the popular assumption that police prevent crime, research shows that the presence of crime in a neighborhood has relatively little to do with the level of police activity in the area. Urban crime rates are the result of deep-rooted economic problems such as unemployment, inequality, and poverty (McGahey 1986; Klockars 1988; Bayley 1988). Consequently,

Despite the fact that for the past fifty years the police have been promoting themselves as crime fighters . . . the best evidence to date is that no matter what they do they can make only marginal differences in it. The reason is that all of the major factors influencing how much crime there is or is not are factors over which police have no control whatsoever. . . . Compared to them what police do or do not do matters very little. (Klockars 1988: 250)

In order to effectively tackle neighborhood crime over the long haul, WON would need to address the problem's complex social and economic root causes.

In light of this, PACT's community-building approach to crime—which aims to provide economic opportunities to local youth—seems much more likely to foster long-term solutions to the neighborhood's drug and gang problems. PACT's crime prevention efforts focused on developing mentoring programs and recreational opportunities for youth, attracting public and private employers to the neighborhood, and strengthening the neighborhood's job training and placement systems.

Although PACT's approach may help to mitigate some of the worst effects of neighborhood unemployment and poverty in the short term, it is unlikely to have any significant long-term impact. While gang membership and drug dealing are largely a function of the lack of economic opportunities in today's inner-city neighborhoods (Wilson 1987; Peeples and Loeber 1994; Anderson 1990), these economic problems are rooted in long-term structural shifts in the global economy (Wilson 1987, 1996; Blank 1996). By trying to develop economic opportunities from within the neighborhood, the most that PACT is likely to achieve is to match individual youth with available jobs. Unless PACT can address the underlying lack of economic opportunities available to youth, its efforts will remain ameliorative at best. And working to attract employers to the Port Angeles neighborhood without creating broader changes in the regional economy is likely to shift economic opportunities away from other similarly struggling neighborhoods.

The limited ability of locally based organizing strategies to address the root causes of urban problems has led some scholars and activists to conclude that community-based organizing is incapable of contributing to long-term social change (see, for example, Harvey 1973, 1976). I disagree. While its direct impacts have historically been limited in scope, I believe that community organizing can provide an essential *building block* for achieving broader structural change.

History suggests that if we want to transform the social and economic arrangements underlying contemporary urban problems, we must build a broad-based social justice *movement*. Scholars and activists have traditionally viewed community organizing and movement formation as distinct—some would even say mutually exclusive—approaches to change. Community-based organizing focuses on the creation of discrete, self-contained, permanent organizations at a local level. In contrast, social movements are broad and diffuse, connecting people at the grassroots across geographic and social boundaries. And whereas community organizing focuses on ameliorating material conditions within the local neighborhood, social movements aim to restructure the established institutional arrangements of mainstream society. But despite community organizing's localized scope, I would argue that it actually provides one of the most effective (and realistic) starting points for movement formation.

Regardless of how globalized our world becomes, local neighborhoods remain the center of most people's lived experience. The neighborhood is where people raise their families, recreate and consume, go through their daily rounds, and intersect with the institutions of government. People's social, financial, and emotional commitments frequently coalesce within the local neighborhood. And, perhaps most importantly, people experience contemporary social problems as they are manifested at a local level. As a result, the most effective way to get people involved in social action of any kind is by engaging them in struggles that relate directly to their everyday experiences in the neighborhood. Locally based organizing thus provides an essential mechanism for getting ordinary people—particularly America's most disenfranchised residents—involved with public life.

In addition, by engaging residents at the neighborhood level, community organizing helps local communities to develop skills and capacities that are essential for the formation of effective social movements. By giving residents the opportunity to get hands-on experience as public actors, community organizing provides them with the political acumen and tactical skills necessary for effective social change work. In addition, as previous chapters have demonstrated, neighborhood-based organizing creates connections among local residents, building their capacity to engage in effective collective action. And while local organizing may not transform society, it helps to ameliorate the often devastating effects of contemporary social, economic, and political arrangements on urban communities, providing residents with the stability and hope necessary to enable them to participate in long-term campaigns for social change. After all, if the threat of violence is so great that residents are afraid to leave their houses, or the housing conditions are so bad that residents feel chronically demoralized and exhausted, then they are not going to be able to effectively contribute to the development of a social change movement.

Finally, even if grassroots organizing is only able to address the *symptoms* of broader social structural problems, it plays an important role in the process of movement formation by pushing these problems to the forefront of the public debate. In the process of organizing, residents may begin to realize the limitations of an entirely locally based strategy. And by setting the wheels of change in motion, local struggles may provide the momentum necessary to propel residents to engage in broader movement work. In the words of Manuel Castells, community organizations address "the symptoms of our contradictions and [are] therefore potentially capable of superseding these contradictions. They are the organizational forms, the live schools, where the new social movements of our emerging society are taking place, growing up, learning to breathe" (Castells 1983: 331).

The question thus should not be whether community-based organizing is relevant to efforts to create social structural change, but rather how we can fulfill community organizing's broader potential. To answer this question, we need to examine the source of community organizing's limitations. Community organizing's limited ability to address the root causes of urban problems can be attributed to two distinct, but related, factors: (1) the limitations of a *community-based* approach, given that the local neighborhood is "neither the site of the causes of its problems nor the site of the power needed to address them" (Fisher 1994: 224), and (2) the limitations of relying on community-based *organizations* as the medium for change. In the remainder of this chapter, I will examine the experiences of my case-study organizations in light of the literature on social movements in an effort to assess the potential for different organizing models to overcome these limitations.

1. OVERCOMING THE LIMITATIONS OF A COMMUNITY-BASED APPROACH

In order to contribute to long-term social structural change, community organizing must be able to both build upon and transcend its neighborhood focus. The organizing models best suited to do this are those that can contribute to the creation of (a) a supra-local infrastructure of well-networked organizations; and (b) an overarching ideological framework that challenges society's dominant economic and political arrangements.

(a) Building a Supra-local Infrastructure

The most obvious way for grassroots organizations to overcome the limitations of their community based approach is by joining together to form wider extra-local networks and alliances (Gould, Schnaiberg, and Weinberg 1996; Hunter 1991; Fisher 1994). Through the formation of broader coalitions with like-minded groups, grassroots organizations can vastly expand their influence within the political sphere. Because the issues that neighborhood groups deal with are often linked to political and economic decisions at the city, state, and national level, if local organizations are going to create broader change they need to be able to mobilize people and resources at all these levels. By building an infrastructure of coordinated local campaigns, organizing groups can have a powerful impact on the public agenda-setting process and the terms of the public debate.

Extra-local alliances are also a way to gain leverage over increasingly powerful, globally mobile economic actors. With the erosion of corporations' traditional connections to specific locales, neighborhood organizations have lost their ability to hold economic institutions accountable to the community's needs. Corporate accountability strategies that may have once brought corporations to their knees are likely to backfire in an era when corporations can hold local communities hostage by threatening to pull out of a neighborhood unless they are allowed to operate on their own terms. In their desperation for jobs and economic investment, this dilemma forces many communities to put up with corporate exploitation of their population and resources. Broad national or transnational alliances can enable local communities to hold such corporations accountable by preventing them from playing one locality against another (Gould, Schnaiberg, and Weinberg 1996). In addition, broader alliances may enable localities to confront economic actors at a scale that matches their scope of activity.

The model of community organizing with the greatest potential to form these kinds of effective extra-local networks is the power-based model. In order to maximize their influence in the public arena, power-based organizations frequently join together to form massive regional or national "interest groups" to fight for specific issues. These networks are built on instrumental ties and selective incentives—the members participate in order to achieve their own individual goals more effectively. In keeping with the networks' pragmatic nature, they are formally and hierarchically structured to ensure high levels of internal accountability and to make it possible to mobilize thousands of participants quickly and efficiently.

Both UNITE and WON are members of regional and national networks that have enabled them to impact political and economic issues at a much broader level. For example, as discussed in chapter 4, through its membership in National People's Action (NPA), WON was able to gain enough clout to impact the public priority setting process within the federal Department of Education and in Congress. By joining with dozens of other NPA members from around the country, WON secured an increase in federal spending for local school maintenance and construction.

These broader alliances also enabled the power-based groups to have greater leverage over major economic actors. UNITE and WON were both members of an ad-hoc citywide coalition of ten power-based organizations in Chicago that successfully pressured First Chicago Bank and Bank One to increase their lending in inner-city neighborhoods. Nationally, National People's Action has worked with neighborhood groups to apply pressure to Marriott Corporation, securing significant commitments for job training and hiring of local residents in various cities in which Marriott's hotels are located.

Through these networks and alliances, the power-based groups have been able to overcome many of the limitations of neighborhood-based action. The networks enable the groups to appeal to residents through their immediate, localized interests, while connecting their local struggles with broader political and economic campaigns: "NPA has put to rest the criticism that community organizing cannot move beyond its local turf to larger issues. The success of NPA is due largely to its dual focus: its commitment to initiating, building and strengthening local organizations so that local groups can win on local issues; and secondly, NPA's commitment to maintaining a national network on issues that have regional as well as national significance" (Dieter 1976: 5).

None of my other case study organizations succeeded in building effective action-oriented, extra-local alliances. The community-building model focuses on rebuilding neighborhoods from within, so while organizations like PACT and CO-OP have created broad networks within the community itself, they are not part of any networks that extend beyond the neighborhood's borders. Similarly, civic organizations are engaged in extremely local, parochial problem-solving and rarely have connections to communities or organizations beyond the immediate neighborhood. The women-centered model focuses on creating small, densely networked teams at a local level, and while both PILOT and TLC are members of loose national networks, these networks exist for the purpose of mutual support and information exchange rather than to impact issues that affect the networks' members at a supra-neighborhood level.

Transformative organizations like JAG recognize the importance of extra-local networks and are linked informally to other organizations around the city, the nation, and the globe. However, while they may view their work within the context of a broader social justice movement, my research suggests they are not likely to be successful in creating networks that can be mobilized toward specific ends. For example, JAG is loosely connected with a number of activist organizations outside the local neighborhood, but these alliances are based primarily on intellectual exchange and analysis rather than strategic action. As a result, these alliances contribute little to JAG's ability to mobilize people and resources for collective action at a citywide or national level.

Even though the power-based organizations are more likely than any of the other organizations to effectively expand their work beyond the local neighborhood, this does not necessarily mean that they are able to fully overcome the constraints of a locally based approach. Although membership in broad networks and alliances is essential in order to move organizing beyond the immediate neighborhood level, it doesn't necessarily translate into campaigns to transform society's underlying economic and political arrangements. The power-based networks are rooted in instrumental ties and a strategic pragmatism that make them an unlikely foundation for a unified social movement. Each power-based organization determines its goals based on the subjectively defined self-interests of its members. Because the organizations take residents' subjective perceptions of their interests at face value and insist on an emphatically "nonideological" approach to change, these goals tend to be framed within the dominant conceptual categories of mainstream society. If power-based organizations join regional and national networks, it is because they see the need for this higher level of organization in order to achieve these locally defined goals. In other words, the networks function by providing selective incentives to each participating organization, not by articulating an alternative vision for society as a whole.

Myles Horton, founder of the Highlander Center—a key catalyst in the formation of several twentieth-century social movements—cautioned that networks that are based simply on instrumental pragmatism and aggregated self-interest cannot provide a foundation for achieving social change: "Organizations with nonstructural reform programs working to achieve limited goals can form alliances, but there's still no qualitative difference and no movement potential" (Horton 1998: 114). In fact, Horton, as well as a number of other critics, suggests that because such networks enable local communities to more effectively achieve their immediate goals—temporarily ameliorating some of the most obvious effects of an unjust social system—they may actually strengthen and legitimate dominant economic and political arrangements rather than challenge them: "Victories that win services or rewards . . . [may be seen as proof] that the existing system is responsive to poor and working people and, therefore, in no need of fundamental change" (Fisher 1994: 229).

(b) Developing the Ideological Foundation for Movement Formation

In order for extra-local networks to contribute to genuine social change, they need to be oriented around a unified vision that goes beyond the overlapping subjectively defined self-interests of the members. Such a vision requires participants to see their problems as more than a mere denial of their fair share of the pie. Instead, they must understand the connection between their own experiences and larger economic and political arrangements. And they must develop a shared ideology or worldview that challenges these dominant arrangements and suggests an alternative vision for society.

What role can community organizing play in this process? All community organizing groups engage in the social construction of reality: they translate participants' experiences in certain ways, leading to distinct definitions of the community's "problems." As discussed in chapter 6, sociologists refer to this process of translation as the creation of "collective action frames"—interpretive schemes that enable residents to explain occurrences in their daily lives in terms of general patterns that attribute causality and assign blame. By providing shared frameworks with which residents can make sense of their individual experiences, collective action frames make community action possible.

Like the power-based model, most community organizing models frame residents' experiences within the conceptual categories of mainstream society. Rather than identifying established institutional configurations as the source of residents' problems, they focus on securing concessions from within those established institutions. Civic organizations posit that residents can solve their problems by working through government-established channels for citizen input. Community-building organizations believe that urban problems can be solved by linking the neighborhood with government resources and mainstream economic opportunity structures. And women-centered organizations suggest that residents can make change by building face to face working relationships with the staff and administrators of public and private institutions. While these frameworks enable the organizations to alter the material conditions of urban neighborhoods in the short-term, they are unlikely to produce meaningful long-term transformations in the institutional arrangements that underlie these problems.

In order to build a collective vision for long-term structural change, community organizations must help residents to develop the critical perspective necessary for understanding the connection between their everyday experiences and these broader structural dynamics. This involves the introduction of "transformative frames"—collective action frames that redefine "activities, events, and biographies that are already meaningful from the standpoint of some primary framework, in terms of another framework, such that they are now 'seen by the participants to be something quite else' "(Snow et al. 1986: 474). Transformative frames provide residents with new lenses through which to make sense of their experiences—lenses that enable residents to perceive the connections between their own problems and broader economic and political arrangements and to conceptualize long-term structural solutions to these unjust arrangements.

By exposing the institutional arrangements underlying a wide range of contemporary social problems, transformative frames illuminate the shared fates of widely diverse social groups and localities, providing a potential foundation for the formation of a unified social movement that crosses lines of geography, race, and identity. In order for such a movement to form, however, these diverse social groups must share the *same* transformative frame — a common understanding of their experiences and a common critique of the dominant social and political structures. Sociologists refer to this shared conceptual framework as a "master frame." A master frame provides a common conceptual vocabulary that enables diverse groups to interpret and understand their experiences in compatible ways: "Master frames can be construed as functioning in a manner analogous to linguistic codes in that they provide a grammar that punctuates and syntactically connects patterns or happenings in the world" (Snow and Benford 1992: 138). This shared vocabulary enables groups to locate the source of their distinct problems within a common set of social structures and dynamics. Thus, in the same way that a shared collective action frame enables individual urban residents to work together with their neighbors to achieve change, a shared master frame enables numerous organizations and groups to work together toward a common social vision, creating the basis for large-scale collective action. Based on this unifying master frame, networks of local organizations can become part of a broad-based social movement.

Of all the models in my study, the one with the greatest potential to contribute to the emergence of such a master frame is the transformative model. Transformative organizations believe it is impossible to address the material problems affecting urban neighborhoods without first challenging their ideological underpinnings. Organizations like JAG utilize popular education and reflection to deconstruct the dominant, taken-for-granted belief systems at the root of contemporary problems, and to introduce alternative conceptual frameworks to help residents recognize the connection between their own experiences and broader social, economic, and political structures. As JAG's approach to urban development demonstrates (see chapter 7), this results in collective action that is explicitly rooted in a transformative frame. JAG's development platform challenges the underlying premises of capitalism and the dominant frameworks of political decision-making in Chicago.[1]

While organizations like JAG can help to introduce transformative frames at the local level, they are often not well positioned to spur the emergence of a broader movement. In order to effectively work toward social change, organizations must not only understand the connection between neighborhood issues and dominant institutional arrangements, they must also have the capacity to alter those arrangements. This requires the formation of broad alliances with other organizations and groups across traditional geographic and social boundaries. But, as discussed earlier, JAG has not been very successful at creating such alliances. JAG's organizer explained, "We've been trying to look at . . . the fact that the immediate problems usually come from something much larger. What we really haven't figured out yet is how a local group that isn't part of a larger network can really tackle those issues on a local level, and that's been a real challenge." JAG's experience demonstrates that just as extra-local networks are not sufficient without an overarching ideology, having an alternative ideology is necessary, but not sufficient, as a foundation for broader social change.

In sum, the power-based and transformative organizations each include some of the features necessary to enable community organizing to overcome its locally based focus, but neither is able to overcome all the limitations of locally based action. With their ability to form strong national networks, the power-based organizations represent the most effective *form* for creating a broad-based social movement. And, with their emphasis on the development of transformative frames, the transformative organizations offer the necessary *content* for such movements. Operating in isolation, however, each of these elements is insufficient for movement formation. It is thus unlikely that organizations from either model, working alone, will provide a foundation for movement building.

This dilemma suggests there may be a fundamental tension between contemporary community organizing models and the formation of social movements. On the one hand, there is no question that community organizing offers significant potential as a building block for broader movements. On the other hand, as currently configured, no organizing model can foster this movement potential on its own. This dilemma becomes even more apparent when we examine the second major limitation of community organizing—its reliance on formal organizations as the vehicle for change.

2. THE LIMITATIONS OF COMMUNITY-BASED ORGANIZATIONS AS THE VEHICLES FOR CHANGE

Community organizing's local focus may limit the scale of its impact, but some critics suggest that its emphasis on building formal organizations represents a far more serious obstacle to movement formation. Alinsky and his followers believed that permanent neighborhood organizations were the only effective vehicle for enabling urban residents to achieve their goals: "A people can participate only if they have both the opportunity to formulate their program, which is their reason for participation, and a medium through which they can express and achieve their program. This can be done only through the building of real People's Organizations" (Alinsky 1946: 196–198). While none of the organizing models in this study are as intensely focused on organization building as Alinsky's power-based model, all of them are committed to the creation of permanent, financially stable, formal neighborhood organizations. But even if formal organizations are an effective way to win material concessions for local communities, are they an appropriate vehicle for achieving more fundamental social structural change?

Some critics argue that the effort to build and maintain stable organizations actually *prevents* the emergence of mass movements. Most notably, Piven and Cloward (1977) argue that community organizing defuses social protest by diverting potentially radical action toward more conservative goals. During moments of insurgency, concerns about organizational survival and growth lead organizers to focus on membership building, a pattern which tends to dampen and subvert the social change potential of popular protest. According to Piven and Cloward, the emphasis on developing a formal membership roster bureaucratizes the mobilization process and inhibits more spontaneous network formation. It also generates competition among organizers who become more concerned with signing up new members than with achieving specific social change goals.

In addition, Piven and Cloward argue that the need for resources drives organizations toward accommodation and cooptation. In the effort to secure funding, organizations divert their potential for radical action toward nonthreatening campaigns for modest reforms within the established institutional order. The dependence on mainstream institutions drives the organizations to frame their work within the conceptual categories and institutional frameworks of mainstream society. "However unwittingly, leaders and organizers of the lower classes act in the end to facilitate the efforts of elites to channel the insurgent masses into normal politics, believing all the while that they are taking the long and arduous but certain path to power" (Piven and Cloward 1977: xxii).

While Piven and Cloward's depiction of formal organizations as obstacles to change seems overly pessimistic in light of my case-study research, the dynamics they identify are real. In order to secure adequate resources for salaries, programs, and operating expenses, most of my case-study organizations couched their work within the relatively narrow frameworks set out by mainstream funding institutions, particularly government agencies and private foundations. Because funders require concrete evidence that recipients are using their resources "effectively," organizations that focus on campaigns with short-term victories and easily quantifiable outcomes are far more likely to leverage the resources necessary for organizational survival than those with longer timeframes and less tangible goals. In addition, most mainstream funders subscribe to a broad liberal populism that emphasizes resident participation and community control but is uncomfortable with serious challenges to the status quo. Almost all of the organizations in my study couched their work within this general framework in order to secure funding to survive. The organizations that resisted this pressure—specifically the transformative groups—had great difficulty leveraging adequate resources. As JAG's director explained,

> Our relationships with foundations right now are problematic. . . . Part of the problem is that part of what JAG is doing is making sure that social justice is part of what we're about. It's not just organizing, it's organizing around social justice issues. And that, I think, is the heart of the problem, frankly. Because when you're talking about social justice you're inherently talking about some kind of restructuring, redistribution, whatever. And the people that we go to for money, regardless of how well meaning they are, are not comfortable with any substantial changes in the status quo.

In addition, competition for members and resources prevented many of the case-study organizations from forming networks and alliances that would have enabled them to address local problems at a broader level. Most of the organizations viewed other community groups—particularly those representing other models—as competitors rather than potential allies and were hesitant to form even short-term alliances because of the possibility that the other organizations would take credit for their work or would steal their members. As observer Ben Joravsky put it, one of the greatest failures of Chicago's organizing groups "has been their inability to coalesce groups from different neighborhoods. Part of the problem stems from existing turf squabbles and rivalries. But tensions are often fostered when organizations compete for grants, newspaper headlines, even members" (Joravsky 1989: 7).

Some organizations focused so much time and energy on their turf battles with other organizations that they lost sight of their own substantive goals, let alone the potential benefits of building broader alliances for social change. For example, when Chicago's Department of Planning and Development proposed that a Tax Increment Financing (TIF) district be created along a several mile long commercial strip that overlapped both UNITE and

JAG's geographical areas, the organizations refused to work together to address the issue. Despite the differences in their organizing styles, both groups were committed to preventing externally driven development that might harm the interests of their members. As a result, they both opposed the TIF, and members of each group spent significant time strategizing about the best approach for preventing its creation. However, when an outsider proposed that they work together to maximize their impact, organizers from both groups summarily rejected the idea. From UNITE's perspective, JAG's small membership size and low capacity meant that the risks of cooperation outweighed any potential benefits. UNITE's organizer summed up the situation when he declared that JAG's members could participate in UNITE's protest if they wanted to, but only if they agreed not to publicly identify themselves as JAG members or let JAG take any credit for the campaign's success. Furthermore, he forbade them to use UNITE's protest as a vehicle for recruiting new members. Conversely, JAG's leaders feared that cooperation with UNITE would force them to water down their ideological agenda, thus undermining their support within the progressive community.

Clearly, community organizing's emphasis on building formal, sustainable organizations at the neighborhood level can pose obstacles for broader movement formation. Despite this reality, however, research on successful social movements of the past indicates that the existence of formal organizations is often essential for the creation of the infrastructure necessary for social-movement formation.

(a) Formal Organizations as the Infrastructure for Social Movements

Formal organizations are essential to social movement formation because they offer a ready-made infrastructure of resources, networks, and leaders. My analysis in the first part of this chapter demonstrated the importance of organizations as the building blocks for regional, national, and international networks. In addition, in the period leading up to social movement formation, organizations can serve as focal points for amassing resources, developing leaders, and building local bases for movement activity. Aldon Morris's (1997) research on the southern sit-in movement during the civil rights era, for example, demonstrates the role played by churches, youth organizations, and local civil rights groups in creating a movement out of isolated incidents of resistance:

> [P]reexisting organizations provided the sit-ins with the resources and communication networks needed for their emergence and development. . . .
> This vast internal organization consisted of local movement centers, ex-

perienced activists who had amassed organizing skills, direct-action organizations, communication systems between centers, pre-existing strategies for dealing with the opposition, workshops and training procedures,
fund-raising techniques, and community mobilization techniques. (Morris 1997: 107)

These organizations provided the infrastructure and capacity necessary for
building a powerful movement for change. In addition, the networks among
these various organizations created linkages between the initial sit-in incidents, building them into a cohesive movement that spread across the
South.

Morris' research not only demonstrates the important role of formal organizations in building the infrastructure for social movements, it also suggests
that the organizations best suited to serve this role are those with strong leaders, stable resources, and substantial internal capacity. But if, as Piven and
Cloward suggest, the drive to build strong, stable organizations forces organizers toward accommodation of the status quo, then the very techniques
that create strong organizations are also the least likely to foster a social
change ideology. What does this mean for movement building?

(b) Informal Organizations as the Ideological Foundation for Movement Formation

Research on social movements suggests that this dilemma can be resolved through a complementary division of labor between large, stable organizations that can provide the infrastructure for movement mobilization
and smaller, less stable groups operating at the margins of society. Because
these latter groups are not as vulnerable to the constraints of formal organization building, they can serve as "cultural laboratories" (Melucci 1989: 60)
for the emergence of radical ideological frameworks.

Most analyses of social movements tend to focus on the visible face of
movement activity, represented by the high-capacity organizational networks that Morris talks about. But, in the words of sociologist Alberto
Melucci, this "overlooks the fact that collective action is nourished by the
daily production of alternative frameworks of meaning, on which the networks themselves are founded and live from day to day" (Melucci 1989:
70–71). Melucci argues that this ideological component of movement formation takes place in "submerged networks" of small, informal organizations that operate at society's margins. Within these "cultural laboratories,"
new ideological and cultural frameworks are developed, and "problems and
questions are perceived and named in different ways" (Melucci 1989: 208).

These submerged networks are often invisible to observers, but they infuse civil society with new concepts and transformative frames, forming the ideological foundation for the emergence of social movements: "The basic thrust of Melucci's conception of submerged networks is the proposition that the initial challenge to the prevailing order takes place principally on symbolic grounds. That is, the status quo must be challenged at the cultural level in terms of its claims to legitimacy before mass collective action is feasible" (Mueller 1997: 160). By challenging dominant conceptual frameworks and generating an oppositional consciousness at the margins of society, these submerged networks foster the development of a widely accepted master frame, thus creating the potential for the emergence of a broader social movement.

This fusion of Melucci's theories with Morris' research on organizational development provides a useful framework for understanding the potential connection between community organizing and social movement formation. Not surprisingly, the two organizing models best suited to serve the roles that Morris and Melucci talk about are the power-based and transformative models. The power-based organizations had the strongest organizational infrastructures of all the organizations in my study, with large grassroots memberships, strong cores of skilled and experienced public leaders, and reliable sources of both internal and external funding. They were also the most stable and enduring of all the organizations in the study, each having existed for more than twenty-five years.

In contrast, the other organizations in my study all had more limited organizational infrastructures. The civic organizations had almost no organizational capacity. The women-centered organizations built participants' leadership skills and had fairly stable funding, but remained small in size and limited in scope. The community-building organizations had resources and expertise within their networks, but they were dominated almost entirely by local institutions and had no direct connection to a local base of residents.

Operating with limited resources, and frequently marginalized by mainstream institutions, the transformative organizations in my study fit closely with Melucci's depiction of "cultural laboratories." With little prospect of receiving support from mainstream funders or government, organizations like JAG are freed from some of the constraints faced by more stable organizations. And, as discussed earlier, JAG's emphasis on popular education, reflection, and analysis makes it ideally suited for generating the alternative ideology necessary for movement formation.

The notion that these two very different kinds of organizations—large, stable networks and small, marginalized, cultural laboratories—could play complementary roles in the process of movement formation helps to resolve the dilemma posed by community organizing's limitations. Even if no single approach to organizing can contribute to the formation of a broad-based social movement on its own, this does not necessarily mean that community organizing is incapable of generating long-term social structural change. My analysis suggests if we can build synergistic relationships between power-based and transformative organizations, we can create the building blocks for the development of a wider movement.

This is not to say that the other models in my study—particularly the women-centered and community-building models—aren't still important and valuable in their own right. Both women-centered and community-building organizations play an essential role in strengthening local communities, building local democracy, and combating the local symptoms of broader structural injustices. This work must be a key component of any effective strategy to create social change. Without the material benefits, collective capacity, and social stability that these local efforts provide, urban residents are unlikely to get involved in broader, extra-local struggles for change. But while these organizations thus serve an essential role at the local level, they do not provide the extra-local infrastructure and transformative frames necessary for broader social movement formation.

What does this analysis mean for the everyday work of community organizing groups? Given the philosophical and practical differences between the power-based and transformative models, is a complementary division of labor realistic? If so, what can we do to foster this broader movement potential?

COMMUNITY ORGANIZING AND SOCIAL MOVEMENTS—BUILDING THE CONNECTION

In order to capture the social movement potential of the transformative and power-based approaches, the practice of community organizing and the environment in which community organizing takes place must change. First, the funding structure for community organizing must adjust to reflect the importance not only of large, stable organizations but also of the informal cultural laboratories that provide the ideological foundation for movement building. As my research demonstrates, transformative organizations are frequently marginalized by funders and philanthropists who prefer to support organizations with short-term and measurable outcomes. But as previous chapters have shown, this lack of financial support makes it impossible for organizations like JAG and CREO to reach the vast majority of urban residents. In order to contribute to the development of an oppositional consciousness among *all* urban residents—not just progressive middle-class activists—transformative organizations must have access to more resources. This is not to say that transformative organizations need to become large, high-capacity, formal organizations. But progressive funders and communities of activists should work to foster the emergence of such organizations throughout civil society and to provide them with the resources necessary to support the long-term educational, cultural, and ideological work that is so important for social change—even if this means forgoing quantifiable, short-term victories.

Second, adherents of both the power-based and transformative models must set aside their turf wars and philosophical disagreements long enough to begin a dialogue about the potential for creating a complementary, synergistic relationship. This does not mean a *merging* of the two models. Critics and observers of community organizing frequently argue that if power-based organizing would simply become less pragmatic and more ideological, it would be able to produce long-term social change (e.g. Fisher and Kling 1990; Kennedy and Tilly 1990). I disagree. Both the transformative and power-based models have unique strengths as well as limitations, and merging them could be very problematic. The power-based organizations' pragmatism and their ability to bring people together based on subjectively defined interests are precisely what enable them to build the infrastructure essential for social-movement formation. Trying to combine the power-based approach with a more explicit ideology would undermine its ability to build large organizations with extensive extra-local networks. Conversely, if the organizations tried to do extensive popular education and consciousness building once the networks were formed, members who had joined for entirely instrumental reasons would not necessarily stay involved. Similarly, it is much easier to foster the reflection, analysis, and deliberation necessary for the development of an alternative master frame within small, marginal groups than within large, bureaucratically structured organizations.

Power-based and transformative organizations should continue to operate independently from one another, but they should find ways to coordinate their efforts, working in a complementary manner toward the formation of a broad, unified social justice movement. In order for this to happen, organizers within both traditions must acknowledge their own models' limitations as well as their unique and complementary roles. And they must begin to work together as colleagues, maintaining ongoing dialogue and communication with one another as well as an open-minded attitude toward one another's work. For example, as transformative organizations in a given locality work to introduce alternative conceptual frameworks into the public debate, the power-based organizations in that same locality should encourage discussion among their members about the concepts that emerge from this process, and the implications of these concepts for local priorities. Over time, if the transformative organizations are able to reach a critical mass of the area's residents—in the process altering their interpretations of their self-interests and the neighborhood's priorities—the decision-making within the power-based organizations will be shaped by these alternative frameworks. Ultimately, if this dynamic occurs on a large enough scale, it will result in the diffusion of a transformative frame throughout the power-based organizations' extensive networks.

Third, in order to foster the emergence of a shared master frame and collective action "program" across diverse organizations and geographic areas, we need to create spaces in which leaders from these various organizations can come together to collectively reflect on their experiences and develop a common vision. The opportunity for shared dialogue and reflection is essential if disparate groups are to move beyond a common opposition to dominant political and economic arrangements toward the creation of a shared proactive agenda and a strategic plan for achieving their goals.

One model for such a space is the Highlander Center, Myles Horton's famous "folk school" in Tennessee. Highlander helped to foster the emergence of several key twentieth-century social movements by bringing together emerging leaders from different organizations for dialogue, reflection, and program development. During the early stages of the civil rights movement, Highlander workshops brought together leaders of local organizing efforts from across the South to develop a shared vision and strategy. For example, in the early 1960s, as seemingly isolated student sit-ins began to take place in various communities, the leaders of the different student groups gathered at Highlander to figure out ways to integrate their independent actions into a broader movement. The students had embraced the sit-in idea as a way to defy unjust laws, but discussions at Highlander made it clear that they had not thought through the broader implications of their actions for movement building. "The new leaders divided into working committees to think through some of the problems and issues raised and to decide on next steps. . . . [Through this process, they] projected the broad outlines of a southern student movement which, in the years that followed, was to profoundly affect the South and the nation" (Horton 1989: 243–4).

Finally, in order to facilitate the mobilization and strategic deployment of these diverse social groups, we need to build coordinating structures that span the various networks within the social movement base. Some of the existing national organizing networks—such as the Industrial Areas Foundation and the Center for Third World Organizing—offer potential models for such a structure. These networks are national in scope, diverse in their composition, and have the capacity to coordinate the strategic planning and mobilization of thousands of residents in numerous communities. However, as they are currently structured, the networks are too insular to provide the kind of broad-based tactical coordination necessary for movement building. Because each network is associated with a very specific organizing model, its primary goal is to strengthen and diffuse its particular model. As a result, the networks are as susceptible to the dangers of formal organization building, such as turf battles and inter-network competition, as are their member organizations. As Gary Delgado, the founder of one such network, explains, "When many of us began organizing, we believed that the organizations we built would form the base for a movement. Somewhere along the line, many of us got stuck in our own brand of organizing. Instead of believing that all of our organizations might have a shot at building a movement, we began to believe that our network was the movement and that everybody else should join, die, or get out of the way" (Delgado 1998: 20).

The coordinating role that these formal networks play is essential to broader movement formation. We should try to build on their successes while working to transcend the narrow dogmatism and competition that has made their effectiveness so limited. One of the primary lessons of this book is the unique and complementary benefits that every model of community organizing brings to the table. If we are to create genuine social change, we must be able to harness and build upon all these strengths. This requires the proponents of particular models to adopt a spirit of cooperation and mutual appreciation. Community organizing can expand its scope, but only if organizing's practitioners are able to overcome their exclusivity and work together.

These proposals are not exhaustive, but they do point to some of the steps that will need to be taken to realize community organizing's broader potential. Creating these linkages will not be easy, but if organizing is to generate long-term impacts, it is absolutely essential. Given the global nature of today's urban problems, recent evidence—at the World Trade Organization protests, and elsewhere—of a growing global social justice movement is encouraging. However, in the United States, this movement has so far been dominated by middle-class, white, leftist activists (Brecher, Costello, and Smith 2000). If this movement is to develop a genuine mass base, it will need to be built upon the leadership and vision of the low-income and working-class communities of color who are most deeply affected by globalization's injustices. The creation of such a broad-based movement is possible only if we start by organizing people at a local level around the issues of immediate concern in their daily lives, using this grassroots organizing as a foundation for building the transformative vision and organizational infra-structure necessary for broader movement formation. Community organiz-ing not only provides an essential vehicle for combating the symptoms of unjust global systems, it may also offer the most realistic starting point for the formation of an inclusive movement for genuine social structural change.

PART IV

CONCLUSION

CHAPTER 9
LESSONS LEARNED

PROJECT of this scope does not lend itself well to a single summary statement or a pithy concluding argument. My intention throughout this volume has been to provide a detailed comparison of the strengths and limitations of the various models, not to uncover the "best" approach or to reveal a single, cure-all solution. Studies of organizing are frequently motivated by the search for "silver bullet" strategies that will magically solve the problems of urban neighborhoods. My research reveals no silver bullets. While some models of community organizing have greater potential than others, no single model fulfills all of organizing's ideal objectives. Instead of searching for silver bullets, my research suggests that we should focus on understanding the benefits and trade-offs of the different models. Toward that end, this chapter offers reflections on how the analysis in the preceding chapters might inform the way we approach the community organizing process—reflections that are meant to inspire further thought rather than to be a final word on the matter.

I begin with a report card on each model highlighting its unique contributions and limitations. These report cards are not intended to provide a comprehensive evaluation of each model; the summaries at the end of each chapter serve that role. Rather, my goal is to identify the distinctive community organizing "niche" that each model fills—the contributions that are unique to that particular approach, and the trade-offs that often accompany these benefits. In other words, while each model offers a wide range of important contributions, my focus here is on the specific contributions that distinguish a particular model from all the other approaches—what this model can do that no other model is capable of. The chapter concludes with a discussion of how these insights might inform the way organizing is practiced on the ground.

THE CIVIC MODEL

Distinctive Contributions

- *Easy to implement:* Of all the models in this study, civic organizations are the simplest to create and sustain. Whereas the other models require trained staff and external resources, the civic organizations typically operate as all-volunteer groups with little to no funding. In addition, the civic organizations are the most informal and unstructured of all the groups. As long as there are enough residents in the neighborhood with the basic skills necessary for keeping the organizations running, civic organizations can operate with minimal investment of time and resources.
- *Connects residents to city services:* Civic organizations link residents to the city's established mechanisms for solving local problems. They provide residents with information about how the city services system works, and they give residents an opportunity to communicate directly with the city services personnel assigned to address specific problems in their neighborhood. By giving residents clear information about city laws and ordinances and direct access to the bureaucracy, civic organizations help to democratize the provision of city services.

Trade-Offs

- *Limited capacity:* The lack of a formal organizational structure constrains the civic organizations' capacity to effectively address the community's problems. Without paid staff or formally designated leaders, the organizations must rely on the personal initiative and individual discretion of each participant in order to get anything done. Combined with the absence of effective mechanisms for internal accountability, this means the organizations are often unable to perform the necessary behind-the-scenes work to move their projects and campaigns forward. As a result, they have the poorest follow through of all the organizations in this study.
- *A forum for the middle class:* With no formal mechanisms for recruiting and training local leaders, civic organizations must rely on the participation of residents who already have leadership skills and experience. As a result, the organizations tend to be dominated by the neighborhood's most privileged residents, particularly landlords, business owners, and middle-class professionals. And because they operate as unstructured forums rather than formal governance mechanisms, the organizations don't provide a way to ensure that the interests and perspectives of all the participants are heard. Because of this dynamic, civic organizations offer

few opportunities for less experienced residents to become actively involved in community life.

- *Potentially divisive strategies:* The civic organizations' homogeneous membership composition and limited size foster an insularity and exclusivity that can undermine the collective efficacy of the community as a whole. The organizations' members don't typically reach out to other populations or social groups outside of their immediate clique, and they rarely work in cooperation with other institutions or organizations. As a result, when civic organizations define the neighborhood's problems, they tend to ignore the interests and perspectives of other social groups within the community. This dynamic can result in strategies that exacerbate social divisions within the neighborhood and limit the community's overall problem-solving capacity.

- *Perpetuates status quo:* The civic model represents an inherently conservative approach to urban problem solving. By framing the neighborhood's problems as the products of social disorder, the model promotes an emphasis on stability and control rather than proactive change. This tendency is exacerbated by the model's orientation to the public sphere. Civic organizations aim to connect residents to existing government channels for citizen input and complaints. While the organizations help residents obtain information about the city services system, they do little to increase residents' influence within the public sphere or to alter the way that government operates. Consequently, residents remain passive consumers of government services rather than active participants engaged in public priority setting.

THE POWER-BASED MODEL

Distinctive Contributions

- *Builds strong organizations:* The power-based organizations' techniques for recruitment, leadership development, and decision-making result in the development of strong, powerful organizations. By recruiting and agitating residents around their most immediate concerns, the organizations are typically able to get large numbers of residents involved in their campaigns. In addition, the use of a hierarchical organizational structure and majority voting enable the organizations to identify neighborhood priorities and develop strategic campaigns quickly and efficiently. Finally, by providing their members with extensive leadership training and logistical support, the power-based organizations create a skilled and disciplined base of leaders.

- *Impacts public decision-making:* Through a well-developed repertoire of techniques, power-based organizations are able to alter the balance of power in urban neighborhoods. By focusing on clearly defined issues and a specific target, the organizations engage large numbers of inexperienced residents in collective action within the public arena. And through the use of aggressive and confrontational tactics, the organizations effectively wield their clout, gaining influence over the public decision-making process. In this way, power-based organizations are able to secure concrete changes in public resources and priorities in order to address the community's needs.

Trade-offs

- *Lack of genuine deliberation:* The power-based organizations are able to move large numbers of residents into coordinated action through the use of a formal, hierarchical structure, majority voting, and a streamlined strategic planning process. However, their reliance on the vote to negotiate among participants' interests can undermine full inclusion of all members' voices. And the imperative to develop winnable strategies through a quick and efficient decision-making process can lead to manipulation of the members and oversimplification of the issues. In some power-based groups, the political process is framed in such a polarized and one-dimensional way that there is little possibility for engaging members in genuine deliberations over public priorities.
- No *structural change:* By strengthening residents' influence at the public bargaining table, power-based organizations are able to alter the distribution of public resources, but they have little impact on the overall structure of local government or the public sphere. In their efforts to become recognized players within the political system, power-based organizations must accept the existing framework of the political decision-making process. Furthermore, by securing concessions from within that process, they may help to reinforce its legitimacy.

THE COMMUNITY-BUILDING MODEL

Distinctive Contributions

- *Builds community's institutional capacity:* Community-building organizations expand the community's internal capacity to address its problems. By developing collaborative partnerships among the neighborhood's institutions, the organizations mobilize the community's existing resources and technical expertise in new and innovative ways. The synergistic relationships that emerge from these partnerships strengthen the community's ability to develop programs, services, and economic development strategies to meet its needs. In addition, through the creation of strong working partnerships with government and the private sector, community-building organizations leverage substantial external resources and support to assist the community in implementing its goals.

- *Comprehensive neighborhood planning:* By working to develop comprehensive plans that address the broad needs and concerns of the community as a whole, community-building organizations take into account the interconnections among the neighborhood's problems. As a result, the organizations' strategies tend to be complex and sophisticated, providing multidimensional solutions to address a broad range of problems. By providing a template for program development and service provision in the neighborhood, the comprehensive plans maximize the effectiveness of the neighborhood's institutions, and they help the community to gain greater control over public and private interventions in the neighborhood.

Trade-offs

- *Limited resident involvement:* Of all the models, the community-building model is most at risk of leaving individual residents who are not the staff and leaders of local institutions and associations out of the organizing process. The emphasis on comprehensive planning and technical expertise privileges the involvement of community-based professionals and administrators rather than the neighborhood's low-income and working-class residents. This dynamic is exacerbated by the absence of any formal mechanisms for holding the member institutions accountable to their constituents or for developing the constituents' capacity as leaders.
- *Collaboration constrains available options:* By building a shared vision among multiple stakeholders, community-building organizations expand the community's capacity to solve its problems. But the pressure to reach consensus among institutions with widely varying interests can limit the potential scope of the organizations' work. In order to get multiple stakeholders to agree on a single vision of the "common good," the vision must be rooted in conceptual categories that all the stakeholders can understand and accept. As a result, the organizations' comprehensive plans tend to be

couched within dominant political and economic paradigms—paradigms that tend to privilege certain interests over others and may not be capable of achieving the community's overall goals.

■ *Accommodation to government:* Community-building organizations require substantial external resources and support in order to implement their comprehensive plans. This creates a dependence on government funding and assistance that forces them to frame much of their work to fit within existing government priorities. As a result, while the organizations are able to shape the way government agencies operate within the community, they have little impact on the government's wider priority-setting and decision-making processes. Furthermore, the dependence on government resources makes the organizations vulnerable to manipulation and cooptation by political leaders who may not share their substantive goals.

THE WOMEN-CENTERED MODEL

Distinctive Contributions

■ *Engage the most disenfranchised:* Of all the models, the women-centered model is the most effective at engaging society's most disenfranchised members in public life. By creating a fluid connection between the personal and public spheres, women-centered organizations are able to reach residents who might otherwise never be involved in the wider community. Through mutual sharing and support, the organizations enable participants to overcome personal obstacles and build collective leadership, making it possible for them to work on broader community issues. And through team-building, leadership training, and an emphasis on the micro-processes of interaction, the organizations help participants to develop the voice and collective capacity to become effective public actors.

■ *Egalitarian and inclusive process:* The women-centered model promotes a highly democratic and inclusive process for decision-making about local priorities and goals. Through the use of formally structured methods of deliberation and a commitment to face-to-face consensus building, women-centered organizations foster genuine resident involvement in neighborhood governance. The disciplined use of methods such as go-rounds and groundrules ensures that all members have an equal voice and that all viewpoints are heard, creating decisions with high levels of legitimacy and member buy-in.

Trade-Offs

- *Limited size and scale:* The emphasis on mutual support and equal voice limits the women-centered organizations' size as well as the breadth of their networks. Efforts to expand their memberships or build wider external ties can undermine the integrity of the women-centered organizations' core teams. Because of this dynamic, women-centered organizations' projects and campaigns tend to be limited in scale and scope. The emphasis on developing hands-on initiatives that are resident-directed and controlled reinforces this tendency, resulting in projects that are valuable and rewarding for the members, but likely to be limited in their broader impact.

- *Process versus product:* The women-centered model's emphasis on internal relationship-building and inclusive decision-making can hinder the achievement of tangible action-oriented outcomes. Providing participants with personal support while helping them to discover the connection between their own problems and public issues can be an extremely time-consuming process, one that frequently slows down the organization's ability to move toward broader action. Similarly, the insistence on including all voices and reaching genuine consensus can make it difficult for women-centered organizations to move efficiently from deliberation to action. And once the organizations begin to take action in the public arena, their emphasis on building face-to-face relationships within local institutions, one person at a time, typically limits their ability to gain meaningful influence over the public decision-making process.

THE TRANSFORMATIVE MODEL

Distinctive Contributions

- *Challenges dominant ideological frameworks:* Transformative organizations work to "demystify" urban residents' perceptions of the social world. Through popular education and reflection, the organizations deconstruct dominant, taken-for-granted belief systems and introduce alternative conceptual frameworks to help residents see the connection between their own experiences and broader economic and political structures. Through this process, the organizations create the ideological foundations within the neighborhood for the emergence of a broader social justice movement.

- *Builds the foundation for social change:* In contrast to the other models in this study, transformative organizations seek to alter the structural roots of the neighborhood's problems over the long term rather than simply mitigate their short-term impacts. While creating genuine social structural change is not something that can realistically happen at a neighborhood level, the transformative organizations do have the potential to alter the structure of public decision-making about local issues—a key step in the broader social change process. By fostering alternative forums for public deliberation and debate over local issues, the organizations challenge the public sphere's traditional agenda-setting process. And by introducing new frameworks and conceptual categories into the public debate, the organizations broaden the choices and options available within the political decision-making arena.

Trade-Offs

- *Limited capacity:* Because of their emphasis on long-term social structural change, transformative organizations have difficulty raising adequate funding to staff their organizing work. With limited staff time and few resources, the organizations are unable to do the long-term popular education and leadership development necessary for engaging low-income residents in their social change agenda. In addition, the effort to recruit and organize residents around a broad agenda for structural change rather than more immediate concerns limits the number of residents who are likely to get involved. As a result, transformative organizations struggle to build enough clout locally to influence the public decision-making process.
- *Difficult to achieve concrete results:* Transformative organizations have a limited impact on the material conditions and quality of life in urban neighborhoods. Trying to achieve structural change from a local level is a difficult—if not impossible—undertaking. The magnitude of the organizations' goals, combined with their relative lack of clout, undermine the transformative organizations' ability to implement a proactive agenda. To the extent that the organizations are able to impact the neighborhood's problems in the short term, it tends to be through opposition to proposed changes in the status quo rather than through the implementation of their alternative vision for society.
- *Tension between education and action:* There is an inherent tension between the transformative model's dual commitment to popular education and public action. Genuine popular education can be an extremely slow, time-consuming process. Disenfranchised residents are fully capa-

ble of developing a complex, systemic analysis of their daily experiences, but this must happen through an organic process in which, after much discussion and reflection, participants develop their own theories and conceptual frameworks for making sense of their experiences. Organizations that try to foster a truly organic process of reflection and analysis may have difficulty moving toward action. Conversely, organizations that try to move participants quickly from analysis to action may end up relying on the leadership of experienced middle-class activists, leaving less experienced participants behind.

IMPLICATIONS FOR DEMOCRACY AND URBAN CHANGE

The report cards on the different models highlight the complexity—and the richness—of the organizing process. Each model has distinctive advantages; but the techniques that make a specific model uniquely suited for achieving certain objectives are often associated with trade-offs that limit its effectiveness in achieving other, equally important objectives. While no single model represents the "right" or the "best" approach for organizing urban neighborhoods, each plays a specific—and vital—role within the urban change process.

The analysis throughout this volume provides a range of tools for assessing the relative merits of different models and for identifying which approach is likely to be the most effective in a given situation. I will close with a brief exploration of some of the ways that practitioners might use these insights to inform their on-the-ground work. These examples are meant not as blueprints for action, but as suggestions that will hopefully generate further reflection.

Thinking Strategically About Different Models' Niches

Knowing each model's unique strengths and limitations allows us to make strategic decisions about which approach to organizing will be most effective in a given situation. The effectiveness of a particular model can vary in response to a wide variety of different factors—the distinct composition of the neighborhood's population, the specific nature of the neighborhood's problems, the political climate, and the primary focus of the organization's goals.

For example, my analysis suggests that of all the models, the civic model is uniquely suited for neighborhoods that have a predominately middle-class, homogeneous population and relatively few social problems. The model provides meaningful leadership opportunities for primarily middle-class residents with preexisting leadership skills and experience, but it does little to include low-income, disenfranchised residents in community life. Similarly, it connects residents to the city services system, but is incapable of addressing complex community issues. Thus, while the model does not offer a very effective vehicle for strengthening democracy in low-income or economically diverse neighborhoods, it could provide an easy way for residents of middle-class neighborhoods to get involved in public life, learn about city government, and solve small problems as they arise.[1]

Just as the demographic composition of a neighborhood's population can influence the effectiveness of a particular model, the specific nature of the neighborhood's problems will often determine which model will be most appropriate in a given situation. For example, both the power-based and community-building models are capable of creating concrete, visible changes in a neighborhood's material conditions and quality of life. But depending on the nature of an individual neighborhood's problems, one model will probably be more successful than the other. The power-based model works best with issues that can be effectively resolved through government interventions or public services—getting new schools built, improving local parks, and changing public policies. In contrast, community-building organizations are best able to address issues that can be solved through the development of locally based programs and services—youth centers, mentoring programs, affordable housing development, and commercial redevelopment projects.

The effectiveness of a particular model in a given situation will also be affected by the local political context. To illustrate, consider once again the example of the power-based and community-building models:[2] In situations where government officials and policymakers are genuinely interested in partnering with local neighborhoods to achieve specific goals, the community-building model provides an effective vehicle for building collaborative relationships while maintaining a reasonable amount of community control. Within such a context, community-building organizations can be an appropriate vehicle not only for developing programs and services, but also for determining the distribution of public programs and resources in the neighborhood. In contrast, in more adversarial political arenas, the power-based model may be the only realistic option for promoting the community's interests within the public sphere. In such situations, the community-building model's conciliatory approach and dependence on government resources make it extremely vulnerable to cooptation and manipulation by local power-holders.

Assessing which model will be most effective in a particular situation also depends on the organizing project's principal objectives. Promoting the community's interests and needs within the public sphere is only one potential goal of the organizing process. If instead our primary goal is to build residents' leadership skills, for example, our assessment of the relative merits of different models will be quite different. To illustrate, let's take another look at the power-based and community-building models. While community-building organizations are extremely effective at building the local community's institutional capacity to solve problems, they are not very effective at connecting these institutions to a local constituency or building a grassroots base of resident leaders. In contrast, the power-based organizations have developed highly effective mechanisms for getting local residents involved in public action and building their individual leadership skills.

Complementary Roles Among the Models

While understanding each model's distinctive niche is a useful way to think about how to approach the organizing process, in many cases no one model will be able to fulfill every objective. After all, most urban communities have a range of different kinds of residents as well as a variety of problems and issues needing to be resolved. Thus, we should also consider the potential complementarities among different organizing approaches. In complex urban environments, the coexistence of a variety of organizations representing several different models offers the potential for addressing multiple objectives and situations simultaneously. For example, since most low-income urban neighborhoods need *both* public services and community-based projects, a neighborhood that has both a power-based and community-building organization could benefit from the synergy between these approaches. The power-based organization could bring residents into the public sphere to fight for improved government services and increased public resources, while the community-building organization could create a coordinated network of institutions to implement community-based programs funded by those resources.

The notion that different models can complement each other by operating in the same neighborhood is consistent with the arguments made by political analysts who emphasize the importance of organizational "plurality". For example, based on an analysis of the organizational culture of one Texas neighborhood, Fisher and Taafe (1997) assert that in a "postmodern" society with multiple identity and interest groups, the coexistence of many different organizations in a single neighborhood promotes broader civic participation. However, while these theorists suggest that having many different organizations in one locality is beneficial, they do not go far enough in specifying how the organizations' coexistence might strengthen the neighborhood as a whole.

My research suggests that simply having a hodge-podge of different organizations in one neighborhood isn't necessarily going to strengthen overall levels of democracy and collective action. Instead, organizations espousing a variety of different approaches to organizing should create cooperative relationships with one another in order to promote specific complementary roles.[3] These relationships should be based on a careful assessment of each model's unique strengths as well as the incompatibilities between different approaches. Chapter 8's discussion of the transformative and power-based models' distinctive contributions to social movement formation illustrates the level of detailed analysis that should inform such an assessment.

The creation of complementary relationships among organizations implementing different models provides a way to maximize the models' distinctive strengths while avoiding their limitations. For example, my analysis in chapter 3 suggests that if we want to maximize the leadership skills of individual residents within a given neighborhood, we could try to harness the potential synergy between the power-based, women-centered, and transformative approaches. Because each of these approaches to leadership targets a different kind of resident and provides them with specific sets of skills, most communities could benefit from the simultaneous existence of all three approaches. The women-centered model brings socially isolated residents into public life for the first time and builds their sense of self-efficacy. The power-based model takes people who are already confident in their own leadership and makes them skilled negotiators and public speakers. Finally, the transformative model helps experienced leaders to develop the capacity to critically analyze the political arena and create a long-term vision for social change. Given that most neighborhoods have residents at various stages of development, creating complementary relationships between the three approaches would fulfill the leadership needs of a wide range of different residents at the same time.

The Potential For Integrating Models

The potential for complementarity among different models also creates the possibility for the development of hybrid organizations incorporating elements of more than one model within a single organizational structure. There is nothing new about this concept—in reality few organizations represent pure examples of any one model. However, theorists and practitioners who promote the strategic combination of different approaches within a single organization typically ignore the complexities of this process. Depicting different models as nothing more than tools in a toolkit, they suggest that organizers should freely pick and choose from among these various tools in order to create the most effective strategies. For example, Jack Rothman (1996) has created a typology of organizing approaches that distinguishes between three different "modes" of organizing along twelve different dimensions of practice, creating thirty-six different variables. He suggests that all organizations reflect a mixture of these different variables, with an almost infinite range of combinations. And he proposes that organizing practitioners should view these different variables as tools that they can choose from in order to help them best meet the demands of a given situation.

My analysis suggests that while the creation of hybrid organizations can be a valuable way to make organizing more effective, it is not as simple as choosing the right combination of tools for the job. Each of the five models has an underlying logic that ties its distinct elements together. Thus, while each model is composed of a variety of different component parts, these parts tend to have a natural affinity for one another. This unifying logic means that while some combinations of these different elements across models are possible, in most cases the elements that make up each model will appear in fairly distinct combinations. Furthermore, in some cases the logics of different models are incompatible, making integration difficult, if not impossible.

Chapter 8's examination of the transformative and power-based models demonstrates this tension between complementarity and incompatibility. My analysis of the two models suggests that both are necessary but insufficient as bases for the formation of a social movement. This means that in order to build a foundation for broader social change, both models must be present. However, attempting to merge both approaches within a single organization would probably undermine much of what each approach has to offer. While the transformative model's explicitly ideological orientation is necessary for challenging dominant social and economic arrangements, the power-based model's "nonideological" approach is precisely what enables it to build the necessary infrastructure for social movement formation. Thus, while building connections between the two models is desirable, it should happen through the formation of complementary relationships between separate, independent organizations rather than the creation of a single hybrid organization.

Even when the elements of different models are compatible enough to make a hybrid structure possible, the integration of different approaches should be handled carefully. The following example illustrates the kind of detailed analysis that is necessary when considering the creation of a hybrid structure: The women-centered and community-building models have enough affinity for one another that the two approaches could potentially be integrated into a single organization. After all, both models are based on partnerships and collaboration, and both strive for the establishment of working relationships with local government. In addition, they both focus on the creation of community-based programs and services to meet residents' needs. And while they involve different organizational structures and decision-making models, both are based on the principles of consensus and shared vision.

Given their mutual compatibility, integrating the two approaches into a single hybrid organization could help to maximize both models' strengths while neutralizing their limitations. Women-centered organizations are very effective at engaging disenfranchised residents in community life, but their ability to create concrete neighborhood change is limited by their small size and scope. Meanwhile, community-building organizations can foster large-scale changes, but offer few avenues for genuine resident participation. If a community building organization incorporated one or more women-centered organizations into its institutional membership structure this would increase the involvement of local residents in the community-building organizations' work; meanwhile, the women-centered organizations would be able to retain the integrity of their closely bonded teams while expanding their capacity to create change.

Despite their relative compatibility, however, the integration of the two approaches would not be unproblematic. The relationship would need to be carefully structured in order to ensure the integrity of the women-centered organizations' internal networks and inclusive decision-making processes in light of the community-building model's communitarian approach. And there would need to be mechanisms in place to deal with the inevitable tensions between the women-centered organizations' inclusive leadership structure and the community-building organizations' necessary reliance on leaders with technical and professional expertise.

Such complexities make it impossible for practitioners to simply pick and choose between different approaches as if they were just a bundle of tools in a toolkit. Even though it is possible—and, in many cases, desirable—for organizations to integrate various features from different models, it must be based on a thoughtful analysis of the complex ramifications of different approaches. My assessment of the ten case study organizations provides useful guidelines for informing such an analysis.

Community Organizing for a More Democratic Society

Over the past decade, the mainstream public policy discourse in the United States has been shaped by widespread concern over the future of American democracy. Warning of a steady decline in citizen participation over the past half century, political analysts have called for a reinvigoration of popular participation in civic life. This book offers insights about the important role that community organizing can play in achieving this goal. In cities across the country, hundreds of organizations like the ones featured in this book are successfully engaging urban residents in public life. Their efforts challenge the prevailing wisdom about American apathy and declining rates of civic involvement, showing that with the right strategies, even the most disenfranchised residents can become active participants in the public decisions that shape their lives.

The book's examination of the community organizing process also challenges the notion that participatory democracy and collective action are naturally emerging phenomena. If we are truly interested in creating a more democratic society, we must build residents' skills as public actors, develop their capacity to engage in collective action, create democratic decision-making structures for identifying community needs and priorities, and develop strategic action campaigns to solve community problems. In the search for effective strategies and techniques for achieving these goals, every model profiled in this book has something valuable to offer.

NOTES

CHAPTER 1

1. For logistical reasons, participant observation in one of the Portland organizations (Central Orland Organizing Partnership) was concentrated into a three-month period, followed by periodic updates for twelve months afterwards. Fieldwork in the other Portland organization (Templeton Leadership Circle) was conducted over a two year period from 1993 to 1995, with interviews conducted in 1998 and periodic updates through 1999.

CHAPTER 2

1. Research on the history of community organizing (Fisher 1994) demonstrates that the frequency with which particular approaches to organizing have appeared in given eras has varied in relation to the national political and economic climate of the time. My experience in looking for case studies for each of the models suggests that the frequency and popularity of a given model also vary considerably in relation to the local political and economic climate of a particular city. It is not surprising, then, given the gritty, confrontational nature of contemporary Chicago politics, that Chicago's community organizing arena includes relatively few examples of the women-centered and community-building models, both of which are consensus-oriented approaches. Conversely, it is not surprising that in Portland, a city known for its open and progressive political culture, examples of both these models abound.

   Despite these variations, the use of an ideal type analysis makes my findings relevant to organizations in any city, regardless of the specific political or economic climate. While each organizing model will be present at different rates in different cities, the basic principles and features of each model remain the same, independent of the external context. By isolating and evaluating the core logics of each model, I provide an analytical tool that can be used to understand the internal dynamics of any organization that adopts a particular model, regardless of its external context. In addition, the ideal type analysis offers an explanatory framework for understanding why a given model is more likely to be present in certain economic or political contexts than others. And it provides the analytical tools for assessing which approach is likely to be most effective and appropriate within a given context.

2. For other studies and discussions of the power-based model, see Alinsky 1946, 1971; Boyte 1990; Boyte and Reissman 1986; Boyte, Booth and Max 1986; Delgado 1986; Fisher 1994; Knoepfle 1989; Lancourt 1979; Marquez 1990; Robinson and Hanna 1994a, 1994b; Rooney 1995; Slayton 1986; Stein 1986; Warren 2000.

3. Despite its connections to Alinsky, the Industrial Areas Foundation no longer represents a "pure" reflection of the power-based model. Much of the IAF's work is now regional in scope rather than neighborhood-based, and it is more nuanced than the straightforward power-based approach utilized by organizations like WON. As a neighborhood-based institutional membership organization, UNITE's approach is reflective of earlier IAF efforts, but it also incorporates some of the newer directions in the IAF's work. The differences between UNITE's approach and the more traditional power-based approach used by groups like WON will be examined, primarily through footnotes, throughout the book.

4. For other studies and discussions of the community-building model, see Eichler 1995; Eisen 1994; Halpern 1995; Kretzmann and McKnight 1984, 1993; Kubisch 1996; Lenz 1988; Medoff and Sklar 1994; Pitcoff 1997, 1998; Shabecoff and Brophy 1996; Spiegel 1981; Stoecker 1994, 1997.

5. The Empowerment Zone program provides funding and investment incentives to selected neighborhoods for a ten-year period. In order to apply, neighborhoods must develop a comprehensive plan that includes the input of multiple stakeholder groups.

6. Throughout the book, I will occasionally use quotes from written documents produced by the case-study organizations — organizational newsletters, unpublished reports, internal memos, and planning documents. In order to protect the case-study organizations' anonymity, I will not provide full citations for these sources. However, I will indicate the kind of document the quote came from. Any quotes that are not attributed to the organization's written documents come from my own original interview and fieldnote data.

7. For other studies and discussions of the civic model, see Berry, Portney, and Thomson 1993; Darian-Smith 1993; Fisher 1994; Hunter 1995; Plotkin 1990; Rabrenovic 1996; Sampson 1995; Wilson and Kelling 1989.

8. For other studies and discussions of the women-centered model, see Belenky, Bond, and Weinstock 1997; Collins 1990; Ferree and Martin 1995; Gutierrez and Lewis 1994; Naples 1998; O'Donnell and Scheie 1999; Stoecker and Stall 1998; Stout 1996.

9. The structure and focus of TLC's work have changed since my research for this study was completed. For the sake of consistency, I will nonetheless use the present tense when describing TLC's work.

10. For other studies and discussions of the transformative model, see Anner 1996; Brill 1971; Delgado 1998; Fisher 1994; Fisher and Kling 1990; Freire 1970, 1985; Gaventa 1980; Horton 1989; Horton 1998; Horton and Freire 1990; Keleher 1997; Kennedy and Tilly 1990; Posner and Kling 1990; Stoecker 1994.

11. Delgado's imagery in this quote is a direct response to the power-based model's proponents, who frequently refer to their approach as "bringing the community to the political negotiating table in order to win their fair share of the pie." In contrast, Delgado argues that we need to challenge the broader political, economic, and social context within which the political negotiating table is embedded.

12. The word "creo" means "I think" or "I believe" in Spanish.

13. Because of this dynamic, my analysis of the transformative model in the chapters that focus on community action and neighborhood change will focus primarily on JAG. However, I will refer to CREO's experiences at various points throughout the book to illustrate the challenges transformative organizations face in combining popular education and action.

CHAPTER 3

1. Belenky, Bond, and Weinstock 1997; Collins 1990; Gutierrez and Lewis 1994; O'Donnell and Scheie 1999; Stoecker and Stall 1998.

2. Logan and Molotch argue that the urban landscape is the product of ongoing struggles between residents—who generally value urban neighborhoods for their "use value," and powerful coalitions of developers, realtors, corporations, government, and other institutional actors—all of whom value urban neighborhoods for their "exchange value."

3. This is particularly the case for organizations like JAG that recruit participants based simply on their common residence in a given neighborhood. Transformative organizations in the United States that recruit participants based on their common position in the economy (e.g. farmworkers, factory workers, etc.) tend to be far more successful at using Freire's popular education methods with their low-income constituents.

4. Most community organizers believe that flyers are almost completely ineffective as a recruitment mechanism. While flyers can help to notify previous participants of an upcoming meeting or event, they are rarely sufficient for getting new members involved. Organizers affiliated with a wide range of different models agree that one-on-one outreach is the only effective way to recruit new participants, particularly low-income and working-class residents.

5. While an emphasis on the leadership of professional staff is most likely to be associated with institutional membership organizations, this does not mean that all such organizations take this kind of leadership approach. UNITE, which is a power-based organization, has an institutional membership structure, but UNITE's organizers work to recruit and train its member institutions' individual constituents to take on leadership roles within the larger organization. In contrast, while both PACT and CO-OP expressed an interest in involving more individual non-staff residents in their work, neither organization did any explicit work to actively involve or develop the leadership of individual constituents.

6. While the transformative organizations in my study had difficulty developing the leadership of low-income, politically inexperienced residents, my analysis

demonstrates the potential for this model to expand the critical thinking skills of residents of all socioeconomic backgrounds.

CHAPTER 4

1. See Granovetter 1973: 1378.
2. There were exceptions to this pattern, but they stemmed more from the cohesiveness of Port Angeles' Latino community than from PACT's network-building work. For example, some of PACT's participants had known each other as high school students or attended the same church, so their relationships tended to be more intimate than the rest of the network's members.
3. Over the past decade, groups affiliated with the Industrial Areas Foundation (IAF), including UNITE, have started to incorporate a more conscious commitment to informal relationship-building and the development of a shared value base among members as a key part of their work. Consequently, while WON's networks are based entirely on instrumental ties, UNITE's networks are more nuanced and complex. This shift within the IAF's work has moved it away from a pure reflection of the power-based approach to incorporate elements from the community-building model.
4. This dynamic is less of a problem with UNITE because of its institutional membership base. With institution-based organizations like UNITE, even though the institutional members join the organization for instrumental reasons, the individual participants tend to be connected to their own institutions through normative ties. For example, many of UNITE's individual participants are the professional staff of social service agencies who are committed to their agencies through normative ties (and, of course, through the instrumental commitment to getting a paycheck). This dynamic increases the stability of UNITE's membership base. As long as the member institutions stay involved with the organization, the individual participants will usually remain committed, even if they do not personally experience ongoing benefits. And even if the individual staff or members of the institutions leave, they are likely to be replaced by other individuals within the organizations.
5. In contrast to the community-building organizations, even though UNITE's membership base is composed of institutions, its networks connect both institutions and residents. UNITE's organizers help the institutions to build direct relationships with their clients, their constituents, or their parishioners and then get them involved with the broader network. As a result, UNITE's grassroots network is even larger than WON's.
6. At a time when, for other reasons, WON did not have enough paid organizers on staff to do the constant recruitment and leadership development necessary for the networks to remain large, its base shrunk to a fraction of its previous size. Once the organization's funding and staffing base stabilized, its numbers gradually returned to previous levels.

CHAPTER 5

1. All the vignettes in this chapter are authentic descriptions of the case study organizations' meetings and are reported as accurately as possible. In a few cases, the vignette is actually a composite of two meetings held on separate occasions, but with the same participants. In some cases, in an effort to shorten the narrative, I have left out some components of the meeting's agenda.

2. While the highly structured decision-making process used by UNITE's Action Council is reflective of most power-based organizations' governance structures, decision-making wasn't quite this formalized at all levels of the power-based organizations' work. In small committees and informal planning meetings, decisions often emerged from a more casual process of discussion and dialogue among the members. However, even in these more informal settings, if conflicts or disagreements arose, the organizations typically resorted to voting in order to resolve the conflict quickly and efficiently.

3. However, UNITE did occasionally hold meetings with participants who were less experienced than UNITE's core members, and at these meetings UNITE's organizer utilized a discussion and decision-making process very similar to WON's standard approach.

4. In the late 1990s, Chicago was embroiled in heated debate over an "anti-loitering law" that had enabled police to arrest anyone who did not disperse from public streets and sidewalks upon police request. The law was eventually declared unconstitutional, and at the time of this CAPS meeting that ruling was in the process of being appealed. CAPS participants frequently blamed the groups that fought the law for causing the city's safety problems.

5. Of course, the determination of which topics are uncontroversial is not neutral in itself, and is likely to reflect a group's unstated biases. Because CAN and CAPS members were predominately middle-class property owners, certain topics and opinions that would have been controversial in other settings were viewed as neutral and acceptable by the organizations' members. For example, during CAN's meetings, the neighborhood's landlords and realtors frequently talked in celebratory tones about the area's rising property values and the conversion of rental buildings to luxury condominiums. Their comments were presented as objective statements about neighborhood improvement and were never censored or rebuked. In contrast, among the neighborhood's eighty-five percent renter population, these statements would have been viewed as controversial and even inflammatory.

6. Empowerment Zones are a federally funded economic development program. PACT unsuccessfully applied for Empowerment Zone designation twice.

7. Redevelopment Areas are one of the City of Chicago's economic development programs. Redevelopment Area designation can be used to achieve some of the same goals as an Empowerment Zone, but with much less funding and fewer tools. For more information about PACT's Empowerment Zone and Redevelopment Area strategies, see chapter 7.

8. The Federal Department of Housing and Urban Development, which sponsors the Empowerment Zone program.

9. CO-OP, my second case study of the community building model, tried to use a highly participatory, individualistic mode of face-to-face decision-making in which the goal was to achieve shared agreements through extensive discussion and sharing of views. With a diverse membership of several dozen organizations, CO-OP's meetings tended to be extremely long and tense, and rarely resulted in agreement. The comparison of CO-OP and PACT's experiences suggests that a less individualistic approach to decision-making, such as PACT's, is essential in order to make this model of governance work.

10. Tax Increment Financing (TIF) is a popular urban development tool that shifts a portion of property tax revenues in designated areas away from traditional taxing bodies in order to fund private commercial and residential development. In Chicago, when an area is designated as a Tax Increment Financing district, the amount of property tax revenue going to the traditional taxing bodies is "frozen" for a period of up to 23 years; during this time period, all tax revenues generated above this frozen base (the "tax increment") are used to fund development projects. In Chicago, many grassroots organizations that are concerned about gentrification have vigorously fought TIF proposals for their neighborhoods.

11. See, e.g., Lukes 1974; Bourdieu 1972.

CHAPTER 6

1. This assumption is implicit in almost all of the contemporary discussions by academics and policy-makers about the importance of social capital and collective efficacy in urban neighborhoods.

2. Institutional membership organizations like UNITE tend to use less aggressive tactics than individual membership organizations like WON. WON's director described the contrast as the difference between guerilla tactics and a standing army. Whereas WON's individual members have no preexisting basis of authority within the political system, and thus have nothing to lose, UNITE's institutional members already have a certain amount of legitimacy that they can leverage, and they usually can't afford to completely alienate themselves from public officials. Thus, groups like UNITE tend to use tactics like public hearings and rallies to demonstrate their numbers and gain media attention.

CHAPTER 7

1. The campaigns depicted in this chapter were selected because they offer good illustrations of each model's distinctive approach to urban change. Each campaign represents a typical example of the case study organizations' day-to-day work. The campaigns chosen to represent different models are not always equivalent in terms of timeline or scope, primarily because some organizations work on discrete, self-contained campaigns, while others work on broader, long-

term initiatives that can not be broken down into individual campaigns. Consequently, the difference in scope between the five examples should not be interpreted as an indication of the organizations' overall levels of activity. For example, even though the power-based campaign depicted in the chapter is relatively small in scope, WON was engaged in more than a dozen campaigns of this size and scale within a single year. In contrast, the campaign used to exemplify the community-building model was the entire focus of PACT's work for a whole year.

2. This dynamic was also linked to the homogeneity and insularity of the civic organizations' bonding networks, as discussed in chapter 4.

3. On the whole, UNITE's institutional membership base enabled it to take on a much wider range of issues than WON. Even though UNITE used the same basic methods as WON for identifying issues and campaigns, its members defined their self-interests based on the mission and values of their institutions rather than their own individual interests as residents. On the whole, the interests of institutions will tend to be more broadly defined than the interests of individuals. In addition, because most of UNITE's members were nonprofit social service or mutual aid agencies and progressive church congregations, they often defined their self-interests in terms of broad policy-oriented issues related to their members' and constituents' needs.

4. Because many of UNITE's institutional members interacted with government agencies and bureaucrats on a professional basis, they took a more nuanced approach to their interactions with government, thereby avoiding some of these pitfalls. Instead of viewing officials as evil or greedy, most of UNITE's members recognized that government officials and agencies face competing pressures from different constituencies and that many policy outcomes stem from these political complexities. As a result, UNITE typically waited to be confrontational with powerholders until it had tried to establish relationships with the relevant government players in order to understand the complexities of the situation and the range of competing demands powerholders were dealing with.

5. "Hancock Park" was one of the first neighborhoods in Chicago to be transformed through gentrification. The upscaling of the neighborhood displaced many existing residents—particularly people of color—and transformed a working-class neighborhood into a middle- and upper-middle class enclave. Residents of the city frequently refer to Hancock Park as a symbol of gentrification.

6. This was PACT's second Empowerment Zone application. The first, four years earlier, was what initially brought the group together, as discussed in chapter 2.

7. A year after the Redevelopment Area project began, PACT's leaders explored the possibility of using a land trust model to protect some of the area's housing from the impact of market forces. A land trust removes land from the private market, preserving the affordability of the housing on that land. In a rapidly gentrifying market, this strategy can protect specific parcels of land from price inflation, but it can't halt the overall gentrification process.

8. This quote is from a story in PILOT's quarterly newsletter.

9. This quote is from a story in PILOT's quarterly newsletter.
10. The terms "Low-Road" and "High-Road" development were first introduced by Bluestone and Harrison (1982). JAG's members were introduced to these terms by members of a citywide labor organization whose director was familiar with Bluestone and Harrison's work.

CHAPTER 8

1. While JAG's approach has the greatest potential for fostering an alternative ideology, my analysis in chapter 3 indicates that the specific methods that the organization has used to transfer this ideology to its constituents have had a limited impact. In order to lay the groundwork for a broad-based social movement, an organization like JAG would need to more effectively foster the development of a critical consciousness among the majority of its constituents, not just experienced middle-class activists. The theories of Freire (1970) and Horton (1998) suggest that this requires a long-term, intensive process of popular education, utilizing structured facilitation and reflection to develop participants' critical consciousness. While JAG recognized the value of such a process, its lack of resources and capacity coupled with the inherently challenging nature of such work forced it to rely on a much more streamlined, superficial process of consciousness-raising and education. The conclusion to this chapter offers guidelines for what it would take for organizations like JAG to be able to do the kind of long-term, extensive popular education necessary for effectively building a mass movement.

CHAPTER 9

1. This finding calls into question much of the recent scholarship on participatory democracy. Emphasizing the importance of voluntary associations for fostering a robust civic life, authors like Putnam (2000) and Etzioni (1993) advocate the creation of organizations that fit my characterization of the civic model—small, informal, all-volunteer organizations that connect residents to official government channels. As politicians and civic leaders increasingly turn to these analysts for guidance in solving America's problems, their attention has focused on the civic approach, to the exclusion of other models. But while such organizations may help to rejuvenate participatory democracy in middle-class neighborhoods, my research suggests that they will do little to bring America's most disenfranchised residents into public life.
2. The concept of "model niche" applies to multiple dimensions of the organizing process and to all of the models. I could have provided a multitude of other examples to illustrate these same points. My emphasis on the power-based and community-building models here is meant for illustration purposes only.
3. In order for these potential complementarities to be realized, organizers themselves—and the networks and training centers that support them—will need to

begin thinking differently about their work. Narrow dogmatism and ongoing turf battles among proponents and practitioners of different models make it virtually impossible to capture the synergy among different approaches. Rather than working to make the practice of organizing as effective as possible, most organizing networks focus instead on the expansion and replication of a particular model. The ongoing competition among different organizations and networks has created hostility, in-fighting, and distrust that limit the broader impact of their work.

BIBLIOGRAPHY

Alinsky, Saul. 1946. *Reveille for radicals*. New York: Vintage Books.
——. 1971. *Rules for radicals*. New York: Random House.
Allison, Graham. 1971. *Essence of decision: Explaining the Cuban missile crisis*. New York: Harper Collins Publishers.
American Civic Forum. 1994. *Civic declaration: A call for a new citizenship*. Dayton, OH: Kettering Foundation.
Anderson, Elijah. 1990. *Streetwise: Race, class and change in an urban community*. Chicago: University of Chicago Press.
Anner, John. 1996. *Beyond identity politics: Emerging social justice movements in communities of color*. Boston: South End Press.
Arblaster, Anthony. 1987. *Democracy*. Minneapolis: University of Minnesota Press.
Arnold, Rick, Bev Burke, Carl James, D'Arcy Martin, Barb Thomas. 1991. *Educating for a change*. Canada: Doris Marshall Institute for Education and Action.
Bachrach, Peter, and Morton Baratz. 1962. The two faces of power. *American Political Science Review* 56: 947–52.
Baladad, R.B. 1996. These beats are made for walking: Organizing a neighborhood walk. *Neighborhoods* 2, no. 3: 6–7.
Baum, Howard. 1997. *The organization of hope: Communities planning themselves*. Albany: State University of New York Press.
Bayley, David. 1988. Community policing: A report from the devil's advocate. In Jack Green and Stephen Mastrofski, eds., *Community policing: Rhetoric or reality*, 225–36. New York: Praeger.
Belenky, Mary Field, Lynne Bond, and Jacqueline Weinstock. 1997. *A tradition that has no name: Nurturing the development of people, families, and communities*. New York: Basic Books.
Bellah, Robert, Richard Madsen, William Sullivan, Ann Swidler, and Steven Tripton. 1985. *Habits of the heart: Individualism and commitment in American life*. Berkeley: University of California Press.
Berry, Jeffrey, Kent Portney and Ken Thomson. 1993. *The rebirth of urban democracy*. Washington D.C.: The Brookings Institution.
Blank, Rebecca. 1996. *It takes a nation*. Princeton: Princeton University Press.
Bluestone, Barry and Bennett Harrison. 1982. *The deindustrialization of America: Plant closings, community abandonment, and the dismantling of basic industry*. New York: Basic Books.

Boggs, Carl. 1986. *Social movements and political power: Emerging forms of radicalism in the West*. Philadelphia: Temple University Press.

Bookman, Ann and Sandra Morgen. 1988. *Women and the politics of empowerment*. Philadelphia: Temple University Press.

Borgos, Seth and Scott Douglas. 1996. Community organizing and civic renewal: A view from the South. *Social Policy*. 27(2): 18–29.

Bourdieu, Pierre. 1972. *Outline of a theory of practice*. London: Cambridge University Press.

Boyte, Harry. 1990. The growth of citizen politics: Stages in local community organizing. *Dissent* (Fall): 513–18.

Boyte, Harry and Frank Riessman, eds. 1986. *The new populism: The politics of empowerment*. Philadelphia: Temple University Press.

Boyte, Harry, Heather Booth, and Steve Max. 1986. *Citizen action and the new American populism*. Philadelphia: Temple University Press.

Boyte, Harry and Sara Evans. 1986. *Free spaces: The sources of democratic change in America*. Chicago: University of Chicago Press.

Brecher, Jeremy and Tim Costello. 1994. *Global village or global pillage: Economic reconstruction from the bottom up*. Boston: South End Press.

Brecher, Jeremy, Tim Costello, and Brendan Smith. 2000. *Globalization from below: The power of solidarity*. Boston: South End Press.

Brill, Harry. 1971. *Why organizers fail: The story of a rent strike*. Berkeley: University of California Press.

Buerger, Michael. 1994. A tale of two targets: Limitations of community anticrime actions. *Crime and Delinquency* 40, no. 3: 411–36.

Burawoy, Michael. 1979. *Manufacturing consent: Changes in the labor process under monopoly capitalism*. Chicago: University of Chicago Press.

Calpotura, Francis and Kim Fellner. n.d. Square pegs find their groove: Reshaping the organizing circle. Oakland, California: Center for Third World Organizing.

Castells, Manuel. 1983. *The city and the grassroots*. Berkeley: University of California Press.

Checkoway, Barry. 1985. Neighborhood planning organizations: Perspectives and choices. *Journal of Applied Behavioral Science* 21, no. 4: 471–86.

Chicago Community Policing Evaluation Consortium. 1999. *Community policing in Chicago, years five and six: An interim report*. Chicago: Illinois Criminal Justice Information Authority.

Collins, Patricia Hill. 1990. *Black feminist thought: Knowledge, consciousness, and the politics of empowerment*. New York: Routledge.

Connell, James, Anne Kubisch, Lisbeth Schorr, and Carol Weiss, eds. 1995. *New approaches to evaluating community initiatives: Concepts, methods, and contexts*. Washington, DC: Aspen Institute.

Consensus Organizing Institute. 1996. Program overview. Boston: Consensus Organizing Institute.

Coser, Lewis. 1956. *The functions of social conflict*. New York: The Free Press.

Couto, Richard. 1999. *Making democracy work better: Mediating structures, social capital, and the democratic prospect*. Chapel Hill: University of North Carolina Press.

Cox, Kevin. 1981. Capitalism and conflict around the communal living space. In Michael Dear and Allen Scott, eds. *Urbanization and urban planning in capitalist society*, 431–56. New York: Metheun.

Crowe, Larry. 1999. Facing violent crime: Boston's success has its roots in community organizing. *Neighborhoods* 5, no. 1: 7–11.

Dahl, Robert. 1961. *Who governs? Democracy and power in an American city*. New Haven: Yale University Press.

Darian-Smith, Eve. 1993. Neighborhood watch—who watches whom? Reinterpreting the concept of neighborhood. *Human Organization* 52, no. 1: 83–88.

Davis, John Emmeus. 1991. *Contested ground: Collective action and the urban neighborhood*. Ithaca, NY: Cornell University Press.

Delgado, Gary. 1986. *Organizing the movement: The roots and growth of ACORN*. Philadelphia: Temple University Press.

———. 1994. *Beyond the politics of place: New directions in community organizing in the 1990s*. Oakland: Applied Research Center.

———. 1998. The last stop sign. *Shelterforce* (Nov./ Dec.): 18–20.

Dieter, Rich. 1976. Introduction. In *A challenge for change: Selected essays on community organizing, leadership development, and citizen participation*, Shel Trapp. Chicago: National Training and Information Center.

Eichler, Michael. 1995. Consensus organizing: Sharing power to gain power. *National Civic Review* (Summer/Fall): 256–61.

Eisen, Arlene. 1994. Survey of neighborhood-based, comprehensive community empowerment initiatives. *Health Education Quarterly* 21, no. 2: 235–52.

Eliasoph, Nina. 1998. *Avoiding politics: How Americans produce apathy in everyday life*. United Kingdom: Cambridge University Press.

Etzioni, Amitai. 1993. *The spirit of community*. New York: Simon and Schuster.

Fainstein, Susan. 1987. Local mobilization and economic discontent. In Michael Smith and Joe Feagin, eds., *The capitalist city: Global restructuring and community politics*, 323–42. Oxford: Basil Blackwell.

Ferree, Myra Marx and Patricia Yancey Martin, eds. 1995. *Feminist organizations: Harvest of the new women's movement*. Philadelphia: Temple University Press.

Ferman, Barbara. 1996. *Challenging the growth machine: Neighborhood politics in Chicago and Pittsburgh*. Lawrence, KS: University Press of Kansas.

Fisher, Robert. 1994. *Let the people decide: Neighborhood organizing in America*. New York: Twayne Publishers.

Fisher, Robert and Joseph Kling. 1990. Leading the people: Two approaches to the role of ideology in community organizing. In Prudence Posner and Joseph Kling, eds., *Dilemmas of Activism*, 71–89. Philadelphia: Temple University Press.

Fisher, Robert and Lisa Taaffe. 1997. Public life in Gulfton: Multiple publics and models of community organization. *Journal of Community Practice* 4, no. 1: 31–56.

Fisher, Robert and Eric Shragge. 2000. Challenging community organizing: Facing the 21st century. *Journal of Community Practice* 8, no.3: 1–19.

Fraser, Nancy. 1992. Rethinking the public sphere: A contribution to the critique of actually existing democracy. In Craig Calhoun, ed., *Habermas and the public sphere*, 109–42. Cambridge: MIT Press.

Freeman, Jo. 1973. The tyranny of structurelessness. *Berkeley Journal of Sociology* 7: 151–64.

Freire, Paulo. 1970. *Pedagogy of the oppressed.* New York: Herder and Herder.

———. 1985. *The politics of education: Culture, power and liberation.* New York: Bergin and Garvey.

Friedman, Warren. 1996a. Building on the progress: Reason for hope/ Room for doubt: The community role in community policing. Chicago: Chicago Alliance for Neighborhood Safety.

———. 1996b. Clinton and community policing. *Neighborhoods* 2, no. 3: 2.

Gans, Herbert. 1962. *The urban villagers: Group and class in the life of Italian-Americans.* New York: Free Press.

Gaventa, John. 1980. *Power and powerlessness: Quiescence and rebellion in an Appalachian valley.* Chicago: University of Illinois Press.

Goetz, Edward and Mara Sidney. 1994. Revenge of the property owners: Community development and the politics of property. *Journal of Urban Affairs* 16, no. 4: 319–34.

Gould, Kenneth, Allan Schnaiberg, and Adam Weinberg. 1996. *Local environmental struggles: Citizen activism in the treadmill of production.* New York: Cambridge University Press.

Granovetter, Mark. 1973. The strength of weak ties. *American Journal of Sociology* 78, no. 6: 1360–80.

Gutierrez, Lorraine, and Edith Lewis. 1994. Community organizing with women of color: A feminist approach. *Journal of Community Practice* 1, no. 2: 23–44.

Habermas, Jurgen. 1962. *The structural transformation of the public sphere: An inquiry into a category of bourgeois society.* Cambridge: MIT Press.

Hallman, Howard. 1984. *Neighborhoods: Their place in urban life.* Beverly Hills, California: Sage Publications.

Halpern, Robert. 1995. *Rebuilding the inner city: A history of neighborhood initiatives to address poverty in the United States.* New York: Columbia University Press.

Handler, Joel. 1992. Postmodernism, protest, and the new social movements. *Law and Society Review* 26, no. 4: 697–731.

Harvey, David. 1973. *Social justice and the city.* Baltimore: John Hopkins University Press.

———. 1976. Labor, capital, and class struggle around the built environment in advanced capitalist societies. *Politics and Society* 6, no. 3: 265–95.

Horton, Aimee Isgrig. 1989. *The Highlander Folk School: A history of its major programs, 1932–1961.* Brooklyn, NY: Carlson Publishing Co.

Horton, Myles (with Judith Kohl and Herbert Kohl). 1998. *The long haul: An autobiography.* New York: Teachers College Press.

Horton, Myles and Paulo Freire. 1990. *We make the road by walking: Conversations on education and social change.* Philadelphia: Temple University Press.

Hunter, Albert. 1991. *National neighborhoods: Communal class politics and the rise of the national neighborhood movement.* New Haven: Program on Non-Profit Organizations, Institution for Social and Policy Studies, Yale University. PONPO Working Paper 164; ISPS Working Paper 2164.

———. 1995. Private, parochial, and public social orders: The problem of crime and incivility in urban communities. In Phillip Kasinitz, ed., *Metropolis: Center and symbol of our times*, New York: New York University Press.

Hunter, Albert and Suzanne Staggenborg. 1988. Local communities and organized action. In Carl Milofsky, ed., *Community organizations: Studies in resource mobilization and exchange*, 243–76. New York: Oxford University Press.

Hyde, Cheryl. 1986. Experiences of women activists: Implications for community organizing theory and practice. *Journal of Sociology and Social Welfare* 13, no. 3: 545–62.

Jacobs, Jane. 1961. *The death and life of great American cities*. New York: Random House.

Jenkins, Craig. 1983. Resource mobilization theory and the study of social movements. *Annual Review of Sociology* 9: 527–53.

Joravsky, Ben. 1989. Alinsky's legacy. In Peg Knoepfle, ed., *After Alinsky: Community organizing in Illinois*, 1–10. Springfield, IL: Sangamon State University.

Judd, Dennis, and Paul Kantor. 1992. The evolution of regimes in American cities, 1789-1933. In Dennis Judd and Paul Kantor, eds., *Enduring tensions in urban politics*, 66–77. New York: Macmillian Publishing Company.

Kanter, Rosabeth Moss. 1972. *Commitment and community: Communes and utopias in sociological perspective*. Cambridge: Harvard University Press.

Katznelson, Ira. 1981. *City trenches: Urban politics and the patterning of class in the United States*. Chicago: University of Chicago Press.

Keleher, Terry. 1997. *Justice by the people*. Berkeley, CA: Chardon Press.

Kennedy, Marie, and Chris Tilly. 1990. Transformative populism and the development of a community of color. In Prudence Posner and Joseph Kling, eds., *Dilemmas of Activism*, 302–24. Philadelphia: Temple University Press.

Klandermans, Bert. 1992. The social construction of protest and multiorganizational fields. In Aldon Morris and Carol Mueller, eds., *Frontiers in social movement theory*, 77–103. New Haven: Yale University Press.

Klockars, Carl. 1988. The rhetoric of community policing. In Jack Green and Stephen Mastrofski, eds., *Community policing: Rhetoric or reality*, 239–58. New York: Praeger.

Knopefle, Peg. 1989. *After Alinsky: Community organizing in Illinois*. Springfield, IL: Sangamon State University.

Kretzmann, John and John McKnight. 1984. Community organizing in the 80s: Toward a post-Alinsky agenda. *Social Policy* (Winter): 15–17.

———. 1993. *Building communities from the inside out*. Chicago: ACTA Publications.

Kubisch, Anne. 1996. Comprehensive community initiatives: Lessons in neighborhood transformation. *Shelterforce* (Jan./Feb.): 8–18.

Lancourt, Joan. 1979. *Confront or concede: The Alinsky citizen-action organizations*. Lexington, MA: Lexington Books.

Laska, Shirley and Daphne Spain, eds. 1980. *Back to the city: Issues in neighborhood revitalization*. New York: Pergamon Press.

Lawler, Edward and Jeongkoo Yoon. 1996. Commitment in exchange relations: Test of a theory of relational cohesion. *American Sociological Review* 61: 89–109.

Lenz, Thomas. 1988. Neighborhood development: Issues and models. *Social Policy* (Spring): 24–30.

Lichterman, Paul. 1995. Piecing together multicultural community: Cultural differences in community building among grass-roots environmentalists. *Social Problems* 42, no. 4: 513–34.

———. 1996. *The search for political community: American activists reinventing commitment.* New York: Cambridge University Press.

Logan, John and Harvey Molotch. 1987. *Urban fortunes: The political economy of place.* Berkeley: University of California Press.

Lukes, Steven. 1974. *Power: A radical view.* Oxford: Macmillian Press.

Lurie, Bea. 1997. Restoring order: Community residents lead the way to safer neighborhoods. *Shelterforce* (March/April): 12–14.

Lynes, David. 1996. Cultural diversity and social order: Rethinking the role of community policing. *Journal of Criminal Justice.* 24, no. 6: 491–502.

Lyons, William. 1997. Reflections on power relations in community policing. *Studies in Law, Politics, and Society* 16: 103–38.

Mansbridge, Jane. 1973. Time, emotion, and inequality: Three problems of participatory groups. *Journal of Applied Behavioral Science* 9, no. 2/ 3: 351–69.

———. 1983. *Beyond adversary democracy.* Chicago: University of Chicago Press.

Marquez, Benjamin. 1990. Organizing the Mexican-American community in Texas: the legacy of Saul Alinsky. *Policy Studies Review* 9, no. 2: 355–73.

McCarthy, John and Mayer Zald. 1987. Resource mobilization and social movements: A partial theory. In Mayer Zald and John McCarthy, eds., *Social movements in an organizational society,* 15–41. New Brunswick, NJ: Transaction Books.

McClory, Robert. 1999. Reviving the energy for action and justice. *National Catholic Reporter,* 15 January.

McGahey, Richard. 1986. Economic conditions, neighborhood organization, and urban crime. In Albert Reiss and Michael Tonry, eds., *Communities and crime,* 231–70. Chicago: University of Chicago Press.

Medoff, Peter and Holly Sklar. 1994. *Streets of hope: The fall and rise of an urban neighborhood.* Boston: South End Press.

Melucci, Alberto. 1989. *Nomads of the present: Social movements and individual needs in contemporary society.* Philadelphia: Temple University Press.

Michels, Robert. 1968. *Political parties.* New York: Free Press.

Miller, Mike. 1993. Organizing and education. *Social Policy* (Fall): 51–63.

Morris, Aldon. 1997. Black southern student sit-in movement: An analysis of internal organization. In Doug McAdam and David Snow, eds., *Social movements: Readings on their emergence, mobilization and dynamics,* 90–109. Los Angeles: Roxbury Publishing Company.

Mouffe, Chantal. 1992. Democratic citizenship and the political community. In Chantal Mouffe, ed., *Dimensions of radical democracy: Pluralism, citizenship, community,* 225–40. London: Verso.

Mueller, Carol. 1997. Conflict networks and the origins of women's liberation. In Doug McAdam and David Snow, eds., *Social movements: Readings on their emergence, mobilization and dynamics,* 158–71. Los Angeles: Roxbury Publishing Company.

Naples, Nancy. 1998. *Grassroots warriors: Activist mothering, community work, and the war on poverty.* New York: Routledge.

National Congress of Neighborhood Women. 1993. *The Neighborhood Women's training sourcebook.* New York: National Congress of Neighborhood Women.

O'Donnell, Sandy and David Scheie. 1999. *Putting families at the center of community action: Report from an exploration of organizations engaged in family-based community action.* Minneapolis: Rainbow Research, Inc.

O'Donnell, Sandy and Ellen Schumer. 1996. Community building and community organizing: Issues in creating effective models. *Shelterforce* (Jan./Feb.): 12–14.

Olson, Mancur. 1968. *The logic of collective action.* New York: Schocken.

Passerin d'Entreves, Marizio. 1992. Hannah Arendt and the idea of citizenship. In Chantal Mouffe, ed., *Dimensions of radical democracy: Pluralism, citizenship, community,* 146–64. London: Verso.

Pecorella, Robert. 1985. Resident participation as agenda setting: A study of neighborhood-based development corporations. *Journal of Urban Affairs* 7: 23.

Peeples, Faith and Rolf Loeber. 1994. Do individual factors and neighborhood context explain ethnic differences in juvenile delinquency? *Journal of Quantitative Criminology* 10: 141–57.

Perlman, Janice. 1976. Grassrooting the system. *Social Policy* (Sept./Oct.): 4–20.

Pililsuk, Marc, JoAnn McAllister, and Jack Rothman. 1996. Coming together for action: The challenge of contemporary grassroots community organizing. *Journal of Social Issues* 52, no. 1: 15–37.

Pitcoff, Winton. 1998. Collaborating for change. *Shelterforce: The Journal of Affordable Housing and Community Building* 97. special section.

———. 1997. Redefining community development. *Shelterforce: The Journal of Affordable Housing and Community Development* 96. special section.

Piven, Frances Fox and Richard Cloward. 1977. *Poor people's movements: Why they succeed, how they fail.* New York: Vintage Books.

Plotkin, Sidney. 1990. Enclave consciousness and neighborhood activism. In Prudence Posner and Joseph Kling, eds., *Dilemmas of activism,* 218–39. Philadelphia: Temple University Press.

Posner, Prudence and Joseph Kling. 1990. Class and community in an era of urban transformation. In Prudence Posner and Joseph Kling, eds., *Dilemmas of Activism,* 23–45. Philadelphia: Temple University Press.

Pratkanis, Anthony and Marlene Turner. 1996. Persuasion and democracy: Strategies for increasing deliberative participation and enacting social change. *Journal of Social Issues* 52, no. 1: 187–205.

Project South. 1998. *Popular education for movement building: A resource guide.* Washington, DC: Project South.

Putnam, Robert. 1993a. *Making democracy work: Civic traditions in modern Italy.* Princeton: Princeton University Press.

———. 1993b. The prosperous community: Social capital and public life. *The American Prospect* 13: 35–42.

———. 1995. Bowling alone: America's declining social capital. *Journal of Democracy* (Jan.): 65–78.

———. 2000. *Bowling alone: The collapse and revival of American community.* New York: Simon and Schuster.

Rabrenovic, Gordana. 1996. *Community builders: A tale of neighborhood mobilization in two cities.* Philadelphia: Temple University Press.

Ragin, Charles. 1994. *Constructing social research: The unity and diversity of method.* London: Pine Forge Press.

Rivera, Felix and John Erlich. 1992. *Community organizing in a diverse society.* Boston: Allyn and Bacon.

Robert, Henry. 1990. *The Scott-Foresman Robert's rules of order newly revised.* Glenview, IL: Scott Foresman.

Robinson, Buddy and Mark Hanna. 1994a. Lessons for academics from grassroots community organizing: A case study—the Industrial Areas Foundation. *Journal of Community Practice* 1, no. 4: 63–95.

———. 1994b. *Strategies for community empowerment.* Lewiston, NY: The Edwin Mellen Press.

Rooney, Jim. 1995. *Organizing the South Bronx.* New York: State University of New York Press.

Rothman, Jack. 1968. Three models of community organization practice. *National Conference on Social Welfare, Social Work Practice, 1968.* New York: Columbia University Press.

———. 1996. The interweaving of community intervention approaches. *Journal of Community Practice* 3, no. 3/4: 69–99.

Rothschild-Whitt, Joyce. 1979. The collectivist organization: An alternative to rational-bureaucratic models. *American Sociological Review* 44 (August): 509–27.

Rubin, Herbert. 2000. *Renewing hope within neighborhoods of despair: The community-based development model.* Albany, NY: State University of New York Press.

Rubin, Herbert and Irene Rubin. 1992. *Community organizing and development.* New York: Macmillan.

Sampson, Robert. 1995. The community. In James Q Wilson and Joan Petersilia, eds., *Crime,* 193–216. San Francisco: Institute for Contemporary Studies Press.

Sanders, Lynn. 1997. Against deliberation. *Political Theory* 25, no. 3: 347–76.

Shabecoff, Alice and Paul Brophy. 1996. Soul of the neighborhood: Community-based groups rebuild the social fabric. *Shelterforce* (May/June): 8–11.

Shuman, Michael. 1998. Why do progressive foundations give too little to too many? *The Nation* (Jan. 12) no.19: 11–16.

Skolnick, Jerome and James Fyfe. 1993. *Above the law: Police and the excessive use of force.* New York: The Free Press.

Slayton, Robert. 1986. *Back of the yards: The making of a local democracy.* Chicago: University of Chicago Press.

Smith, Neil. 1996. *The new urban frontier: Gentrification and the revanchist city.* New York: Routledge.

Snow, David and Robert Benford. 1992. Master frames and cycles of protest. In Aldon Morris and Carol Mueller, eds., *Frontiers in social movement theory,* 133–55. New Haven: Yale University Press.

Snow, David, Burke Rochford, Jr., Steven Worden, and Robert Benford. 1986. Frame alignment processes, micromobilization, and movement participation. *American Sociological Review* 51: 464–81.

Spiegel, Hans. 1981. The neighborhood partnership: Who's in it? Why? *National Civic Review* (Nov.): 513–20.

Stack, Carol. 1974. *All our kin: Strategies for survival in a black community.* New York: Harper and Row.

Staggenborg, Suzanne. 1995. Can feminist organizations be effective? In Myra Marx Ferree and Patricia Yancey Martin, eds., *Feminist organizations: Harvest of the new women's movement*, 339–55. Philadelphia: Temple University Press.

Stein, Arlene. 1986. Between organization and movement: ACORN and the Alinsky model of community organizing. *Berkeley Journal of Sociology* 31: 93–118.

Stoecker, Randy. 1994. *Defending community.* Philadelphia: Temple University Press.

———. 1997. The CDC model of urban redevelopment: A critique and an alternative. *Journal of Urban Affairs* 19, no. 1: 1–22.

Stoecker, Randy and Susan Stall. 1998. Community organizing or organizing community? Gender and the crafts of empowerment. *Gender and Society* 12, no. 6: 729–56.

Stone, Rebecca. 1996. *Core issues in comprehensive community-building initiatives.* Chicago: Chapin Hall.

Stout, Linda. 1996. *Bridging the class divide and other lessons for grassroots organizing.* Boston: Beacon Press.

Tocqueville, Alexis de. 1971. *Democracy in America.* New York: Washington Square Press.

Trapp, Shel. 1976a. *A challenge for change.* Chicago: National Training and Information Center.

———. 1976b. *Dynamics of organizing.* Chicago: National Training and Information Center.

———. 1986. *Basics of organizing.* Chicago: National Training and Information Center.

Tropman, John, John Erlich, and Jack Rothman. 1995. *Tactics and techniques of community intervention.* Itasca, Illinois: Peacock Publishers.

Tucker, Robert, ed. 1978. *The Marx-Engels reader, 2nd edition.* New York: Norton.

United States General Accounting Office. 1995. *Community development: Comprehensive approaches address multiple needs but are challenging to implement.* Washington D.C.: United States General Accounting Office.

Van Den Bergh, Nan and Lynn Cooper. 1995. Introduction to feminist visions for social work. In John Tropman, John Erlich, and Jack Rothman, eds., *Tactics and techniques of community intervention*, 74–93. Itasca, IL: Peacock Publishers.

Vidal, Avis. 1992. *Rebuilding communities: A national study of urban community development corporations.* New York: Community Development Research Center, New School for Social Research.

Warren, Mark. 2001. *Dry bones rattling: Community building to revitalize American democracy.* Princeton, NJ: Princeton University Press.

Weber, Max. 1978. *Economy and society.* Berkeley: University of California Press.

Williams, Michael. 1984. Two models of community organizing. *Urban Affairs Quarterly* 19, no. 4: 568–75.

Wilson, James and George Kelling. 1989. Making neighborhoods safe: sometimes 'fixing broken windows' does more to reduce crime than conventional 'incident- oriented' policing. *The Atlantic* 263, no. 2: 46–47.

Wilson, William Julius. 1987. *The truly disadvantaged: The inner city, the underclass, and public policy.* Chicago: University of Chicago Press.

———. 1996. *When work disappears: The world of the new urban poor.* New York: Alfred A. Knopf.

Wypijewski, JoAnn. 1997. A stirring in the land. *The Nation.* (Sept. 8), no. 15: 17–25.

Zald, Mayer and John McCarthy, eds. 1987. *Social movements in an organizational society.* New Brunswick, NJ: Transaction Books.

INDEX

CONCEPTS AND NAMES